POLISH WRITERS
on Writing

Polish Writers on Writing captures the brilliance and originality of a literature rightly considered one of the most important and influential of our time. These writers are branded by the political realities of their country — creating literature out of the brutality of the Second World War, under the inhibiting and numbing Communist reign, and finally within a free society, but one burdened by its history.

No common denominator, not even the easy one of "Polish twentieth-century authors," does justice to the variety of talents, styles, and experiences in this collection. "All of the writers have lived in the same house," Zagajewski says, "in the house of a shared history and a shared language, but the windows of their apartments face quite different directions."

CONTRIBUTORS

Stanisław Barańczak
Miron Białoszewski
Stanisław Brzozowski
Józef Czapski
Witold Gombrowicz
Julia Hartwig
Zbigniew Herbert
Gustaw Herling
Paweł Huelle
Anna Kamieńska
Ryszard Krynicki
Bolesław Leśmian
Czesław Miłosz

Sławomir Mrożek
Tadeusz Peiper
Julian Przyboś
Tadeusz Różewicz
Adolf Rudnicki
Bruno Schulz
Jerzy Stempowski
Jan Józef Szczepański
Wisława Szymborska
Aleksander Wat
Stanisław Ignacy Witkiewicz
Adam Zagajewski

THE WRITER'S WORLD
Edward Hirsch, SERIES EDITOR

The Writer's World features writers from around the globe discussing what it means to write, and to be a writer, in many different parts of the world. The series collects a broad range of material and provides access for the first time to a body of work never before gathered in English. Edward Hirsch, the series editor, is internationally acclaimed as a poet and critic. He is the president of the John Simon Guggenheim Foundation.

Irish Writers on Writing (2007)
EDITED BY Eavan Boland

Mexican Writers on Writing (2007)
EDITED BY Margaret Sayers Peden

Polish Writers on Writing (2007)
EDITED BY Adam Zagajewski

Trinity University Press gratefully acknowledges the generous support of the following Patrons of The Writer's World:

Sarah Harte and John Gutzler
Mach Family Fund, Joella and Steve Mach

POLISH WRITERS

on Writing

EDITED BY
Adam Zagajewski

TRINITY UNIVERSITY PRESS
San Antonio, Texas

Published by Trinity University Press
San Antonio, Texas 78212

© 2007 by Adam Zagajewski
Complete copyright information continues on page 253.

Cover design by Karen Schober
Book design by BookMatters, Berkeley

♾ The paper used in this publication meets the minimum
requirements of the American National Standard for
Information Sciences—Permanence of Paper for Printed
Library Materials, ANSI Z39.48-1992.

Printed on 100% post-consumer waste recycled text stock.

Library of Congress Cataloging-in-Publication Data
   Polish writers on writing /
   edited by Adam Zagajewski.
      p.   cm.
   Includes bibliographical references and index.
   ISBN-13: 978-1-59534-030-6 (cloth : alk. paper)
   ISBN-10: 1-59534-030-0 (cloth : alk. paper)
   ISBN-13: 978-1-59534-033-7 (pbk. : alk. paper)
   ISBN-10: 1-59534-033-5 (pbk. : alk. paper)
      1. Polish literature—20th century—History and
   criticism.   2. Authorship.   I. Zagajewski, Adam,
   1945–
   PG7053.A89P65   2007
   891.8'5090073—dc22   2006037500

11   10   09   08   07   C   5   4   3   2   1

Contents

Preface

Adam Zagajewski

For Polish literature the twentieth century was a time of painful experiences, mixed influences, and various, sometimes contradictory, intellectual tasks. From a European perspective it was the nineteenth century that constituted, in a sense, an anomaly. Then, the act of writing was often considered as a kind of a collectivist gesture and was judged more in the light of patriotic expectations than as a purely aesthetic object. Writers and their oeuvre seemed to belong to the society, to the nation, and thus privacy was not allowed. Poland as a country had lost its sovereignty toward the end of the eighteenth century, at the same time the United States had gained its independence. Poland had been partitioned between the three neighboring states: Russia, Prussia, and the Hapsburg empire.

At this time Poland had no central unifying institutions — except for literature and art and sporadic political and military actions planned by both exiled and nonexiled activists and patriotic aristocrats. Major writers and outstanding poets stayed abroad during this period, mostly in Paris, producing poems, dramatic works, poetic novels, and manifestoes that were then smuggled into the divided territory and studied, both as works of imagination and as inflammatory political tracts. As it developed in Western Europe and Russia in the eighteenth and nineteenth centuries, the realistic, objectivist novel came to Poland much later. Gustave Flaubert, had he been a Polish writer, wouldn't have written about Ms. Bovary; rather, he might have composed a book about Ms. Poland. The same for Baudelaire: no cats, no spleen, no balcony, just the Great Cause. This was the nationalism of the weak, always prettier than the chauvinism of the strong.

But the beginning of the twentieth century in Poland saw a literary revolt against this self-imposed burden. The rebellion took place before the country's political predicament had ended. (In 1918 maps of Europe again carried the silhouette of Poland, although the country had changed its shape, moved to the West; a similar change would occur once again in 1945.) This rebellion became an important ingredient of the new Polish literary modernism. The twenties and the thirties stood under the sign of a liberation from the collective mode of writing and thinking. But soon the outbreak of World War II with its disastrous consequences for Poland put the old question back on the agenda: should writers under the burden of this new catastrophe simply revert to the nineteenth-century model of social/patriotic commitment or should they modify it completely?

Having said this, however, this anomaly happened to a literary tradition that in many other respects — and in other periods as well — had followed a general pattern of almost all European national literatures: the Polish literary tradition emerged from the Latin Middle Ages, invented the vernacular as a literary vehicle when the medieval mentality was on decline, and was steeped in Greek-Latin-Italian models and genres. Polish poets knew and admired Horace, Virgil, and Dante, and they were mostly interested in universal questions. Sixteenth-century Polish writers had studied in Padua and other Italian cultural centers of the Renaissance. The poet Jan Kochanowski, for example, the greatest among them, was a Renaissance man, one of those minds in which the culture of the time came to full fruition. European connections to the Polish literary tradition were so strong that the energy of its growth had been extremely complex. The turn to a narrower national subject, which happened in the nineteenth century, was never met without at least some hesitation, resistance, or doubt.

Let's return to the intellectual dilemma occasioned by the tragedy of World War II. This dilemma is in many ways the focus of this book, although of course the time span the volume covers is broader. Early in the anthology we explore the work of Stanisław Brzozowski, a fervent philosopher and prolific prose writer who died young (1911), much too early to be able to respond to the problems that arose in the 1940s. The same is true for

Bolesław Leśmian, an eminent modernist poet who died before 1939 after a long literary career. The war — for many Polish writers and readers alike it is *the* war — was a pivotal event for Stanisław Ignacy Witkiewicz (who willingly used the pseudonym "Witkacy," a more frivolous version of his family name), an avant-garde playwright and prose writer. It was also so for Bruno Schulz, an experimental, visionary fiction writer.

The war was a fatal event for Witkiewicz and Schulz: Witkiewicz killed himself in September 1939 after hearing the news that the Red Army had entered Polish territory from the east (while the Nazis had already conquered a vast quantity of it coming from the west, south, and north); Schulz was killed by an SS man in the ghetto of his native Drohobycz in 1943. These two deaths were highly significant: they marked the violent end of a short-lived era of liberated imagination in Polish literature. Not that imagination evaporated completely, but from then on it had to be channeled differently.

For the majority of the writers represented in this volume, World War II constituted a decisive threat and challenge, not just for their private lives, for their sheer survival, but also as far as their literary ideas and dreams were concerned. I would argue that many of these writers faced a choice not very different from the one their nineteenth-century predecessors were confronted with: namely, should the new catastrophe be understood and dealt with as a national disaster, or should it be approached as a global event provoking an answer couched in universal terms? Their choice went toward the universal, not toward the local, thankfully. They — here I mean the generations more or less directly affected by the war, as opposed to younger writers, to my generation or to my younger colleagues — acted as free agents, free spirits, writers and thinkers who even in this time of distress wanted to save their individual artistic freedom. They understood their situation as perceived against the backdrop of the world's literature, not merely in a parochial, nationalistic context.

And yet, free as they were and passionately interested in universal questions — and we know that those things are mostly contemplated in the profound solitude of a writing studio or a walk under a starry sky — these writers seem to have talked to each other all the time. In selecting texts for this book, I've ultimately dealt with a family of writers, with a tribe of artists who confronted each other through time, shaping each other's ideas accordingly, dialogically, to use a modish term, not as monks separated by the thick walls of their individual cells. I've found among these writers more communality than isolation, more conversation than silence.

When Schulz — a solitary, mysterious writer living in the provinces, in his tiny Drohobycz — proceeds to define his own art, he does so while exchanging letters with his literary friend, Witold Gombrowicz, who himself lives in Warsaw, the very center of prewar Poland. When much later Gombrowicz — by then a "resident alien" in Argentina, an exile having few ties with the local literati — tries to better understand his own artistic stance, he does so by circumscribing Czesław Miłosz's poetic and philosophical imagination. And Miłosz spends his creative time responding to Gombrowicz's portrayal of himself and to the end of his days will be fascinated and sometimes scandalized by Gombrowicz's ideas. Jerzy Stempowski, an outstanding essayist and critic, another exile, living in Switzerland — a lot of these exchanges happened as correspondence between exiles — writes long letters to Miłosz, telling him how he sees and understands Miłosz's oeuvre.

Anna Kamieńska, not an exile — not everybody left the country, after all — in her beautiful poetic diary referred often to her colleagues, other Polish poets. Sławomir Mrożek formulated many of his ideas in a correspondence with Jan Blonski, one of the most brilliant critics of the postwar period. (Interestingly, as Mrożek lived in Italy at this time, he wrote to Blonski only when Blonski stayed in France, not when the critic returned to Krakó, then Kraków, so that the Medusa's eye of the correspondence censor didn't peruse their letters.) When Jan Józef Szczepański, a well-known prose writer, composed his programmatic essay (included in this book), he meant it as a dialogue with at least two authors — one a classic (Joseph Conrad); the other, an outstanding fiction writer who was the addressee of this text written in the form of a letter (Julian Stryjkowski).

The communality of Polish letters is unique in many ways. Aleksander Wat's best known book, *My Century*, a monument of lucidity, was created in many sessions of an endless conversation with Miłosz (as readers of this anthology would know), taped and later, much later, posthumously published. Even Wisława Szymborska, who is famous for shunning any direct programmatic utterances and who endeavors to say everything within her poems, was compelled by the pressure of the Nobel Prize tradition to deliver a lecture on her understanding of poetry — another example of a dialogue; a mandatory exercise in this case. Let's cite yet another author: when we read the essay (or story — the genre is debatable here) by Adolf Rudnicki, a well-known writer of short stories and literary diaries, describing a walk in the occupied Warsaw — an important walk, an important conversation — we realize quite rapidly that the other writer and conversationalist here is, once again, Miłosz.

Perhaps somebody with a talent for diagrams and drawings could try to produce a map capturing the structure of all these exchanges, dialogues, and polemics. We wouldn't be amazed, I think, had we found in the middle of this web the figure of who else? Miłosz, of course. Indefatigable correspondent, commentator, helper, polemicist, at times doubter and believer, poet, essayist, and fiction writer. Somebody who held himself responsible for the very shape of Polish letters, for the "household" of Polish poetry (the metaphor is his).

So here's the innocent paradox of this generation. These brilliant writers understood that in bad times they should keep their inner freedom, their individual voices, and their passion for infinity and not bend under the nationalistic yoke. Yet the weight of the Polish nineteenth-century model was such that they needed a constant consultation, a constant conversation to withstand this pressure. Their solitudes needed company, discussion, encouragement. When I say those writers had postulated a "universalistic" stance, I mean that for them the debacle of the mid-century, World War II with its Auschwitz and Kolyma, had to be contemplated as a global catastrophe, not a problem of merely one nation. And, they thought, the disaster struck everywhere, destroying not only human lives and beautiful cities, churches and roads, railways and theaters, but also damaging — in a different way — human souls, as well as fiction and poetry.

If the reader of this book finds in some chapters, in the majority of them probably, a tone rarely heard elsewhere, a tone having more to do with the notion of the moral responsibility of literature, of the seriousness of poetry, than with purely technical considerations — or with the postmodern conviction that reality is hopelessly inaccessible, as language always confuses and is meaningless — then maybe the muted influence of the Polish nineteenth-century "anomaly" can be detected right here, this time having a beneficial impact.

But after all, our poets and prose writers, those who speak in this book were — *are* — individual writers. No common denominator, not even the easy label of "Polish twentieth-century authors," will ever render justice to the variety of their talents, styles, and experiences. Yes, all of them had — or have — lived in the same house, in the house of a shared history and a shared language, but the windows of their apartments faced quite different directions. It's true that many of these writers paid attention more to a common fate of their society than to the private lives of isolated individuals, and yet their work differed wildly.

Stempowski, a great erudite in love with both the age of the European Enlightenment and the delicate poetry of figures of Late Antiquity, couldn't be more different from Miron Bialoszewski, the secular, urban, and somehow modern mystic, largely a self-taught man. Or Jan Józef Szczepański, it has to be either Jan Józef Szczepański or simply Szczepański, a declared realist, a fiction writer who patiently explored modern history, trying to find in it patterns of moral behavior — what did he have in common with Miłosz, a religious poet who always claimed he loved and craved reality but in his artistic practice couldn't help but fall prey to the charm of poetic forms, structures, and unrealities? Let's not forget Zbigniew Herbert either — his unique sense of humor, the distinctive combination of a respect for the Ancients with a contemporary irony.

Even within this broadly labeled war generation, however, many Polish writers produced their intellectual categories, the vessels of their imaginations, much before the actual war broke out. Thus Gombrowicz — a writer fascinated with theories that he invented and developed throughout his career — had already proposed his visions of Form (which enslaves all of us in the society) and Immaturity (a weapon against the societal tyranny) in the thirties and later. In the second half of his life Gombrowicz tried to apply these notions to the new state of the world. Miłosz's imagination worked in a different way, but he also entered the dark years of war with a mind already filled with ideas and with a solid sketch of his aesthetic. The same is true for Józef Czapski, a painter and writer who had already witnessed the cruelties of the war and the Russian revolution.

Not so, of course, for the younger writers like Tadeusz Różewicz or Herbert or, in a slightly different way, Szymborska. They all emerged from the Great War somehow conditioned by its inhuman power, refusing to

carry on what they considered the grandiloquence of the previous generations. These writers wanted to be — and they were — terse, ironic, antiro-
mantic, skeptical. Tadeusz Borowski, who is not represented in this book,
also belonged to this generation — a tragic figure and the brilliant author of
the Auschwitz prose (*This Way to Gas, Ladies and Gentlemen*) that was exceptional in its intentional, painful cynicism.

But both for the former as for the latter, for the older and the younger
among these writers, one thing is true: their spiritual situation can be seen
as a kind of a fight, an uneven duel between Imagination and History (yes, I
know how imprecise these big words are) — or between their Imagination
and their perception of History. And perhaps this struggle is the most interesting thing here, the fierce combat between two completely different elements of the human environment — the artistic dream on the one hand and
the brutality of history on the other. Isn't this what literature is all about?
Measuring the strangeness of the external world with the fragile instruments of interiority?

Of course, I should add, the decades after World War II were also marked
by another, very strong presence of historic actuality: by the changing,
sometimes more and sometimes less dictatorial pressure of the communist
state. At first, in the late forties and early fifties, the state came up with a
normative doctrine of socialist realism — a disaster for artists and writers
(and for their readers as well!). Later it mellowed and contented itself with a
more lenient policy; socialist realism had been abandoned. The weapons
writers used against this powerful antagonist — the state — were not rifles
and grenades but Imagination, Irony, and Metaphor, yet another set of skir-
mishes between the outer and the inner worlds.

The choice of fragments proposed in this volume certainly is not the only
just and exhausting presentation of twentieth-century Polish writers' programmatic pronouncements. I'm sure some readers will criticize my selection of the authors and their texts, suggesting that X has been omitted and
Y given too much space. This seems to be the inevitable destiny of every
anthology: to make some readers happy and some angry. Let's hope the proportion between the two won't be worse than the ratio between the length
of the day and the night in June. And if to somebody it seems more like
November, the responsibility is mine.

Acknowledgments

I would like to thank several people who assisted me with their advice while this book was taking shape. Alissa Valles not only translated many of the chapters; she also helped select the pieces. So did Anna Czabanowska-Wróbel, Daniel Gerould, Wojciech Karpiński, Ryszard Krynicki, and Marian Stala.

I would also like to acknowledge the generous help of the Blessing Way Foundation in New York, which contributed to the completion of the project.

Bolesław Leśmian

(1877–1937)

Bolesław Leśmian was a provincial notary, a shy and inconspicuous person
("from an empty carriage stepped out Bolesław Leśmian" a well-known
anecdote has it). He was famous in a quiet way between the wars, elected
to the short-lived but prestigious Polish Academy of Literature. In Poland
today he is hailed by many as the greatest poet of the twentieth century. For
some this highest ranking is meant politically (directed against Czesław Miłosz,
or another poet), but for others this statement is an expression of genuine
admiration.

Leśmian's poems are wonderfully dense; they make language work and
glisten. He was a late and ironic symbolist, a poet who didn't quite believe in
the symbols he employed but immensely enjoyed the half-playful, half-tragic
game of creating new and daring mythologies. As readers, we don't know
who Leśmian was as a human being: his poems never reveal the author's
face; they're more ambitious, they aspire to revealing the face of the Universe,
though in a humorous mode. His command of poetic language was amazingly
subtle; fragments of his poems could be put together as an anthology of the
best metaphors and similes in twentieth-century Polish poetry.

Philosophically Leśmian grew out of the early-twentieth-century crisis,
when some thinkers—like Henri Bergson, whom Leśmian read and loved—
tried to rescue the fragile human territory from the fangs of omnivorous
science.

Metamorphoses of Reality
1910–11

In any given time, reality is not what *can* be asserted but what does not *need* to be asserted.

By that token, various gods constituted a varied reality up to the point when they began to be asserted. Each of us possesses a sense distinct from the other senses: a sense of reality. The more this sense accompanies our other senses or thoughts, the more value the latter acquire in our eyes.

But we cannot take in the whole earth without remainder with that one sense. It is either too small or too large: either it cannot attain, or it overshoots the boundaries of the world accessible to us. Today certain objects seem real to us, tomorrow others. And that which yesterday was still reality, today has a rainbow variety of insults hurled at it: delusion, appearance, a tin of soap.

The lower a man's spiritual level, the larger is the field of his reality. For Flemish painters of the period of decline, reality is a precious silk dress, a lamp lit in a room, the room itself and its furnishings. That is why they take such care to polish every detail, not giving precedence to any single one and believing in the sublimity and realness of all. This is realism on a broad field, naive realism quite indifferent to what lies within that field: whether a typical potbelly holding a glass of wine, or God with the cross on his shoulders, or a masterfully woven basket with parsley and carrots, or a yellow canary in a green cage. Everything is equally true and real.

But the more we reflect and investigate, the more we look more deeply into the essence of the thing and listen to the faint whispers of existence, the more our sense of reality becomes discriminating, the more its field visibly narrows. It is easier for us to believe in that which occupies as little space as possible in the illusionary spheres of brittle matter, which once entranced us with its apparent accessibility and tangibility. That is why, on the one hand, the canvases of our paintings become less roomy, less accommodating to the whole stampede, the whole mob of once honored things; but, on the other hand, they become more receptive to a multitude of penetrating perceptions and intuitions.

We do not believe in the reality of the precious silk dress itself and the preciousness of the silk, but we search it for a particular play of light and shadow, colors and shades, because the latter express something lesser in terms of space and something greater in terms of hints about a reality of which we have inklings.

Long ago we were satisfied with man captured as a type — that is, as the most common product of customs and daily habits and of life lived by the greatest number. We believed in his reality. The commonness and everyday-ness of such a man increased the field of reality itself. How jolly it must be to live on such spacious ground!

But to be only a type in the presence of the universe — that is rather risky! . . . We found a rarer but more certain value in ourselves: character. But when that too ceased to be enough for us, we looked deeper into our selfhood and singularity in a relentless hunt for the least flimsy, for the most real. Belief in selfhood, deflecting our eyes from many objects outside us, thinned the field of visible reality even further, concentrating it into senses not spatial. The struggle with the world and with other people was trans-formed into a struggle with ourselves, our predicament; into a mood, anatomy (bone and body) — into colors and shades. But beyond the self there exists some tone in the soul; some elemental *song without words*, wait-ing for the necessary words to come in a creative hour, but for which these words are always something other than itself. Capturing that tone, that song without words, makes it possible for pupils to follow a master and allows the master to be himself, unveils to him his own worlds, hands him the right words and rhythms, teaches him what no experience can teach.

That song without words does not originate in the realm of logic where every word originates but in other, nonlogical realms, where it is possible to exist without words and where the concept of existence — freed from the bonds of grammar and syntax — ceases to be a logical proposition, with its obligatory subject and predicate, its beginning and end, its birth and death.

What is that tone? What is that song without words? We intuited it, but let us beware of definitions. A definition is a funeral shroud we spread over dead things, things gone for ever. A definition is a transparent glass tomb, in which embalmed holy remains are laid to rest. Man seen as a song without words eludes our definitions. He knows, however, that in order to become real, he has to find his tone, he has to draw out his song without words. It is his only, his truest reality. A reality barely resembling, in its cross-sectioned or abbreviated form, the words with which it must at some point be filled, in order to translate its own essence into a common, interhuman language. This will always be only a translation, an interpretation — never the original, never the prototype.

Here we have come to the original, the prototype, the least subject to the criticism of our logical mind. We removed our reality as far as possible from its potential enemies, we narrowed its field until it was nothing but a space-less tone, in order to protect it from the danger menacing it from flimsy materiality and in order to believe in it with our oversensitive faith that doesn't endure gods with too definite lines and too broad surfaces.

But that reality also dissolves into nothingness before our eyes, like a dream, of which we don't know who is dreaming it. And instead of naked bodies, instead of characteristic faces, instead of expressions of mood, we see a landscape on the canvas as if man didn't exist at all. A landscape like man resting from himself, like the best harbor for his weariness and his ceaseless travels, like a return to nature, where a patient and nameless reality outside him is waiting, a reality unlike himself and attracting him by that very unlikeness.

But there, among flowers and greenery, in the shade of trees, on the banks of streams, a longing for himself is sitting in ambush, a longing for his own forms, his own body. He looks with anxiety and alarm at the division, the dark abyss that opened up between him and his body. And once again he desires to believe in the reality of his being, the reality of his existence, in the power of his spirit. He wants to return to himself, to greet himself on the threshold of his own dreams, to hear his own voice, behold his own face in the mirrors of the house he abandoned.

And he returns full of new experiences and discoveries, loaded down with the memories of long wanderings on the many ways of life, manly in his long-ing and faith in himself, placated in his anger and petulance about the changeability and ephemerality of old faiths, prepared for new work of love and passion for that strange delusion which in the universe carried the name of man and that is to be his reality once again from now on.

Then slowly, after short mornings of ecstasy and long evenings of meditation, he will be granted once more that hour of childhood delights, when all objects that until now elicited unbelief acquire charm and meaning in his eyes again — and the soul fills up with them as if with words to one always invigorating song. And again, the whole world, from the pasque flower to God, becomes reality. And again, his heart is willingly maddened by a faith summoned from nowhere, faith in people, animals, plants, roadside stones, bees pollinating flowers, the lit windows of a lonely country cottage, the knots of pine trees glittering in the sun, in the dawn and dusk, in the sailing of a boat on the waves of a familiar lake . . .

And this whole world, repeatedly retrieved from oblivion, seems to him a hundred times more precious and enchanting than a sudden doom met, than a reality bought by bloody labor.

What is this reality? By what measure should it be measured? By none other than the one with which we measure the bloody labor of our spirit, the degree of effort of our creative powers.

Just as the vestal virgins fed the holy fire, so we must feed our reality, summon it with a strained, inspired effort of the spirit so it lasts, for its lasting is our lasting also; its volatility, our volatility; its complete eclipse, our eclipse.

Reality is subject to the same evolutionary changes as life is, as the human spirit carried by this life.

What then does realism look like in literature and art, the realism that appears to impose on everything the idea of one inalterable truth, one inalterable form, in which that truth is expressed? It is merely a misunderstanding no smaller or greater than many other misunderstandings.

Every age and every particular artist has a different reality of his or her own.

For Tolstoy, reality is recalling things seen and sensed. For Dostoevsky, the discovery of unusual and unexpected psychic states. For Kasprowicz, the raised voice of human suffering. For others, a nobleman's coat of arms and a girl's cheek flushed with the cold.

Yes, everyone has his or her own reality. Schopenhauer finds it in the Universal Will liberated from the burdens of phenomena. Kant, in the thing in itself that is inaccessible to our thinking. Bergson, in the ceaseless and elusive tide of existence.

The followers of realism are in error when they consider it a kind of indivisible and universal institution, where everyone can find a piece of a general truth, if only he has the desire to do so.

No such institution exists, nor did it ever. In fact, the true realist is obliged to create what is real for him, his own reality.

It is created a little by everyone who loves, hates, is sad and happy, picks some flower or other in a field, and gazes at some star or other in the sky. . . . But for us the greatest temptation and terror and joy is the moment when some hand until then unknown knocks at the gate behind which a new longed-for reality is concealed.

At a moment like that, the whole earth seems to be listening to which of its creatures is being called by name and surname when the gate opens — who and what is to become reality from now on? . . . And who and what are to fall into nothingness?

And the gate opens to the delight of some and the despair of others, for not all have a right to live, although all have a right to die . . .

Translated by Alissa Valles

LETTER TO ZENO

PARIS 1912 [?]
VAVIN 13

Dear Zeno,

Thank you for your card. All the same, I am waiting for ampler indications and more specific comments on my collection, because I would like to put it to press. The cycles *Near the Sun* and *Under Guard of Evenings* are indeed arbitrary and were assembled in haste. I did not have sufficient time before my departure. Tell Mortkowicz to bring the manuscript back and show me by title the poems you think should be taken out and the ones I should add to other cycles. It seems to me you must have mixed up two titles: "The Distant" and "Angels," because you advise me to shorten "Angels," but that cycle cannot be shortened. Besides that, it rather seems to me that "The Distant" does not fit in the collection. I will not add any more poems to this book because I am working on another collection that will be different, more varied, and will contain a long poem, quite peculiar and unexpected. I don't know if this first collection is what I wanted to make it. It seemed to me that — after going astray many times — I returned to nature, anew, once again affirmed in me and seen to the core; to nature, which during my oblivion transformed itself and acquired the ability to look into me just as I looked into it. I was bored by the conceptual and idea-driven treatment of things, which in our poetry have long ceased to be themselves. A flower is not a flower but let's say an author's longing for his beloved. An oak is not an oak but what have you — a superman's straining toward the sun, and so on. In a word, our poetry became driven by world views. Instead of the world — an idea, a world view. I felt a desire to enter the world — nature, flowers, lakes, the sun, the stars — to enter so completely that I would have the right to pronounce higher words without the justification of ideas, without any idea as an epigraph, hanging knowingly over the words. Fashion lends charm to every such epigraph, but what is made within the range of that epigraph evaporates with time as something to be understood in a historical context and requiring a commentary for generations with different ideas. I longed for everything in me to sing again, to flower and fill with fragrance. I began to look for the world outside us, an epic-tragic world. That was only a beginning — and no one will guess. Only this way will what I said be in my dramas and long poems. I add in passing that I understand the epic as a song — a song not of oneself. As to the element of song in the drama, it probably doesn't need stating. Hence, I began in a song what I will unfold in the same song. Only a flower "sung from within" lives in us and summons up the flower outside of us. Only a man "sung from within" is what we care about in art. The rest is not epic or drama or art, but realism, everyday colloquial speech.

I write in bursts — on intuition, because I think that will do. Because my first collection is the first gate — which I opened for myself in the lap of nature — I would suggest as a general title: *Open Gate* or *Roadside Crop*, or *Harp in the Chasm*, or *Crossroad Orchard*, or *Sun Watch*, or *Green and Purple*, or *Spring Unrest*, or *Mirrored Toil*, or *Rose Homestead*, or *Cornflower Patch*, or *April Fulfilled*, or *Through Singing*, or *Fire of Clouds*, or *Resurrection of Flowers*. I want this first collection to have fullness, scope, prodigality, generosity. That is why, if it is too short, I prefer to add (I would send them right away) if only two or three fine cycles. If you think it is a good idea, write to me immediately, because later it will be too late. Did you notice that the poem "Evenings" (*Under Guard of Evenings*) turns out to be the last in the cycle? I will wait for clarification on the question of "Angels" and "The Distant." I send warm regards and await your reply. I have to start the printing of the collection, a great deal depends on it.

B. *Leśmian.*

It seems to me best to call it *Cornflower Patch*.

Translated by Alissa Valles

Stanisław Brzozowski

(1878–1911)

Stanisław Brzozowski influenced not one but at least two generations of Polish writers and philosophers. He was born and lived in the Russian part of Poland (remember that the country was partitioned between the late eighteenth century and 1918). Brzozowski was in turn influenced by the intensity of Russian cultural debates and by the sudden explosion of Friedrich Nietzsche's ideas. Literary criticism was his main area (he also wrote novels); he was one of those critics who tend to be potent cultural legislators rather than patient commentators on novels and poems. His books read like feverish, inflammatory manifestos. For him literature was an indispensable tool for social reform, a courageous gesture of a collective self-healing. He asked the most fundamental questions concerning links between society and artistic consciousness.

Brzozowski's questioning played an important role in the difficult process in which an enslaved nation (a partitioned nation) was trying to wake up from the complacency of political nonbeing. From the aura of a quasi-Marxist worship of labor and work, of a frantic *vita activa*, he moved toward Catholicism, which he understood to be a demanding and beautiful church that disciplined but did not abolish individualities. His last philosophical hero was Cardinal John Henry Newman.

Brzozowski spent the final months of his short life in Florence. The pages quoted here are taken from his posthumous *Diary*, where regrets mix with aperçus, accusations, and noble dreams.

DIARY ENTRIES

DECEMBER 10, 1910

This is undoubtedly a crucial time for me: my youth has quite gone now and the time has come in which I cannot merely be promising but I must offer things capable of existing, possessing at least certain rights to existence. And, at the same time, all the shortcomings in my preparation, all the negligences come more and more clearly to the fore. Despair is an easier thing than a calm and cold eye for things as they are. What weighs more heavily and is more dangerous than any cultural shortcomings is my inner disorder of will, my growing lack of courage. To a certain degree that lack, seeking a justification for itself, creates the sense of other shortcomings, although it would be ridiculous to deny that they are horrifying.

Strive not to let a single day pass without raising the mind to fundamental aims and tasks. The principle of "leveling" has too much power over me, the common too easily levels me — that is, the place where all points of view intersect, the point of their absolute neutralization.

Don't be discouraged, don't be discouraged, by the fact that there is no perspective, sense, or use for me in the future, that all action seems merely a personal eccentricity, a mania. Don't be discouraged, but try to free yourself from this state. — Pray. Pray by lifting your mind every day, even if only for a moment, to the realm where your questions become visible. Try to have them nearer, so that you don't need to derive chastening encouragement from their presence, the fact that they are in you. So that this isn't a separate moment in you — a decoration or the certificate of a parvenu. Have your own preoccupations constantly present.

My God: Why was there such an effort to destroy my mind? Don't suppress bitterness but don't yield to it either. Try to understand the actions of your own intellectual nature — construct its freedom — you have no right at all to write freely. Search. Search not with the idea that one's nature is something easy, something that comes without effort. No, a nature is a state of mind, a totality of aims, measures, and ideals whose confluence (?) is the work of all our abilities and which develops those abilities, but the totality itself is a work of construction and will.

Renan, Sainte-Beuve, Hegel, Balzac — doubtless I would draw encouragement if I were able to work on them. To force that awkwardness which is spreading in me. Pray. Prayer is to be present in the realm of law and aim, immersion in the sphere where laws and aims exist. That is where the boundary is. From that realm one can think about God without idolatry.
    Try to live by prayer, not by polemic and opposition. Strength is lost in that friction and a certain light is not born.

Blake has an unequaled significance for me. He is for me a great witness. It is enough to think about him to rise to the level of high thoughts.

To understand properly the English poetry of such figures as S. T. Coleridge, Blake, Keats, Meredith, Shelley, one must never lose sight of the conviction of the metaphysical essence of poetry, one must see it as essentially *Poesis*, the creation of life, new facts of the human soul, its new organs, new spiritual entities. Only such a view protects us from anecdotalism and sentimentalism in poetry. Poetry comes into being where a *synthetic* picture of the world, a totality of thought, word, a *particular* spiritual entity, a particular ideal form of humanity is felt as joy and maintains itself by the power of its magic over the soul and minds, over all of life — and thus when a certain ideal form of humanity is created, drawn out from the very inner heart of life; in judging it we are concerned precisely *with this form*, its quality, scope, and only when standing firmly on that ground can we attain freedom from a quantitative point of view, only then do we understand that in fact one poetic fragment of Keats has a potential value equal to the multivolume works of happier poets. Remember this if you want to keep a proper orientation. Moreover, remember that this *view* — writing this I have to use ridiculous oppositions — cannot be reconciled with any neglect of the "sensual enchantment of poetry." On the contrary, that enchantment is what makes poetry above all a profound work of life, in the magic of form lies its creative element, in the existential, metaphysical sense. For that reason one cannot speak of any correspondence of form and content, of richness of content and poverty of form. *Poetically*, content is form; in order to be poetry, content has to become a joyful fact of life. The more it is itself, the more it takes in all of life. Every element of indifference that dwells in us, that can exist at the moment of poetic expression, diminishes the depth of poetry, acts to its detriment. *Poetry must be seen as the creative self-definition of man.*

December 16, 1910

What do we find on arrival? The lives of former human generations and our attitude to them. That is the point of departure for my philosophy and its basis, determining its methods, its character, its relation to other movements.

Hence flows a completely different horizon for criticism, biography, history. Criticism above all.

Every excellent person, every person powerfully alive changes something in the postulates that are the germ of all certainties, all of human reality. In such a person we seize these new tones, values, new properties of life in the act of being born. Criticism is the analysis of our breathable air. It exposes the genesis of its elements and their value.

Daily care in the life of a thinker and a poet can be a source of inspiration and, at the very least, a sort of precious current of blood in that inspiration. That's where Balzac got it, and Dostoevsky.

The quiet triumphs of lens-grinding, constant and serene, patient and laborious, don't you sense them in the pathos of the *Ethics*?

A thought must always be supported by something existential; here the links can be very strange.

Don't speak ill of daily care.

Intellectual honesty is the most difficult thing. A person attains anything more easily than the understanding that he thinks only what he thinks and how he thinks, that there is no way of getting anything more from one's own thought process than what it contains — from the nature of the inner content of our life and the totality of its relations to the life processes preceding us and contemporary with us.

I don't know how it is in painting, music, other branches of art. I know how it is in literature — in all art forms creating in the word. Here the dependency on the age, the connection to it, are extraordinarily subtle, they branch off into the most intricate network of imperceptible veins and tissues. Irzykowski! He just doesn't want to face up to the facts. When we want to create in the word, it always manifests itself to us as it is in the society we know. — The word has a meaning arising from the life that surrounds us, and when we want to give it another, a different meaning, not met with in this life, it is an almost inhuman labor, perhaps unattainable. It is a hard and resistant material. The meaning of a "word" grows in us by the very process of life — it is for us what that life made it into. I beg you: try to write a comedy now à la Ben Jonson, a drama à la Massinger, à la Racine; to the extent that you are a person of any depth and sincerity, you will be unable to create even a satisfactory appearance of one. Life would be an easy matter if we could be so *vogelfrei* [free as a bird]. Sadly, we in fact find the world, ourselves, but in a different sense than the one Avenarius presents us. A cultured man can't learn to think biologically about his life, about himself, as if about something not only serious but immeasurably real, in the sense John Henry Newman wants to emphasize when he says he has only himself and can't reject himself, because he has nothing with which to replace himself. He himself doubtless already extended this to collective life (the text in which he speaks of reproaching one's own age as of a weakness), and this idea must be penetrated properly, but it is hard even to understand it well at all: that we can't reject our epoch, we can't reject history — human history as the final and deepest work, because we don't have anything with which to replace it. It is all man has. The word has no absolute extra-historical meanings. It is always an infirm and limited creature of life: infirm and limited even when we consider it as a creature of the whole species, but a single one. The reality of man is relative, provisional, unfinished; there is no ready, finished, closed reality.

JANUARY 4, 1911

Yesterday I finished the first volume of my novel. I had moments of desperation, for it seemed to me all of the characters were incurably papier-mâché and I didn't care about them in the slightest. But yesterday that most difficult thing happened: blood started circulating between me and the work. There are things that are right in being said. Now I would like to enter a different way of looking at the world, but it will be untrue if it is said that this novel doesn't have its own way of seizing on existential reality. I would prefer that seizing to be different; in me it is in fact already different, but my writing always remains outside of me and expresses what is my past. One could even use this as a reproach against my writing, that it sets me back and in the main I am inclined to believe something of the kind, not only for myself but in general. In those who live a powerful moral life — that is, who transform themselves — art is always a return or a delay: something is consolidated here, something that we once were or even something that we still are, but in any case something not a pure dynamic creating one's own being, curing it, reconstructing it. Art is dependent on the elements that change the slowest, on what moves us, what we feel, and its connection to our self-sympathy, becoming a moment of the drive to self-impression. So when we begin to write, it is not *will* that revives in us and gains the advantage of us, but *nature*: nature becomes will. These moments, then, contain the ethical justification of art. It guards against one-sidedness, in that even what we do not want to and did not dare to achieve by will, becomes will in spite of us. Our self-knowledge is sharpened and to the extent the current of life is strong in us, we come out of the holding back strengthened, deepened, and more broadly true to ourselves.

However, herein also lies the source of the fact that I am powerless against what I write. I can't go back. Each thing I write is for one time only. A state and a disposition that doubtless exclude perfection, but Blake was never able to correct his work. I hope that there will come a time in my life for serene creation, but that will not be before I become fully integrated in truth. Then, when the process of interpenetration of ethics and psychophysiology (I know what I mean when I write this) is completed, will I be able to write differently. Now it would be vain to dream of an aesthetics of another kind. I still have to follow in the footsteps of Dostoevsky.

Browning is so profitable to me because he is akin to Dostoevsky but he is also more safeguarded. This safeguarded-ness is not necessarily superiority. In any case, it is necessary to reflect on where the boundary lies between these two artists.

Today's critic is like Socrates, only instead of a small Athenian world, he has all of humanity.

Translated by Alissa Valles

Stanisław Ignacy Witkiewicz

(1885–1939)

Son of a well-known architect and writer, Stanisław Ignacy Witkiewicz (nicknamed Witkacy) entered the world of art and literature early on. A personal tragedy (the suicide of his fiancée) sent him abroad; together with Bronisław Malinowski, who would become well known as a leading anthropologist of the time, Witkiewicz traveled to Australia. His military service in the Russian (tsarist) army during World War I encompassed a murky period of his life, as he was then technically a Russian citizen, given the fact that his family lived in the part of Poland that through the partitions had become a segment of the tsar's empire.

His artistic action and influence culminated in the twenties and thirties. His plays slowly gained recognition during this period, his feverish manifestos ignited many younger minds, his paintings—many of which he regarded as being only alimentary—sold. Witkiewicz's mind represented an unusual fusion of an avant-garde imagination (indeed, his plays do not resemble classical theater) and of a conservative philosophy: he dreaded the demise of what he called "metaphysical feelings," foreseeing the advent of an anthill-like, dumb mass society. It is probably this fascinating anomaly that makes him so interesting now. Also, there is a fascinating contrast between his theory of pure form and the robust, Rabelaisian language of his prose.

Witkiewicz's last powerful statement was his death: he killed himself in

September 1939, after having learned that not only had Hitler invaded
Poland, but that Hitler had been joined in this by Stalin (on September 17),
a consequence of the Ribbentrop-Molotov Pact.

Chapter 3 from
The Decline of Art

November 13, 1918

In the closed cultures of antiquity the great artistic styles whose beginnings
are lost in the mists of history developed extremely slowly; these styles consisted of two fundamental elements: ornamentation and the presentation of
religious images under pressure from the menacing conditions of life and a
profound and implacable faith. The religious content of the sculpture and
painting that adorned the temples was directly connected to the form;
there was no difference between Pure Form and external content because,
being close to its primeval source, metaphysical feeling in its purest form,
the directly expressed unity in plurality was not divided from its symbol: the
image of a fantastic deity. At that time there were not, in our sense of the
term, any separate artists forging a style of their own. Rather there was a
throng of workers within the context of a style that evolved slowly as the
result of a collective effort to which each of them contributed certain relatively minor alterations. . . .

As religion grew superficial and gods were likened to men and the intellect developed in pace with social democratization, there was an immediate
effect on art. This process reached its height in Roman sculpture, and then
there was a total decline of Art. . . . When Christian mysticism arose, there
was fertilization of the human spirit with regard to art. . . .

But from our point of view, the Renaissance was a defeat for true Art. . . .
Painting declined rapidly, and its ideal became fidelity in copying the external
world. . . . The true revival of Pure Form took place in the last decades of the
nineteenth century in France starting with the Impressionists who, however,
did not leave behind them works of great value besides a riotous outpouring

of color, which had been previously killed off by classicism. Even though it stopped being a soulless and even sentimental imitation of nature, painting during this period was not connected with a generally valid metaphysics in the form of religion but was rather the expression of a private, secret, and more or less deliberate metaphysics on the part of individual artists. . . .

The value of a work of art does not depend on the real-life feelings contained in it or on the perfection achieved in copying the subject matter but is solely based upon the unity of a construction of pure formal elements. . . .

Today we have come to Pure Form by another road; it is, as it were, an act of despair against life, which is becoming grayer and grayer, and for that reason, although art is the sole value of our times — excluding of course the technology of living and universal happiness — present-day artistic forms are, in comparison with the old ones, crooked, bizarre, upsetting, and nightmarish. The new art stands in relation to the old as a feverish vision in relation to a calm, beautiful dream. . . .

Nowadays an overworked person has neither the time nor the nervous energy for any thoughtful absorption in works of art, the understanding of which demands leisurely contemplation and inner concentration proportionate to the slow maturation of the works themselves. For people nowadays, the forms of the Art of the past are too placid, they do not excite their deadened nerves to the point of vibration. They need something that will rapidly and powerfully shock their blasé nervous system and act as a stimulating shower after long hours of stupefying mechanical work. This can best be seen in the theater, which, as most dependent on an audience, has most rapidly reached a point of decline from which most probably nothing can ever rescue it, despite efforts at restoring certain old forms. Irrevocably past are the times of metaphysical experiences in the theater, as was the case at the beginnings of Greek tragedy, and all attempts at extricating oneself from mindless realism by means of a "revival" of old forms are an impoverishment of what is and not the natural simplicity that was an expression of strength and spiritual equilibrium.

Today's theater cannot satisfy the average spectator; only the dying breed of theatrical gourmets appreciate the revived delicacies, whereas cabaret on the one hand and cinema on the other are taking away most of the audience from the theater. . . . Cinema can do absolutely everything that the human spirit might desire, and so if we can have such frantic action and striking images instead, isn't it well worth giving up useless chatter on the stage which nobody needs anymore anyhow; is it worth taking the trouble to produce something as infernally difficult as a truly theatrical play when confronted by such a threatening rival as the all-powerful cinema? . . .

Today, like everyone else, the painter as artist is compelled to live in the same atmosphere as other people. He is born in it, from childhood he's been exposed to all the masterpieces ancient and modern in reproductions, something which previously was quite unknown; while still a youth, he grows literally blasé about all forms, he succumbs to the general acceleration of life through the necessity of experiencing it with the frantically gesticulating people all around him, he becomes caught up in the feverish tempo of it all, even if he were to live in the country, drink milk, and read only the Bible; and his nerves are so frayed that metaphysical anxiety in his works assumes forms at the sight of which the general public . . . without understanding their profound substance, roars with laughter and the critic talks about the decline of art. . . . Such an artist either dies of hunger, embittered by the world's failure to understand his tragedy, or one or more gentlemen appear to take him on as an enterprise and launch his career . . . and make a pile of money out of him; and then the same critic who previously had virtually wiped the floor with him . . . now will write about him with wild enthusiasm, while the artist himself, after having created his own style at the age of twenty-eight, will long since have been in the cemetery for suicides or in the hospital poisoned by some drug, or calmed down in a straitjacket on a bed, or, what is still worse, alive and well, but imitating himself in ever-cheaper editions for business purposes. . . . Nowadays painting is teeming with hyenas and clowns, and it is often very hard at first sight to distinguish between clever *saltimbanques* and the true geniuses of our rabid, insatiable form. . . .

We do not maintain, however, that to be a genius one has to drink oneself to death, be a morphine addict, a sexual degenerate, or a simple madman without the aid of any artificial stimulants. But it is frightful that in fact whatever great occurs in art in our agreeable epoch happens almost always on the very edge of madness. . . .

In our opinion, true artists — that is, those who would be absolutely incapable of living without creating, as opposed to other adventurers who make peace with themselves in a more compromising fashion — will be kept in special institutions for the incurably sick and, as vestigial specimens of former humanity, will be the subject of research by trained psychiatrists. Museums will be opened for the infrequent visitor, as well as specialists in the special branch of history: the history of art — specialists like those in Egyptology or Assyriology or other scholarly studies of extinct races: for the race of artists will die out, just as the ancient races have died out.

Translated by Daniel Gerould

SECOND RESPONSE
TO THE REVIEWERS OF *THE PRAGMATISTS*

1922

It is more difficult to prove something than to be ironical, although injecting a certain amount of vitriol into one's arguments is perhaps the best way of carrying on a discussion. . . .

In a work of art the important thing is the proportion of real-life and formal elements, and not the systematic elimination of the former for the sake of the latter. There is no denying that the judgments we make in evaluating these proportions will, within certain limits, be subjective. . . .

I have no wish to deprive words of their meaning, nor actions of theirs. Both these composite elements have a basic sensory and signifying component: the articulated sound and the conceptual significance of the word, and the visual image and the significance of the action. The novelty of my theory lies in treating the signifying components of words and actions as artistic elements, i.e., as elements capable of creating formal constructions, acting directly, as though they were simple elements, qualities, and their complexes. . . .

In general, I am pleased with the variety of opinion about my work. For some I am a "nihilistic bourgeois," for others (the critic Stanisław Pieńkowski) a kind of Bolshevik agitator. Quite a wide range of options! For some my art is "religious" (the director Wilam Horzyca interpreted my theory as an attempt to return to the mysteries), for still others it is absolute, even deliberate nonsense. We shall see how the future will judge. The one thing I could ask for is an understanding of my theory before criticizing it. Perhaps that will come with time. As of now I have lost faith in the value of carrying on any further polemics. I not only have not found any followers, but I cannot even discover a worthy opponent. My plays will certainly not be staged for a long time (and perhaps never).

Still, if any theater does decide on staging any of my plays, I would like to ask the director and actors for (a) as unemotional, straightforward, articulate delivery of the lines as possible, (b) as *mad* a pace of performance as possible, consistent with the adherence to the preceding condition, (c) as strict an observance as possible of my "directorial" indications as to the placing of the characters, as well as about the settings according to my descriptions of them, (d) no attempts to make anything *stranger* than it already is in the text by means of setting-atmosphere-hit-them-in-the-guts gimmicks and an abnormal method of delivering the lines, (e) minimal cuts. . . .

As a formal construction, Pure Form acts directly, calling forth in us — at the moment when the plurality of elements is integrated into a unity — heightened "metaphysical feeling," or in other words it brings out the quality of unity per se against a "confused background," the unity of our individuality. That is why I have defined a work of Art as a kind of narcotic. Just as the visions are not contained in a dose of hashish preserves but rather are produced under its influence, so "metaphysical feeling" is not contained in the signification of the content of a work of art in Pure Form, which produces an immediate effect. The signifying content is given indirectly in signs — it is rendered intelligible in the context of the permanent associations of the sign with the signifying complex. The formal content of a work of Art (to the extent that we can so characterize a formal idea, given the actual unity of the plurality of elements), is directly given *without any symbolic function of the particular elements.*

Translated by Daniel Gerould

LETTER TO BRONISŁAW MALINOWSKI

MAY 11, 1929

Dear Malinowski:

How can I explain the total lack of your letters and your not coming to see me the last time you were in Zakopane, when you spent time with that bloody and damned Chwistek and called me a Don Juan (as he told me with pleasure). Write at once or "taste not the Pierian Spring."

Yours Truly
Witkacy

Rules of the S. I. Witkiewicz Portrait-Painting Firm

1928

Motto:
The customer must be satisfied.
Misunderstandings are ruled out.

The rules are published so as to spare the firm the necessity of repeating the same thing over and over again.

1. The firm produces portraits of the following types:
    1. Type A — Comparatively speaking, the most as it were, "spruced up" type. Suitable rather for women's faces than for men's. "Slick" execution, with a certain loss of character in the interests of beautification, or accentuation of "prettiness."
    2. Type B — More emphasis on character but without any trace of caricature. Work making greater use of sharp line than type A, with a certain touch of character traits, which does not preclude "prettiness" in women's portraits. Objective attitude to the model.
    3. Type B + s (supplement) — Intensification of character, bordering on the caricatural. The head larger than natural size. The possibility of preserving "prettiness" in women's portraits, and even of intensifying it in the direction of the "demonic."
    4. Type C, C + C_0, E, C + H, C + C_0 + E, etc. — These types, executed with the aid of C_2H_5OH and narcotics of a superior grade, are at present ruled out. Subjective characterization of the model, caricatural intensification both formal and psychological are not ruled out. Approaches abstract composition, otherwise known as "Pure Form."

5. Type D — The same results without recourse to any artificial means.
6. Type E — Combinations of D with the preceding types.
   Spontaneous psychological interpretation at the discretion of the firm. The effect achieved may be the exact equivalent of that produced by types A and B — the manner by which it is attained is different, as is the method of execution, which may take various forms but never exceeds the limit(s). A combination of E + s is likewise available upon request.

   Type E is not always possible to execute.
7. Children's type — (B + E) — Because children can never sit still, the purer type B is in most instances impossible — the execution rather takes the form of a sketch.

   In general, the firm does not pay much attention to the rendering of clothing and accessories. The question of the background concerns only the firm — demands in this regard are not considered. Depending on the disposition of the firm and the difficulties of rendering a particular face, the portrait may be executed in one, two, three, and even up to five sittings. For large portraits showing the upper body or full figure, the number of sittings may even reach twenty.

   The number of sittings does not determine the excellence of the product.
2. The basic novelty offered by the firm as compared to the usual practice is the customer's option of rejecting a portrait if it does not suit him either because of the execution or because of the degree of likeness. *In such cases the customer pays one-third of the price, and the portrait becomes the property of the firm.* The customer does not have the right to demand that the portrait be destroyed. This clause, naturally, applies only to the pure types: A, B, and E, *without supplement(s)* — that is, without any supplement of exaggerated characteristics, or in other words the types that appear in series. This clause was introduced because it is impossible to tell what will satisfy the client. An exact agreement is desirable, based upon a firm and definite decision by the model as to the type requested. An album of samples (but by no means ones "of no value") is available for inspection at the premises of the firm. The customer receives a guarantee in that the firm in

its own self-interest does not issue works that could damage its trademark. A situation could occur in which the firm itself would not sign its own product.

3. Any sort of criticism on the part of the customer is absolutely ruled out. The customer may not like the portrait, but the firm cannot permit even the most discreet comments without giving its special authorization. If the firm had allowed itself the luxury of listening to customers' opinions, it would have gone mad a long time ago. *We place special emphasis on this rule, since the most difficult thing is to restrain the customer from making remarks that are entirely uncalled-for.* The portrait is either accepted or rejected — yes or no, without any explanations whatsoever as to why. Inadmissible criticism likewise includes remarks about whether or not it is a good likeness, observations concerning the background, covering part of the face in the portrait with one's hand so as to imply that this part really isn't the way it should be, comments such as, "I am too pretty," "Do I look that sad?" "That's not me," and all other opinions of that sort, whether favorable or unfavorable. After due consideration, and possibly consultation with third parties, the customer says yes (or no) and that's all there is to it — then he goes (or does not go) up to what is called the "cashier's window," that is, he simply hands over the agreed-upon sum to the firm. Given the incredible difficulty of the profession, the firm's nerves must be spared.

4. Asking the firm for its opinion of a finished portrait is not permissible, nor is any discussion about a work in progress.

5. The firm reserves the right to paint without any witnesses, if that is possible.

6. Portraits of women with bare necks and shoulders cost one-third more. Each arm costs one-third of the total price. For portraits showing the upper body or full-figure, special agreements must be drawn up.

7. The portrait may not be viewed until finished.

8. The technique used is a combination of charcoal, crayon, pencil, and pastel. All remarks with regard to technical matters are ruled out, as are likewise demands for alterations.

9. The firm undertakes the painting of portraits outside the firm's premises only in exceptional circumstances (sickness, advanced age, etc.), in which case the firm must be guaranteed a secret receptacle in which the unfinished portrait may be kept under lock and key.

10. Customers are obliged to appear punctually for the sittings, since waiting has a bad effect on the firm's mood and may have an adverse effect on the execution of the product.

11. The firm offers advice on the framing and packing of portraits but does not provide these services. Further discussion about types of frames is ruled out.

12. The firm allows total freedom as to the model's clothing and *quite definitely does not voice any opinion in this regard.*

13. The firm urges a careful perusal of the rules. Lacking any powers of enforcement, the firm counts on the tact and good will of its customers to meet the terms. Reading through and concurring with the rules is taken as equivalent to *concluding an agreement.* Discussion about the rules is inadmissible.

14. An agreement on the installment plan or by bank draft is not ruled out. Given the low prices the firm charges, requests for reductions are not advisable. Before the portrait is begun, the customer pays one-third of the prices as a down payment.

15. A customer who obtains portrait commissions for the firm — that is to say, who acts as "an agent of the firm" — upon providing orders for the sum of 100 złotys receives as a premium his own portrait or that of any person he wishes in the type of his choice.

16. Notices sent by the firm to former customers announcing its presence at a given location are not intended to force them to have new portraits painted, but rather to assist friends of these customers in placing orders, since having seen the firm's work they may wish something similar themselves.

Warsaw, 1928
The "S. I. Witkiewicz" Firm

Price List

Type A = 350	Type C = without price
Type B = 250	Type D = 100
Type B + s = 150	Children's type = 150–250
Type E = 150–250	

Translated by Daniel Gerould

Tadeusz Peiper

(1891–1969)

A tragic and interesting figure of the avant-garde movement, Tadeusz Peiper spent several years in Spain as a young man. After his return to Poland, he created a legend (perhaps based on fact) of a lost suitcase that was supposed to contain manuscripts that would revolutionize Polish poetry. During World War II, Peiper was arrested in the Soviet Union, later released and eventually allowed to return to Poland. His literary activity was gradually paralyzed by mental malady; in the final years of his life, poor and derelict, he would be seen in the streets of Warsaw carrying with him barely readable manuscripts of his diary.

Peiper is remembered for his vigorous writings from the twenties and thirties. His position was close to futurism, though much more rationalistic and constructive. His programmatic essays have had the charm of a great architect's vision and have remained more accessible than many of his poems. Even so, Peiper's poetry—marred by his dry approach to the metaphor that he saw as a "pseudonym"—has moments of beauty, and his idea of a "blossoming poem" has been an inspiration for younger poets.

That

1972

That, that worlds inside my walls, that worlds will shriek inside
  my walls,
worlds of cities, of cities like a sea, a sea not of people but of stars,
a sea of song, a song straining the sky, straining it on syllables of
  pride,

through lights new as the springtime lit up by fashion,
and that I don't see the hands to which I opened my doors
and that I don't see the minds into which I lay my worlds
and that, and that, that I am not amongst you.

I adored paths by which a mist of gold enters the city amid
  tarnished rainbows,
I adored days so close that if they had no dusk, she would have no
  tomorrow,

I adored sated evenings, robust nights, and love which doesn't
  poison you,
I adored pages of unknown beauty
held in hands, shocking young eyes,
I adored the propellers of questions and short answers born on
  the go,
I adored the holy infantophagy of the spirit:
mouthfuls of matter created by man, fruit and food of the spirit,
I adored every creature with which the world is enriched, not
  cluttered,
I adored every greatness unfolding in a yawning lap,
I adored, adored, it didn't change a thing.
The walls remained firm, so the fruits rot.

But, after all, I spoke so clearly that every pear could catch flame!
my sentences, which sometimes were as crooked as a carpenter's
  thumbs,

since, when I crookedly seized the tree of matter, fruits, branches,
    and leaves found their way into my sentences too,
and every stump, touched by me, said as much as it meant.
But for you my act crumbled, like a nut crushed too hard,
but know: the faults in my work are most fragile
when they originate with you.
Your sky, not mine, shrouds me in dread.
To believe in my words, it's enough for me to look at the clock,
to think, enough to defend myself,
    but to act, I need cities in which a spark feeds on the fat of praise,
and where there are those who would dream what I dream like me.

So I regret
that I don't see the minds for whom I opened a door
and that I don't see the hands in which I lay my worlds
and that, and that, that from my dreams I won't make our dreams,
I, I the mayor, I the mayor of homeless dreams.

Translated by Alissa Valles

Bruno Schulz

(1892–1942)

Born in Drohobycz, a town not far from Lvov, a place that had its moment of economic boom (with petrol) but then slumbered in the reminiscences of past glory, Bruno Schulz made his living as a modest art teacher at a local high school. The publication of his prose made him well known, however, and he suddenly found himself among the elite of Polish writers. He traveled to Warsaw and attracted many admirers—some of whom would later become apostles of his work (Jerzy Ficowski, for instance, would become the future editor of Schulz's letters and a great connoisseur of his oeuvre).

The fantastic world of Schulz's prose, his lush poetic language, the slowness and improbability of his narration, set him radically apart from other fiction writers. His is the narration of a poet, of a painter (or draftsman) who is more interested in the act of displaying his unique props than in efficient storytelling. His writing polarizes readers; you can only worship or reject him—no leafing through his books is possible.

His tragic death in the Drohobycz ghetto—he was Jewish—at the hand of an SS man occurred apparently on the eve of Schulz's planned escape. This death was turned into a spiritual victory by those who spent their lives saving Schulz's work from oblivion. One of the most relevant programmatic texts written by Schulz was a result of a half-humorous, half-serious exchange of letters with Witold Gombrowicz. In this chapter we include both Gombrowicz's provocative note and Schulz's response.

An Essay for S. I. Witkiewicz

1935

The beginnings of my graphic work are lost in mythological twilight. Before I could even talk, I was already covering every scrap of paper and the margins of newspapers with scribbles that attracted the attention of those around me. At first they were all horses and wagons. The action of riding in a wagon seemed to me full of weight and arcane symbolism. From age six or seven there appeared and reappeared in my drawings the image of a cab, with a hood on top and lanterns blazing, emerging from a nocturnal forest. That image belongs to the basic material of my imagination; it is a kind of node to many receding series. To this day I have not exhausted its metaphysical content. To this day the sight of a carriage horse has lost none of its fascination and troubling power. Its schizoid anatomy, sprouting antlers, whorls, knotholes, outcroppings at every extremity, was arrested in its development, as it were, at a time when it still wanted to reproduce and branch into other forms. And the wagon is a schizoid structure, too, derived from the same anatomical principle — multiarticulated, fantastic, made up of sheet metal warped into flipper shapes, of horse hides and huge clattering wheels.

I don't know how we manage to acquire certain images in childhood that carry decisive meanings for us. They function like those threads in the solution around which the significance of the world crystallizes for us. Another of those images for me is that of a child carried by its father through the spaces of an overwhelming night, conducting a conversation with the darkness. The father caresses the child, folds him in his arms, shields him from the natural element that chatters on and on, but to the child these arms are transparent; the night cuts straight through them, and over the father's soothing words he hears its sinister blandishments without interruption. And oppressed, full of fatalism, he answers the night's importunities with tragic readiness, wholly surrendered to the mighty element from which there is no escape.

There are texts that are marked out, made ready for us somehow, lying in wait for us at the very entrance to life. This is how I absorbed Goethe's ballad, with all its metaphysics, at age eight. Through the half-understood German I caught, or divined, the meaning, and cried, shaken to the bottom of my soul, when my mother read it to me.

Such images amount to an agenda, establish an iron capital of the spirit, proffered to us very early in the form of forebodings and half-conscious experiences. It seems to me that all the rest of one's life is spent interpreting these insights, breaking them down to the last fragment of meaning we can master, testing them against the broadest intellectual spectrum we can manage. These early images mark out to artists the boundaries of their creative powers. The works they create represent drafts on existing balances. They do not discover anything new after that, they only learn how to understand better and better the secret entrusted to them at the outset; their creative effort goes into an unending exegesis, a commentary on that one couplet of poetry assigned to them. Art, for that matter, does not resolve that secret completely. The secret stays in a tangle. The knot the soul got itself tied up in is not a false one that comes undone when you pull the ends. On the contrary, it draws tighter. We handle it, trace the path of the separate threads, look for the end of the string, and out of these manipulations comes art.

If I am asked whether the same thread recurs in my drawings as in my prose, I would answer in the affirmative. The reality is the same; only the frames are different. Here material and technique operate as the criterion of selection. A drawing sets narrower limits by its material than prose does. That is why I feel I have expressed myself more fully in my writing.

The question of whether I'd be able to interpret the reality of *Cinnamon Shops* in philosophical terms is one I would much rather avoid. It is my opinion that rationalizing one's awareness of what inheres in a work of art is like unmasking actors, means the end of enjoyment and impoverishes the problems inherent in the work. The reason is not that art is a crossword puzzle with the key hidden, and philosophy the same crossword puzzle solved. The difference lies deeper than that. In a work of art the umbilical cord linking it with the totality of our concerns has not yet been severed, the blood of the mystery still circulates; the ends of the blood vessels vanish into the surrounding night and return from it full of dark fluid. A philosophical interpretation only gives us an anatomical sample dissected from the total body of the problems involved in the work. Just the same, I am curious how the philosophical credo of *Cinnamon Shops* would sound in the form of discourse. It would have to be an attempt to describe the reality given there rather than a justification of it.

Cinnamon Shops offers a certain recipe for reality, posits a certain special kind of substance. The substance of that reality exists in a state of constant fermentation, germination, hidden life. It contains no dead, hard, limited objects. Everything diffuses beyond its borders, remains in a given shape only momentarily, leaving this shape behind at the first opportunity. A principle of sorts appears in the habits, the modes of existence of this reality: universal masquerade. Reality takes on certain shapes merely for the sake of appearance, as a joke or form of play. One person is a human, another is a cockroach, but shape does not penetrate essence, is only a role adopted for the moment, an outer skin soon to be shed. A certain extreme monism of the life substance is assumed here, for which specific objects are nothing more than masks. The life of the substance consists in the assuming and consuming of numberless masks. This migration of forms is the essence of life. Thus an all-pervading aura of irony emanates from this substance. There is an ever-present atmosphere of the stage, of sets viewed from behind, where the actors make fun of the pathos of their parts after stripping off their costumes. The bare fact of separate individual existences holds an irony, a hoax, a clown's stuck-out tongue. (Here, it seems to me, we have a point of contact between *Cinnamon Shops* and the world of your paintings and plays.)

What the meaning of this universal disillusioning reality is I am not able to say. I maintain only that it would be unbearable unless it was compensated for in some other dimension. In some sense we derive a profound satisfaction from the loosening of the web of reality; we feel an interest in witnessing the bankruptcy of reality.

There has been talk about the book's destructive tendency. From the viewpoint of certain established values, this may be true. But the work operates at a premoral depth, at a point where value is still *in statu nascendi*.

As a spontaneous utterance of life, a work of art poses tasks for ethics, not the reverse. If art were merely to confirm what had already been established elsewhere, it would be superfluous. The role of art is to be a probe sunk into the nameless. The artist is an apparatus for registering processes in that deep stratum where value is formed. Destructive? But the fact that these contents express themselves as a work of art means that we affirm them, that our deep perception has spontaneously declared in their favor.

To what genre does *Cinnamon Shops* belong? How should it be classified? I think of it as an autobiographical narrative. Not only because it is written in the first person and because certain events and experiences from the author's childhood can be discerned in it. The work is an autobiography, or rather a spiritual genealogy, a genealogy *par excellence* in that it follows the spiritual family tree down to those depths where it merges into mythology, to be lost in the mutterings of mythological delirium. I have always felt that the roots of the individual spirit, traced far enough down, would be lost in some matrix of myth. This is the ultimate depth; it is impossible to reach farther down.

I later found an imposing artistic realization of this idea in Thomas Mann's *Joseph and His Brothers,* where it is carried out on a monumental scale. Mann shows that beneath all human events, when the chaff of time and individual variation is blown away, certain primeval patterns, "stories," are found, by which these events form and re-form in great repeating pulses. For Mann, these are the Biblical tales, the timeless myths of Babylon and Egypt. On my more modest scale I have attempted to uncover my own private mythology, my own "stories," my own mythic family tree. Just as the ancients traced their ancestry from mythical unions with gods, so I undertook to establish for myself some mythical generation of forebears, a fictitious family from which I trace my true descent.

In a way these "stories" are real, represent my way of living, my personal fate. The overriding motif of this fate is profound loneliness, isolation from the stuff of daily life.

Loneliness is the catalyst that makes reality ferment, precipitates its surface layer of figures and colors.

Translated by Walter Arndt and Victoria Nelson

THE MYTHOLOGIZING OF REALITY

1936

The essence of reality is Meaning or Sense. What lacks Sense is, for us, not reality. Every fragment of reality lives by virtue of partaking in a universal Sense. The old cosmogonists expressed this by the statement, "In the Beginning was the Word." The nameless does not exist for us. To name something means to include it in some universal Sense. The isolated word as a mosaic piece is a late product, an early result of technology. The primeval word was a shimmering aura circling around the sense of the world, was a great universal whole. The word in its common usage today is only a fragment, remnant of some former all-embracing, integral mythology. That is why it possesses a tendency to grow back, to regenerate and complete itself in full meaning. The life of the word consists in tensing and stretching itself toward a thousand connections, like the cut-up snake in the legend whose pieces search for each other in the dark. This thousand-formed but integral organism of the word was torn apart into syllables, sounds, everyday speech; and in these new forms, adapted to practical needs, it was handed down to us as a handy code of communication. In this way the life of the word, its development, was shunted onto a new track, the track of mundane life, and subjected to new rules of order. But if for some cause the restrictions of pragmatic reality loosen their grip, if the word, released from its restraint, is left to itself and restored to its own laws, then a regression, a reversal of current, occurs; the word strives for is former connections, wants to complete itself with Sense. And this striving of the word toward its matrix, its yearning for the primeval home of words, we call poetry.

Poetry happens when short-circuits of sense occur between words, a sudden regeneration of the primeval myths.

As we manipulate everyday words, we forget that they are fragments of lost but eternal stories, that we are building our houses with broken pieces

of sculptures and ruined statues of gods as the barbarians did. Even the
soberest of our notions and categories are remote derivatives of myths and
ancient oral epics. Not one scrap of an idea of ours does not originate in
myth, isn't transformed, mutilated, denatured mythology. The most fundamental function of the spirit is inventing fables, creating tales. The driving
force of human knowledge is the conviction that at the end of its
researches the sense of the world, the meaning of life, will be found. It
seeks out sense at the very top of its scaffoldings and artificial stackings of
level upon level. Yet the building materials it uses were used once before;
they come from forgotten, fragmented tales or "histories." Poetry recognizes these lost meanings, restores words to their places, connects them by
the old semantics. In the poet's mind, the word remembers, so to speak, its
essential meaning, blossoms, unfolds spontaneously according to its own
inner laws, regains its wholeness. Thus all poetry is mythologizing and
strives to restore myths to the world. The mythologizing of the world is not
over yet; the process was only halted by the development of knowledge, *sci-
entia,* diverted into a side channel where it courses on without understanding its identity. But science, too, only fabricates its own world myth because
myth is embodied in the very elements themselves, and there is no way of
going beyond myth. Poetry reaches the meaning of the world intuitively,
deductively, with large, daring shortcuts and approximations. Knowledge
seeks the same meaning inductively, methodically, taking into account all
the materials of experience. Fundamentally, one and the other are bound
for the same goal.

The human spirit is indefatigable in supplying glosses to life by means of
myths, in "making sense" of reality. The word itself, left to its own devices,
gravitates toward sense.

Sense is the element that involves mankind in the process of realization.
It is an absolute given that cannot be derived from other givens. Therefore
what makes sense to us cannot be defined. The process of imparting meaning to the world is closely bound up with the word. Language is man's metaphysical organ. Nonetheless, in the course of time the word becomes static
and rigid, stops being the conductor of new meanings. The poet restores
conductivity to words by new quasi-electric tensions that are produced by an

accumulation of charges. Mathematical symbols are the extensions of the word into new realms. The image, too, derives from the primal word, the word that was not yet a sign but myth, story, sense.

We usually regard the word as the shadow of reality, its symbol. The reverse of this statement would be more correct: reality is the shadow of the word. Philosophy is actually philology, the deep, creative exploration of the word.

Translated by Walter Arndt and Victoria Nelson

CORRESPONDENCE WITH WITOLD GOMBROWICZ

JULY 1936

Open Letter to Bruno Schulz

My good Bruno,

Bogusław would like us to write for him in *Studio*; wouldn't it be better to write in *Studio* for oneself — or still better, to write each other? — yes, writing letters back and forth is really the most pleasant, but how much more enticing still to take aim at a concrete person than to shoot off into empty space a bulletin that is addressed to everyone and therefore to no one. For a long time I've racked my brains over what kind of thought I could fire off to you, dear Bruno, but absolutely nothing occurred to me until yesterday [when] I bumped into the opinion of a certain doctor's wife whom I once met by accident on Line 18. Bruno Schulz, she said, he's either a sick pervert or a poseur, but most probably a poseur. He's only pretending. — She said this and got off, for the streetcar had just stopped at Wilcza Street.

Thus I shoot you with this woman's opinion; I hereby inform your personage publicly and formally that this doctor's wife regards you as a madman or a poseur. And I challenge you to take your stand against this woman. So: a specialist's better half, whose opinion you already know, lives in Wilcza Street. There, in Wilcza Street, she lives and has a negative opinion; there, she circulates it to chance acquaintances who take her at her

word. There, Bruno, at 102 Wilcza Street, this unpleasant opinion grows
and prospers, the unfavorable view of a member of a vast social and cultural milieu who is very decided in her notions. What are you going to do
with her opinion? Will you, following the example of the overwhelming
majority of your literary colleagues, assume a pretentious attitude, that is,
an attitude full of demands and complaints against the general public
because of its lack of understanding and too-low level? No, Bruno, not for
a minute did I suspect of you the shamelessness and banality of a com-
monplace reaction by a hack whose sacred reputation has been injured.
And neither do I believe that you will blush naively and cry, as happened
in France to one of our most popular female writers when she was told that
Polish literature was rather lowbrow. . . . Or perhaps, indulging in your
masochistic tendencies, you will humiliate yourself and fall at the dainty
toes of the satisfied doctor's wife. That way you would at least be able to
enjoy the female and, against her will, get some sensual pleasure out of her.
Hey, Bruno, I join you officially and formally in holy matrimony with the
verdict of this woman, I deliver her verdict on you, I load it on your shoulders and buckle you up with it, I ram into the consciousness of Bruno
Schulz the verdict of a woman, marry this man with a spouse through the
legal bond of her verdict. What will this Bruno Schulz of yours do, then,
in such a situation — this very Schulz whom you write books to and who
must represent you, how will you wind up your Schulz and put him in position facing this person? My God, I have no desire to give form to my
thoughts, it's hot, the devil composed this letter; if Bogusław hadn't gotten
sick, then we wouldn't have to do it. But consider: the cruelty of a thing
lies in the fact that all objective arguments serve scarcely any purpose.
How, in effect, is one supposed to argue to a woman met by accident that
one is neither crazy nor a poseur! Here it is a question not of content but
rather form. Before the tribunal, which is composed of some accidental
readers of *Studio,* I challenge you to a formal fight with a woman who is,
like the others, also accidental. The tribunal will not concern itself with
your argument; for that we have neither time nor common, generally rec-
ognized criteria. There are too many of our own matters to be carefully
dealt with for us to deal with other matters as well. We will simply have a
look and determine if that Schulz who was taken by surprise on a flat road

by a silly run-in with a woman is capable of preserving good, sovereign form or if he, to our malicious pleasure, is compromised. And remember that your attitude must not only be subjectively right but, worse, must have the appearance of correctness for people who observe from the outside. If, for example, you explain that the opinion of the doctor's wife didn't faze you at all, we will not believe you, for on what basis are you supposed to be less touchy than we are? The tribunal that must pass judgment on you will judge you according to its own standards.

With complete premeditation I present you and no one else with just this question. Your philosophical, artistic, and poetic style does not predestine you to a squabble with mothers of doctors' children. Your form is manifested *in excelsis*! Get back down here on earth! Dance with an ordinary woman! Show how you defend yourself against a chance encounter! Show what style you use to destroy her or lift yourself above her or keep your distance; show us this expression on your face, give us one look at it, how gentle Bruno shakes off the opinion of the doctor's wife from Line 18. What good would your form be if it were only being put into use at two thousand meters above the level of life? One must play the game with people on every level and in every possible situation. Our attitude toward matters of stupidity is perhaps even more important than our attitude toward the great, wise, principal problems.

That damned Bogusław! Good-bye, Bruno.

With deepest respect,
Witold Gombrowicz

Open Letter to Witold Gombrowicz

To Witold Gombrowicz

You'd like to lure me into an arena, dear Witold, beset on all sides by the curiosity of the mob, you would like to see me as the enraged bull in pursuit of the doctor's wife's fluttering banner; her flimsy amaranthine peignoir is supposed to serve as your cape, behind which the thrusts of your sword await me.

It would have taken a more provocative color, dear fellow, an arrow with more poison on it, and a poison that works more fatally than the spit of the doctor's wife from Wilcza Street. You would have had to launch a much cleverer doctor's wife at me, a more seductive woman, one it would be worth taking on one's horns. You somewhat overestimate my sensitivity, trying to foist this rag-stuffed puppet on me. Scarred old bull that I am, with the best of will I can't do more than lower my head and glare with threatening bloodshot eyes around the picador's lances you have stuck me full of. Alas, I lack the noble fire and that blind tempestuous fury that might have plunged me forward, as you planned, into a magnificent assault. And you had staked out the territory for me ahead of time, closed and barred the side exits in order to get me smack in the middle of the arena. You spoiled the contest for me from the start, you handpicked the audience, fine-tuned the acoustics of the place, laid out in detail what was expected of me. But what would have happened if I had turned out to be an unconventional bull, a bull without honor or ambition in his breast, if I had spurned the audience's impatience, turned my back on the doctor's wife from Wilcza Street you are pushing me on and, tail up for battle, made a rush at you instead? Not to bump you off your feet, O noble toreador, but to take you on my back if this is not megalomania — and carry you out of the arena, beyond the confines of its rules and statutes.

Because, to put it plainly, I don't believe in the sacred code of arenas and forums, I despise and deprecate it whereas you, who are dazzled by it, have filled it margins with brilliant glosses full of mockery — truly a strange form of worship, that manages to leap on top of its idol with somersaults of irony!

You'll agree, then, dear Witold, to call off this curious tauromachy, leave the ripped-up puppet lying on the sand and, with the mutters of the disappointed crowd rising behind us, walk side by side at an easy gait, bull and toreador, to the exit, freedom, absorbed in intimate conversation even before we leave behind the outer circle of the arena.

Really, what kind of paradox is this? You a defender of the public arena and its massive acoustics! What, after all, are the acoustics of forums and arenas, what truths and arguments find expression there, and what gives them such an irresistible appeal to our hearts and convictions? What part of our essential selves hurries to meet them, full of affirmation and nodding approval, against our better judgment? Do you admire and cherish that popular joke, the joke with crowd appeal, the joke that hits the enemy from behind his reasons and arguments, sentencing him to mockery, knocking the weapon out of his hand without any crossing of swords on its merits? Are you reduced by directness of effect, the immediate irrational solidarity of all doctors' wives from Wilcza Street, the applause of all those people who are ordinary, flesh-bound, and mediocre? What's more, aren't you able to sense, aren't you astonished at this involuntary sympathy and solidarity with what at bottom is alien and hostile to you growing out of the depths of your being? Let me tell you, then, that what appears to you as some sort of malign force transcending the individual is only a weakness of your own nature. It is the mob within us that applauds, dear Witold; the mob deeply rooted inside, casting spells, gives off its collective grunt, smothers our better knowledge and causes our hands to life convulsively with blind acclamation. These are reflex motions of the herd that dim our clear judgment, introduce archaic and barbaric modes of reasoning, open the arsenal of an atavistic and discarded logic. This kind of joke appeals to the mob in you, at this signal a dark, inarticulate mob rises up in you, like a bear trained to the sound of a gypsy's flute.

The doctor's wife from Wilcza Street! Did you mean to upset my plans, confuse my feelings, confront me with a representative of a consolidated tight, powerful guild and lay out the grid for our contest right next to the well-marked battlefront of sex? Did you plot, in your craftiness, to lure me into that marshy border region you know so well, where the compass needle of our feelings begins to whirl, where the magnetic poles of moral values switch charges in a strange ambivalence, and hate and love alike lose their clarity in a great general confusion? Oh no, dear Witold, I have liberated myself from this sort of thing; I've learned by this time how to counteract this great confusion, to separate and seal off what is alien to me. Certainly, I appreciate and admit with all my heart that the doctor's wife has beautiful thighs, but I put this matter in its own place. I can ensure that my worship of the doctor's wife's legs does not filter down into a totally inappropriate area. And the steadfastness of this worship does not prevent me from nourishing a sincere contempt, on the intellectual level, for her philistine dullness, her prefabricated thinking, her entirely alien and hostile mentality. Of course — I confess it frankly — I hate the doctor's wife from

Wilcza Street, a creature leached void of any substance, the pure distillate of a doctor's wife, the textbook case of a doctor's wife or simply of a wife . . . though on an altogether different plane I find it difficult to resist the charm of her legs.

Granted, this iridescent ambivalence, this Januslike duality of my nature, which changes depending on whether I happen to consider the doctor's wife as the owner of her legs or of her intellect, is a puzzling phenomenon that gives cause for reflection, provokes philosophical generalizations and metaphysical perspectives. It seems to me that here we may have caught redhanded one of the basic antinomies of the human soul, as if we had struck a quivering metaphysical nerve.

I am not in favor of easy simplifications, but until psychology can shed more light on these matters I propose we accept, as a provisional hypothesis, that our sexuality together with its whole ideological aura belongs to another era of development than our intellectuality. I generally think that the organization of our psyche is not uniform at all in the matter of the developmental levels of different spheres, and that its antinomies and contradictions may be explained by the coexistence and overlap of many simultaneous systems. Here is the source of the confusing, multitrack nature of our thinking.

I have deliberately descended into the realm of sexuality because under the pressure of everyday life we have long been accustomed to keeping its transactions under separate accounts. But at this spot the multilayered structure of our psyche is quite evident. It becomes less evident in the realm of general moral, biological, and social value formation, and here I encroach on your highly personal domain. I recognize your peculiar irritability regarding this topic, your frankly pathological (and therefore creative) anxiety. This is a sore point where your hypersensitivity reaches it's peak, it is your Achilles heel that itches and rankles you as if some new organ wanted to sprout from it, a kind of new hand more prehensile than the other two. Let us try to confine and isolate this especially painful and sensitive place, locate it with surgical precision, even if it is metastasizing and starts spreading in all directions. I have the impression you are troubled and disoriented by the existence of some unwritten code of values, some anonymous Mafia, something evading the control of *consensus omnium*. Behind the official values that we sanction and profess lies hidden some unofficial but powerful conspiracy, an elusive underworld system — cynical and amoral, irrational and mocking. That system (for it does absolutely possess the features of a consistent system) lends its sanction to the untruths of a perverse woman, sets up paradoxical hierarchies, gives shattering force to a shallow joke, gathers us up against our will or wisdom under the power of a collective guffaw. This intangible system that cannot be localized anywhere, that slips between the cells, as it were, of our value judgments, evades responsibility and eludes every attempt to capture it or pin it down. Anything but solemn or serious this unsolemn and unserious system kills with the powerful weapon of ridicule; it is indeed a peculiar and troubling phenomenon. I don't know if anyone is free from its fascination.

I consider it a great service that you were the first to direct our thoughts and feelings to these matters. If I am not mistaken, you were the first to succeed in smoking out the dragon from it myriad hiding places and bringing him within arm's length. I'd like to crown you ahead of time with the laurels of the dragon's future slayer, for I consider that anonymous system as something evil that must be overcome. That is why I worry about your all too protracted collusion with it, your long-winded whispers and shady dealings, your whole two-faced muddled policy. For heaven's sake, come to your senses! Shake off this blindness! Understand finally where the enemy is and where the friend! You, predestined dragonslayer, armed by nature with formidable instruments of murder, you with your fine sense of smell that tracks the enemy to its deepest hiding place — lay hold of him by his lying tongue, twist it in his maw with two snaps of the teeth, seize, choke, tear out his throat!

No, really, Witold, I believe you. You are only charming him with a magician's sleight-of-hand, fumigating him with the incense of praises, hypnotizing and immobilizing him in the pose of timeless idol you impute to him. Oh, well, I will second you in this. Let us enthrone the doctor's wife from Wilcza Street, hosanna, hosanna, let us prostrate ourselves before her. Let her sprawl, push out her white belly, swell up with pride — the doctor's wife from Wilcza Street, the timeless idol, object of all our yearnings, hosanna, hosanna, hosanna. . . .

While she sits there all carried away, overflowing her banks, with sky-blue eyes that flicker over us unseeing, let us analyze her face, test her expression, sink a prove to the bottom of that unfathomable visage.

You say this is the face of life? You say not only that we, the brighter and better, have the right to make fun of the doctor's wife, but also that you acknowledge her equal right to scorn, disdain, and ridicule? In that case you stand on the side of inferiority against superiority. Your try to compromise our actions by casting before our eyes the massive torso of the doctor's wife, and you identify with her thick-headed chuckles. You claim that in her person you defend vitality and biology, against abstraction, against our detachment from life. If this is biology, Witold, then you must mean the force of her immobility; if this is vitality, you must mean her heavy passive mass.

But the avant-garde of biology is thought, experiment, creative discovery. We, in fact, are this belligerent biology, this conquering biology; we are the truly vital.

Don't laugh. I know what you're thinking, what a low opinion you hold of our life. And that pains me. You compare it with the life of the doctor's wife, and that life seems real to you, more firmly rooted in the soil, whereas we, creating up in Cloud-cuckoo-land and devoted to some chimera under hundreds of atmospheric pressures of boredom, distill our products that are useful to almost no one. Boredom, Witold, blessed boredom! It is our lofty asceticism, our high breeding, that doesn't allow us to dine at the lavish banquets of life; it's the incorruptibility of our taste, pledged to new and unknown sensations.

In conclusion, permit me to tell you in a few words where I would like to see you, where I see your rightful place and proper station. You have the stuff of a great humanist. What else can your morbid sensitivity to antinomies be if not a longing for universality, for the humanization of the not yet human realm, for the expropriation of separate ideologies and their annexation to a single great unity? I don't know how you will bring it to completion, but I think that this is the positive meaning and sanction of your efforts which, until now, were no more than a routing out and forcing into the field of fire the game of that half-human preserve.

With greetings to you, I am
Yours
Bruno Schulz

Translated by Walter Arndt and Victoria Nelson

Jerzy Stempowski

(1893–1969)

Regarded by many as the most influential twentieth-century Polish essayist, Jerzy Stempowski seduces his reader through a rare combination of virtues. An erudite who seems to have read the entire Western literature in original languages, he is never academic or purely didactic in his writing. Formed by the tradition of the Enlightenment, he never succumbs to a rationalistic dryness of style. Just the opposite: he is a poet always able to elevate his discourse by a sudden turn of phrase, by a metaphor, a rare simile. He is an aesthete with strong political opinions, somebody who hates tyranny and totalitarianism but believes that a writer should be elegant even when dealing with tyrants.

Stempowski's life was cut in two by World War II, after which he became an exile in the Swiss city of Bern, which he liked and even loved. There's something touching in the modesty of his exile existence, even in the scarcity of his literary output (though balanced by his numerous letters having a rococo charm and bearing witness to Stempowski's brilliant intelligence). A highly civilized voice that could easily be drowned in the barbaric noise of the twentieth century, his work was saved by the France-based exile magazine *Kultura*. Today his work enjoys a well-deserved popularity among more sophisticated readers.

LETTER TO JÓZEF CZAPSKI

MURI/BERNE
APRIL 12, 1947

Dearest Józio,

Early this morning I received the first issue of *Kultura* and right away read your essay on Bonnard. After reading it, I would like to give you a big hug. I've never heard anything so simple and at the same time so penetrating about Bonnard. Because Switzerland draws artists and paintings with all its money, I've seen many paintings of his here in the past few years and have often wondered how to place them in the history of my time and what makes their individual, distinct charm. That is why I read your recollection with such joy. It's wonderful. It will certainly be the best thing written on him this year.

I was very struck by what you write at the end in the form of an apostrophe to your Kapist friends and in general to Polish painters. I am also continually disturbed by such thoughts. It seems to me that I could not write a single word beyond the actuality of today, even writing on pastures and mountains. I feel it as you do, though the thought means something different to me.

I would like, for example, to answer the question: In what degree were the artists of the Renaissance children of their time, dwelling in actuality? The more I call to mind their paintings in galleries, the more does their connection to their contemporaries seem roomier to me. That terrible image of Renaissance Italy that emerges from Machiavelli and Guicciardini is not to be seen in the painters. It was a time of the ruination of all law and order, the disappearance of the remainder of Christian morality. In that time the Holy Father himself could fall into the hands of a brash thug by the name of Gian Paolo Baglione, who let a Pope and thirty cardinals go just because — as Machiavelli tells the story — he was a little tyrant, deprived of greatness even in his crimes. From that time almost nothing remained in painting, perhaps apart from the tumultuous biographies of a few dozen painters.

In the art of the Baroque there are also no immediate allusions, although that art penetrated further into the heart of nations and the heart of Europe than any other.

What [Stanisław] Brzozowski says is only partly true. Writers are linked to their age by a common vocabulary and an array of concepts, by the image a given generation has of the world and of humankind, but not by events they witnessed. This distinction lies at the foundation of the division of history into political and cultural history. Artists live in the latter and are connected to it, even if they appear privately in the former.

At this point I think of the example of Virgil, who wrote virtually on the steps to the throne. There are reasons to believe that his Georgics, for example, were written on commission by the then minister of agricultural reform, with the aim of encouraging military settlers to hold on to their garden plots. At the same time, how often down the ages have the Bucolics and the Georgics not been invoked and studied, always with the aim of distancing oneself from thrones and events, in praise of life in the wilderness, in the outback, far from the insanities of those holding power. Such a reading of Virgil is not without foundation and arises from his own thought. I cite it as a proof that although Virgil personally was not able to walk away from the throne and the highest actuality, as an artist he was continually putting himself at a distance from it and passed for centuries as the paragon of such distance.

Perhaps the fact that artists take distance from the contemporary world means only that the contemporary world wasn't worth much to them.

Another side of this question occurs to me — namely, that a work of art presents a world better ordered with respect to value than the world we know from common experience. Every kind of art contains a certain kind of prescription serving to order the world with respect to value. A melodrama divides contemporaries into black and white, although experience tells us that characters are strangely mixed: Because thou art neither cold nor hot, I will spue thee out of my mouth. Comedy divides its characters according to a much more subtle borderline between what is serious and what is ridiculous, though we know: *du sublime au ridicule il n'y a qu'un pas* [it is but one step from the sublime to the ridiculous]. The process of ordering according to value itself necessarily distances the artist from his time, in which he himself is an actor full of doubt, most often precisely in the area of evaluation.

In a poem by Vladislav Felitsianovitch Khodasevitch there is this stanza:

> Later, when your muse
> is slightly disenchanting,
> praise a simple cup of tea,
> dust on a butterfly's wing.
> Write in calm and grace,
> bend the obedient word,
> bless and curse a world
> reflected on in peace.

It seems this has been the prescription of all times: curse or bless after proper reflection, in tranquility.

Those who don't create art themselves but live with it are another matter. For them art is close to actuality; they have a pressing need for it. There has been a drawing by Hogarth hanging above my bed for several months. It shows an old man with wings — evidently, before the end of the world, according to Hogarth, people learned to fly — lying on a pile of rubble and puffing out a last curl of smoke from his pipe. In the curl there is the inscription *finis*, and a white clay pipe is broken in his hand. Next to the old man a will lies, on which you can read the last words: "the rest I leave to CHAOS making him main executor; witnesses: Klotho, Lachesis, Atropos." Life's drama lies in the trash, visible are only the final words: *exeunt omnes*. All of which together is, extremely surrealistic. Every day I look at this sketch with great pleasure. If a fire broke out in my house, I would save this sketch before anything else, although its place in the history of art is known and clear to me. It's just that the events of the past years have brought me so close to this sketch that it has become my friend and companion. But to what actuality was it linked for its author? That's not entirely clear. Goya also didn't get his *Los Desastres* from nature, or the man with bowed head in jail, under whose silhouette he wrote "*mejor es morir*." Perhaps I'm wrong, but it seems to me that the artist's point of view is different from the spectator's. Because you yourself are not only an artist but also an extraordinarily receptive spectator, both points of view are joined in you and you do not make a choice between them. That doubleness creates certain complexities. Thanks to it, you are dear to me and I feel close to you. Without it, you might be like an archangel, blessing or cursing, standing on one of the earth's poles, splendid and remote.

About other matters I'll write another time. I'll only add that illnesses and the operation are behind me, I'm sprightly and dream of scribbling. I embrace you, dearest, most warmly, your sincerely devoted

Jerzy

Translated by Alissa Valles

LETTER TO CZESŁAW MIŁOSZ

NYDEGASSE 17, BERNE
JULY 7, 1960

Dearest Czesław,

Thank you very much for your letter. I read *Native Realm* with the greatest interest, not only literary but also in some sense personal interest. In your background, as you describe it, there is much that is familiar and close to me and that has a particular interest for me at the moment. To say something about that, I have to begin as usual with a brief introduction.

I've been thinking for a while now about writing a sociological essay in which I'd like to refresh certain ideas of a now forgotten Krakowian, a professor in Graz, Ludwik Gumplowicz. In Italy and Switzerland, where there exist historical stratifications in the population — some are descendents of Romans, others barbarians of various shades — a close observer can pick up several otherwise inexplicable models or "patterns of behavior," as the jargon of sociology has it. Amid general prosperity one sees, for example, people living like monks, in complete abnegation. However, the most striking difference is the one between the descendents of the original Roman population, who gave the earth's surface its visible form until now and erected innumerable buildings — and the descendents of the conquerors who drove the farmers of old from their holdings and settled in their houses, until they mucked them up so badly that they couldn't stand to live in them any longer themselves. There are excellent descriptions of these historical processes in fifth-century texts. A certain power of observation can trace the attitudes, gestures, behavior of the people now living here to one of these two types: to the original population, which created Western civilization, and to the conquerors, in whom the dream of violence had not been extinguished, who didn't feel comfortable in civilization (Freud calls it *das Unbehagen in der Kultur*, "civilization and its discontents") and who liberate themselves in acts of violence and lawlessness. In trade customs, at meetings of supervisory councils, and in hostels — everywhere one can make out these two types of behavior. After Sorel, Mussolini and Hitler tried to educate their peoples to be conquerors. The fate of those experiments differed. On Germany's terrain there was less of an older original population and it was easier to return to barbarism. In Italy the descendents of the invaders are in the minority, and even those who put on black shirts were merely skeptical opportunists. Looking at the former Fascist admirals and generals gathered together on the occasion of a certain trial, a court reporter could write: Even Mussolini himself couldn't turn these polite officials into conquerors.

In Poland there were no such lines of division. It lacked the historical conditions for the formation of this sort. The nobility did not derive from invaders and nomads but from the same settled population as the serfs. Models of behavior crystallized in a different way. Those we saw in our time did not arise along an atavistic route or a Mendelian return to elemental types; rather, they were the result of a long differentiation of groups and individualization of persons. That's why they carry so many delicate, subtle, often elusive features. Chalasinski, in his pamphlet reproaching the Polish intelligentsia for modeling themselves on the nobility, did not manage to say what constitutes the behavior of the nobility. And I won't try in this letter either.

To be brief, I will say only that your background is strikingly aristocratic and that its many features are characteristic of a significant part of the Jagiellonian borderland nobility. Your horror of nationalism, of every kind of herd activity and mentality is one such feature. A nobleman on a borderland

homestead didn't have much to pin his hopes on beyond "All together, gents";
he was alone and had to keep a clear head. The way you describe subtle intellectual experiences and processes is also aristocratic. Today's literature is
wholly egocentric, navel-gazing; writers no longer describe experiences other
than their own. But a borderland nobleman had to be able to read the
thoughts of the Belorussians, Ukrainians, Jews, Old Believers, Caraites, gyp-
sies, and so on, as well as the thoughts of governors, police superintendents,
and majors. That was his daily business, a crucial skill. You haven't lost anything of that gift of your ancestors. That trait links you to Conrad, who also
understood all island dwellers. I think of Conrad here because, like you, he
lacked another trait connected to the former — namely, the ability to negoti-
ate and mediate. He who understands everybody is made to be a negotiator
and an intermediary, an explorer of middle roads, on the condition, however,
that he also possesses a lightness and ease in contact with people, what in
French is called *entregent*. I'm sure you do not lack that gift, but you have it to
a lesser degree than your background might lead one to expect. In me, for
example, that borderland trait is more clearly present. Perhaps it matters less
to writers — like Conrad and you. It may also be that it was less developed in
the Lithuanian nobility than in the Ukrainian. The Lithuanian nobility was
more taciturn and cautious, the Ukrainian more inclined to caprice.

Native Realm is an incomparable mine of observations concerning the
aristocratic background. It strikes me that in recent years you have returned
to your native parts as Mickiewicz returned to Soplicó. I understand this
insofar as Paris — from which I have kept a safe distance for seven years,
despite my proximity to it — is a barren place, which doesn't say anything
new these days. Its frightening clamor is like a silence in which one hears the
gibberish of one's own dreams. At the end of May, I was there for ten days on
business and was very happy when I got back on the train at the Gare de
l'Est. From the time that *laboratoire central* vanished, one sees that the city is
nightmarishly ugly. Nothing has taken the place of Paris either. Europe has
simply become a province, and the conversations in it remind one of
Machnowiecka Street in Berdyczó, where the nobility exchanged the last
gossip in front of Szafnagel's store. My acquaintance with Berdyczó manners
is often very helpful in orienting myself in the Europe of today. In the fall I

will have to go back to Paris for a few days. I will be very glad to see you. Then I'll say more about *Native Realm*. I send you warm greetings, Czesław.

Your devoted
Jerzy Stempowski

Translated by Alissa Valles

On Scribbling

1957

Writing is not a novelty to me, but I never had a high opinion of it as a way of spending time. I always had the sense, today to a greater degree than ever, that it requires from me some special motivation or justification. I assume I am not alone in this sense and that a lack of justification — more than any opportunistic angle — has spurred writers to judge what they do from the point of view of social utility.

I spent a significant part of my childhood and youth among people writing, correcting proofs, and devoting themselves to other literary pursuits, which rarely produced any noteworthy results. In our age they are probably the by-product of printing machines and paper factories, which — like machines in general — cannot go unused.

From my early acquaintance with the mechanics of writing and printing, I derived the belief that there was no need to multiply the vast production of the printed word. Even the most studious reader won't manage to exhaust the program of reading he's chosen. So I virtually counted it to my credit that I refrained from scribbling.

I began writing late, when I was thirty-six, for accidental reasons, in a period particularly deprived of entertainment. Looking at it today, in retrospect, I'm not sure I would have started writing at that time if I had had the opportunity to pursue music more systematically or set out on a long journey. I might have soon tired of these entertainments, but perhaps they would have satisfied me in the period I expended on my first experiments with the pen.

It may be tactless to write about this in a book that may be read by literati, but writing throughout the ages has been an occupation of the *minorum gentium*. Admittedly, it was taken up by those who had ruled by the grace of God, in moments of reverential remorse at the sight of the miserable results of their rule, by ministers in disfavor, ambassadors obliged to live on a meager pension, as well as parliamentary representatives whose mandate was withdrawn when the people sent a better demagogue to the capital, and who had to wait several years for a new election campaign to begin. But the main core of writers were people who looked for compensation in the word for everything that life had denied them or could not offer anyone.

The skill of putting signs on paper, like a kind of black magic, always held the potential for creating fictions dazzling to the experimenter himself. In my youth I saw dadaists solemnly sticking on a wall phrases, clipped from newspapers and mixed up in a hat. From these phrases something resembling poems were composed, full of startling associations. The surrealists took these possibilities seriously, attempting so-called *écriture automatique*.

Even signs assembled at random can cause a jolt of surprise, let alone words polished by literary virtuosos! The phrases they compose tear themselves free from their author and take on a life of their own, like precious stones, talismans and fetishes containing the promise of an imaginary fortune, buried jealously in memory.

> *L'étoile a pleuré rose au coeur de tes oreilles,*
> *L'infini roulé blanc de ta nuque à tes reins,*
> *La mer a perlé rousse à tes mammes vermeilles*
> *Et l'homme saigné noir a ton flanc souverain.*

> The star has wept rose in the shell of your ears,
> Infinitude flowed white from the nape to the hip,
> The sea has budded pearly at your . . . breasts,
> And man has bled black in your sovereign lap.

The power of composing linguistic formulas that still absorb our long attention dozens or hundreds of years later and leave indelible traces on the passing hours is no doubt worthy of the power of command. And so it has indeed been seen, because those who possessed it have been granted in all times the honors rendered to leaders and rulers. So Martial is surely wrong. When speaking of the career of a wealthy shoemaker. he reproaches his parents for having given him only a literary education: At me *litterulis stulti docuere parentes*. For that matter, all the successors of Martial and Horace up to Tuwim have been bursting with pride at their possession of magical power over the word, also modestly called the poetic craft.

But all of this is true only of poetry. Prose doesn't derive its force from magic but from clarity of thought ordering the chaos of phenomena. Here the black magic of the word is a subordinate thing. Even rhetoricians agree that the most eloquent is he who has the most important matter to convey, even if he speaks an uncouth dialect. The need to order and master surrounding phenomena by thought would appear to be an automatic function in any case, not provoking any immediate impulse to write. The urge to propagate one's ideas and impose them on others is an entirely different matter, and the proof of this is the fact that it does not usually favor clarity and sincerity of expression. Flirting with clarity of thought and surrendering to all other motives constitute the inner contradiction of prose.

The exit from silence, which would seem to be the proper gesture of thought, is a certain kind of deviation from its ambition. It requires one to make one's living off the word, an uncertain material, alternately too resistant and too fluid, obeying laws other than the laws of thought and giving off unexpected sparks and scrapings when handled.

To live off the word, particularly the written word, which doesn't yield either hallucinations or exact understanding, requires one to renounce many ambitions and become as simple as a cook who, in a spirit of simplicity, not knowing any chemistry or physiology, mixes in a pot the victuals he has brought back from the market.

Translated by Alissa Valles

Józef Czapski

(1896–1993)

One of the most amazing figures in contemporary Polish culture, Józef
Czapski was born not far from Minsk (in what is today called Belarus) into an
aristocratic, cosmopolitan family. He traveled through the twentieth century
in many disguises, sometimes even in a military uniform, but most often as an
independent and rather poor painter and writer. After World War II, Czapski
settled in France, where he co-edited an important exile monthly, *Kultura*, a
magazine that made it possible for the most distinguished exile writers
(among them Czesław Miłosz, Witold Gombrowicz, Gustaw Herling, and Jerzy
Stempowski) to regularly publish their works in Polish.

As a painter, Czapski belonged in a loose way to the *école de Paris*, within
which he developed an individual aesthetic. As a writer, he created his own
personal idiom that achieves a striking originality in his *Diary*, which so far
remains largely unpublished. He wrote about his life, art, books, and ideas; he
portrayed his friends and his time. The fact that Czapski was a painter who
wrote—and not a "professional" writer—gave him an additional freedom of
judgment and style. Among his writings there is a little book on Marcel
Proust, the fruit of a series of lectures given in a grim place: a Soviet POW
camp (where the inmates were Polish officers taken as prisoners in the fall of
1939). Another of Czapski's books describes in detail his experiences in the
Soviet Union, where he met all kinds of people, among them Anna
Akhmatova, who later wrote a poem about their encounter.

Czapski's work contrasts between art and horror, goodness and inhumanity. He was able to sustain the tension between the more political aspects of his writing and the purely aesthetic quality of his paintings. This tension became his personal signature.

The Russian Background

From 1939 to 1942: the war, the camps — Starobielsk, Pavlishchev Bor, Gryazovyets, the formation of the Polish army in the Soviet Union. Here I include excerpts from my diary, written during a journey from Moscow to Tashkent in 1942.

In the camp at Starobielsk I was classed as a consumptive, and I was very careful not to fall out of this category, in which I had in fact been placed by mistake. Not used for any important work apart from peeling rotting potatoes, washing the stairs, and carrying out big bedbug hunts, I had time not only for reading but also for writing and even, in Gryazovyets, for daily drawing, with a bad pencil, on wretched cottony paper — that was my salvation. I even managed to get little caps of children's paint, and for a few weeks in a row, I made "portraits" of my friends in small patches of aquarelle paint, or painted still-lifes — the big wooden tub at which all of us washed, with a section of wall. Thanks to that almost daily work, I didn't daydream about drawing and painting — a dangerous kind of dreaming, in which one "soars about the heavens without decent feathers." Cézanne wisely said that it is dangerous to think about painting without a palette in hand. I was kept in check by the consciousness that I couldn't draw, that I couldn't paint. Thus I was absorbed by the overcoming of concrete difficulties. And that period convinced me for good that the driest drawing — without a trace of "music," the drawing the most miserably slavish to nature, deepened every day, sharpened, brought to the limit of one's capacity — is for me, and I stubbornly think, for every painter, a vital source.

In the cozy Fitzwilliam Museum in Cambridge, in a little room as narrow as a corridor, filled with precious drawings, there is a small Claude Lorrain. A few stones and grasses drawn with a fine line on gray paper, the drawing is

underscored with a light white gouache, there isn't a trace of any advance
intention for any one form or another, apart from maximum precision of
observation. What does a drawing like this have in common with the "ideal"
vegetation of his classical paintings, which would not have existed without
the preparation of these nature studies? Looking at that drawing a few
weeks ago, I thought, but yes, that is how I desperately wanted to draw
grasses in Gryazovyets, little serrated clover leaves, the wooden tub, or the
hand of a friend holding *Pravda*. At that time I dreamed of Corot's drawings,
his studies of shrubs and trees, a withered iris, stony landscapes and little
birds, those small aquarelles I saw a decade ago in the Escorial in a half-dark
room in which Philip II died. They were hung squeezed into one frame, the
only sign of the king's earthly interests amid faces of saints, hellfire, and torture instruments painted with equal precision and realism by Flemish
painters.

Can one arrive at art in the full sense without following this narrow path
of absolute humility, this reverence for the world seen by the eye, without
this work allowing objective control of the precision of eye and hand?

In the camps, though it was rare to find paper, I wrote a great deal. I did-
n't manage to bring anything with me from Starobielsk. But I do still have a
series of notebooks filled with tiny handwriting, mostly in pencil, from
Pavlishchev Bor and Gryazovyets. Notes on painting, preparations for a few
dozen lectures I gave there on art and even on French literature (only my lectures on Proust, copied out by friends, were published in *Kultura*). I don't
have the patience to read them, though much there concerns themes that I
touch on now, almost twenty years later, with the difference that there I
illustrate them with other examples and write about them from a different
perspective.

Gryazovyets had a slender but precious library that we prisoners
devoured: it included Russian classics, among other things a few volumes of
a big Tolstoy edition. There were sketches for *Anna Karenina* that were not
used in the final version, there were nineteenth-century French writers, a lot
of Balzac (luckily Marx loved *La Comédie Humaine*), Flaubert's *Éducation
Sentimentale* with an excellent introduction illuminating the era, with the
inevitable Marxist twist, there was even Thomas Hardy. I don't think I ever
read with such attention. The awakening of Stiva Oblonsky in his study after

his wife discovers his infidelity, the faces of peasants in the strike scene in Balzac's *Paysans*, as if painted by Ribera, and above all the scene in *Tess of the d'Urbervilles* where Tess, in the depths of despair, wakes up on the edge of the forest and sees traces of blood nearby and further on bloodied, wounded pheasants. As I said then with shame, it was as if those experiences of literature for which I hungered were often more powerful than the fall of Paris or the bombing of London, which the Soviet radio reported with evident satisfaction, because at that time I didn't know how to touch or see those events with living imagination.

Books helped me by awakening "involuntary memory." Though I have a dreadful memory for so many things, I could call to mind texts, fragments of other books, that I hadn't had my hands on for many years; I *saw* all sorts of paintings with the eye of my imagination. For me personally, the fact that recollections surfaced that seemed long lost bordered on a miracle. We lived cut off from the world (the camp), in conditions of malnutrition though not of hunger, amid warm friendships (there were also disputes, dozens of matters of honor to be settled by duels in a free Poland), with a handful of books, a patch of northern landscape: birches against a pale sky, splendid gleaming magpies hopping around in the dry leaves, glorious weeds of supernatural size that exploded in the spring, the incomparable charm of the luxuriant northern spring. We didn't only preserve ourselves from despair, but in that second year of imprisonment a new suspect comfort was born: It was as if the fierceness, the brutal dangers of the world — where men had to fight and couldn't be passive or pure for even a moment, if they weren't dying — were covered with a cloud, one's responses slackened, one acquired distance, and even resignation was becoming less impossible.

June 1941. We were wandering around the camp grounds. To this day the wild cry of exuberant enthusiasm thrown out by a scruffy colonel bending his whole upper body from the window is ringing in my ears: "Hitler attacked Russia!" For us that meant once again fever, life, and all hope. Barely a few weeks later, we were already back in the Polish army in formation. Yesterday we had been base bourgeois from a feudal Poland never to exist again — now we were the sons of noble and invincible Poland, allies of the Soviet Union and the great Stalin.

The steppe, the wooden houses like houses of cards in the summer camp at Totsk, frost and gales, relentless waves of human shadows in rags — on their way to the army.

After a few weeks, transferred to headquarters in Buzuluk, I am head of the search office for Polish officers and soldiers missing in Russia: Kuibyshev, Chkalov, Kuibyshev, Moscow, then again Kuibyshev, and finally Yangi-Yul near Tashkent. I described all of that in *On Inhuman Land*. Ferocious work, unrelenting pressure, a constant responsibility for human fates and lives, material conditions in large part a hundred times worse than in Gryazovyets, not a single moment for "contemplation" — not to mention drawing — for thinking in any categories but those of immediate action.

"You suffered so much in Russia!" I never know what to say to that; the mere fact that I was alive, that I could achieve or fight for something, for somebody, that was happiness then.

In Moscow I tried to get through to Soviet dignitaries (I was an ally, an emissary of General Anders, and courtesy toward him was official policy), to the closed offices at the Lubyanka prison with their heavy curtains and soft couches. I was carrying memoranda with demands for missing friends (who had been killed long before). I still believed that the people who received me then with icy politeness held in their hands the power of decision and salvation.

On my way back to the army, with a suitcase stuffed with gifts from Torgsin — sausage, tea, cheese (the highest privilege). I travel more than ten days by train from Moscow to Tashkent in an upholstered car with a *platskarta,* a reserved seat. There are four of us in the compartment. Every day Tanya and Manya, two railway employees, prepare warm soup with kasha for us; at stations they brutally chase hoards of civilians with luggage from the steps, as well as "heroic defenders of the fatherland" sent from hospital for a short leave with their families. A likeable captain, a Ukrainian, manages to get hold of kasha and bread to share among us; I share my Torgsin products and amid sincere or insincere but always equally patriotic hymns of praise to Stalin, omniscient and benevolent, I settle into the greatest comfort: a warm corner, apart from which I am sated, I have a few books, paper, and the eternal pen, and I only catch one flea on my bunk. Regarded at first with suspicion — they must have thought I was a top spy because I wrote constantly, and later perhaps that I was a madman — in the course of days spent traveling together and kasha eaten together, we become friends.

Those days, torn from a feverish routine, from obsessive activity, I now remember as happy ones. Is there any place, any Gehenna, where a man freed from physical suffering, hunger, and cold, or even from the feverishly harried responsibility of work, would not be capable of experiencing a quarter of an hour of happiness? (Simone Weil wept when she read *in the newspaper* about hungry children in China; she was probably incapable of such quarter hours at *such* times). After all, I was on a mission whose hopelessness was becoming more and more evident, which concerned thousands and thousands of people, among some of whom were dear friends; in Moscow I beat my head against the wall, yanked at eternally closed doors!

In the warm, contented compartment I looked through the icy windows at the red sun setting, the snow drifts that stopped us every so many dozens of hours, blocking the tracks, at the ruined domes of churches with broken crosses standing in black villages; and then in the steppe beyond the Volga, a snowy desert, where across four roads from Kuibyshev a snowy plain stretches out from Jeletsk to the Aral Sea, without a single tree, almost without buildings, almost without people. Around broken down stations, a few low mud houses with little statues of Lenin and Stalin. The Aral Sea, heaps of salt covered with straw.

I can only barely see a few Kazakhs in the snow, under big fur hoods. Fascinated by the world outside the window, by my travel companions, reading and making notes constantly, I wrote these remarks on technique in art, attempts to bring together, to formulate what seemed to me the most essential in my experience after two and a half years taken away from work. There are echoes and reflections here of polemics with the Polish artistic climate that we Kapists found in Poland after our return from Paris. On varying fronts we tried to struggle with the form of thoughtlessness in Witkacy [S. I. Witkiewicz], Czyżewski, Strzemiński, and a few others.

It seems to me though that now those notes are even more against the prevailing views, though from an entirely different angle. At the present, with very rare exceptions, painters look at nature with hostility or indifference, while I am forever writing about the study of nature!

Almost twenty years after writing those notes in a Soviet train compartment, my "warm-up" as I call it there, with studies of nature and my turning away from nature, happens at an earlier stage; I mostly paint from memory these days. If I had to write about my practice as a painter now, I could write more about the next stage, when a painter turns from the immediate study of nature. But even now I couldn't arrive at true painting, as opposed to secondhand painting, without constantly returning to nature, without turning back to analytical work from nature, so what I wrote then I still sign off on today.

Translated by Alissa Valles

ON INTERVALS IN WORK

During intervals a certain greater or lesser progress can be made in *consciousness*, but upon returning to work one is always surprised anew by the fact that independently of progress in consciousness, in practice one has *regressed* in the real work. A painter has to start again, and not even at the point where he broke off, but much further back. If a painter doesn't feel like obeying this truth and yields to the illusion that progress in consciousness is already progress in the capacity for the work itself, he condemns himself to a road immeasurably longer, to a harmful illusion that is a conscious or unconscious *lie* to oneself, the destruction of laboriously won foundations for the work, sometimes forever.

This common fate of Polish painters, the slow but steady regression of once capable artists, is due to the fact that they take their own inner experience for a premise allowing them a creative leap in realization, a premature leap over a whole sequence of stages not worked out properly.

These skipped stages demand time, which isn't taken into account; a lot of sweat, labor that quite often turns out to have been fruitless, which we consciously or subconsciously try to shirk. The faster a painter can humble himself, once again determine his actual regressed position and start working again from that place without any rush, the faster he will be able to reach beyond what he has attained as the result of his previous work.

But with every subsequent step he will still have to put on the brakes as he moves forward, putting the emphasis the whole time on achieving a *work temperature*, a continuity, qualitative growth (depending on the individual and the stages, now a greater, now a lesser *quantity* in terms of work hours, a constantly changing technique, not just in work but in life).

In France probably fewer talents perish, while with us they almost as a rule go to waste, because from Poussin through David, Delacroix, Degas, Cézanne, and so many others, there is in France a continuously enriched and deepened tradition of "secret knowledge": how to work, not just in the superficial sense of facility of execution but in the sense of a deep "breath" in painting, a connection between a vision and the *realization* of that vision.

In France there was never the superstition, so popular in Poland, that a painter has a right to be stupid.

Translated by Alissa Valles

ON VISION AND CONTEMPLATION

We paint only one percent of contemplation.

—NORWID

What is vision? A certain synthetic, singular way of looking at the surrounding world. A moment of such vision always comes unexpectedly, like grace. Sometimes without any preparation, without any capacity to give it embodiment, sometimes after many years of work, as a reward — always incommensurate and even incongruous with the effort we put in. Sometimes it arrives inconspicuously and manifests itself slowly and more and more effectively in a work begun without vision, or almost without vision.

If we read the medieval mystics, we find striking analogies there with the artist's vision, the paths leading to that vision and the paths that lead to states of ecstasy, to what Saint John of the Cross calls *contactus Dei*. I don't want by any means to collapse the infinitely more sensual, material experience of the artist with the ecstasies and states of prayer of Saint John and others, but nevertheless the analogies are so striking, the graph of these states is so often identical in its fits and lags, in the conscious return to more matter-bound prayer, that the most secularly inclined artist should give it some thought. Prayer techniques, methods for bringing oneself to these higher prayer states were elaborated by mystics of very different religions. I've never made a more thorough study of this, but it's enough to read the life of the Spanish Saint Teresa, or even more Saint John of the Cross's *Summary of Mystical Doctrine*, published in Saint Maximin, to see how much that reading has to offer to a painter. That dry handbook, written almost in the style of a high school textbook, what an aid it can be in distinguishing in oneself real from artificial, delusory, induced fits and inspirations, which result in opaque, falsified art. I want to be understood well: I'm not talking about religious art at all, in the sense the phrase is usually employed. I mean art in general, in contrast to nonart, to everything that in the guise of effects, tricks, originality, or ordinary imitation gives itself out to be one or another art form. I'm talking about the art of both Dürer and Cézanne, Degas or Gierymski.

It seems to me that the paths to inspiration are infinitely varied, that there aren't and can't be any obligatory theories or methods, that every new experience grows from innumerable new combinations of feeling, genius, consciousness, work (as far as religious inspiration goes, how many mystics have not been suspected of heresy?); nevertheless, coming to know the varied paths involved in the creative mechanism that in others brings these states to another, higher plane, can help us and purify and deepen our work. Artists who build everything on talent, waiting in cafés for inspiration, unbound by awareness or any more profound tradition, can very easily lose the potential for any development, just tread water and thus regress.

It was Norwid who said that we paint one percent of contemplation. Thinking through, carrying through the analogy between religious contemplation and, for example, Cézanne's contemplation might be a point of departure for art's use of the whole treasure-house of knowledge about contemplation that we can find in mystical literature. But who reads it? Priests, monks, maybe psychologists and pathologists, for whom art is a largely alien world — painters don't read much, and if they do, it's not the mystics.

Translated by Alissa Valles

Fertile Indolence

Nietzsche said that a human being is first a camel, then a lion, then a child. For camels, fertile indolence is probably a closed book. It concerns lions and children. In life, this Nietzschean sequence of succession often changes and becomes entangled. A person is already a lion or even a child and then he becomes a camel again, though it seems there are happy people who never have lived through "camel" periods and perhaps didn't need them.

An understanding of fertile indolence is probably one of the most important kinds of knowledge for an artist and, if it isn't given, perhaps one of the most difficult. It must be a continuous, acute consciousness, although even that doesn't always help; we must be constantly, subconsciously, instinctively vigilant in order not to allow fertile indolence to transform itself into wasteful indolence, which weakens and annuls any project instead of enriching it.

In a camel phase, the most apparently wasteful work, any burden to carry, is better than indolence, because at such a time indolence is pointless and only sinks one deeper into the void. We feel this then and, whether we want to or not, we walk the difficult joyless path of the camel. But tired and as if steeped or cleansed by our great exertion, we come out of it capable of greater attention, higher temperatures, with deeper sensibility. At this time observation ceases to be merely an act of will or the muscles and so a constraint, and it gradually becomes a reflex, later almost second nature; only then can one speak of fertile indolence, only then is a day of inaction the repose Norwid spoke of, and one returns to work after one's inactive day enriched, with recharged batteries. A person capable of such indolence is threatened by a kind of fall, a peril: an urge to prolong the state, because it is a happy state. But that happiness of passive contemplation, when it is attained, with time imperceptibly loses its force of vibration, the sharpness of the senses dissolves or loses color. Every attempt at the realization of some project is so fraught with difficulties, so menaced are we by the necessity of passing across a barren field, returning to a camel's state in which we lose the taste of the original experience which drove us to work, which made us fruitful, that we are tempted to withdraw further and further into passivity. Why torture ourselves when we are happy simply lying in bed and contemplating the shadow of the easel on the ceiling? That capacity for passive happiness brings some artists in the end to an infertile decrepitude of the state which happiness created. Here we are saved only by an *inner independence of pleasure as well as pain*, the trait or creative element that won't allow us to rest, though that is what we desire.

This inaction is a dream with open eyes, a state only seemingly restful: the creative instinct is more awake than at any other time, the "facultés en éveil," the alert faculties, rolled into a ball, are awake, waiting to throw themselves on the first catch, to leap forward at full speed but also with a full, cold, calculating consciousness.

The artist truly imbued with work and the thought of work makes use of everything. There is no desert, no bleak, impoverished place where he would not find riches for his sensibility. When Gauguin left to paint on Tahiti, Renoir is supposed to have said: "I don't see why he has to go so far — can't you paint in Bagnolles?"

The old Delacroix said that after a day of work, a game of cards with the concierge from the building across the street was enough to give him complete happiness. I know this is only one kind of artist, that there were others, like Chateaubriand and Byron, who were tormented by boredom and had to have constantly new and sharp impressions and experiences, which could never satisfy them. They were also great artists — but how much more worthy of emulation and respect do I find the humble Delacroix with his old servant Jenny, old Cézanne immersed in his uninterrupted labor, in the remote French provinces.

Translated by Alissa Valles

On Leaping and Flying
In order to attain anything it is not enough to walk, one has to fly.
—LIFE OF SAINT TERESA OF AVILA

I wrote about the harmfulness of haste and of false, destructive leaps; nevertheless, I don't see how it's possible to achieve anything without a leap. "Leap" is the word that expresses most accurately what you feel when the creative moment arrives, the moment of vision, the lightning flash that transforms one's relation to the work, which is suddenly governed by an entirely different law: from the measured, almost logically calculated approach of slowly warming and widening exertion, from the dog collar of reason and various restraining mechanisms — the artist is suddenly torn away, *not because he wants to be*, but because he can't resist a certain force acting in him.

If this leap is not an inner necessity, one should guard against it.

And suddenly all the forms elaborated, not just by me but by a long chain of tradition, cease to be axiomatic; we really do leap into the unknown: What we see, how we see, how we try to realize our vision, is sometimes the complete opposite of the experience accumulated so far and of our technique. "Every artist is a little like Lope de Vega," writes Théophile Gautier, "who at the moment when he was writing his comedies, locked up the rulebook with six keys — *con seis claves* — and consciously or not forgot about systems and paradoxes in the blaze of work."

An example from my work: For months I work analytically. To the degree that there is a heightening of the sharpness of vision, the eye's precision, the analysis becomes very exact, the number of colors and shades grows to the degree that I feel the *limitlessness* of the numbers of increments, between ochre and burnt sienna, for example, mixed with more or less black and white paint; the limitlessness of related, now warmer, now cooler shades; the distribution of paint in warmer and cooler patches becomes more and more precise, from a small comma I move to a spot, from a spot to a point more and more microscopic. (The smooth gray wall in the small picture by Vermeer in the Louvre, *Embroidress*, seen through a magnifying glass, shows a series of points, each drowned in other warmer and cooler points). And just then, when I've turned away from every other task, immersed in that endlessly expanding inner world of shades of color, when after a varying period of work I've constantly discovered anew that a few colors on a palette can yield millions of color combinations, then suddenly (the later the better) comes the opposite kind of vision of the surrounding world — a synthetic vision. I begin to operate not with little spots but with large ones, patches, movements not in small, discrete touches connected with a line and a more rational connection to the whole but a combination of color and form so intimately connected that there is no line separate from color and no color separate from line, so that every spot has a form, the form is organically unified by line and color, the form is natural, instinctive, governed by the composition of the whole, and what a moment ago might have seemed the strangest distortion becomes the only true expression of my vision, for the most part departing wholly from a photographic naturalism. (But this is purely personal; with another painter the vision could stand in an entirely different, infinitely closer or more distant relation to naturalism.)

Manet said that he felt with each new painting that he was throwing himself into an abyss. That is precisely the leap, the dangerous flight I'm writing about: Up until the last minute we don't know if we have wings to carry us or whether we will crash into the abyss.

We know Cézanne's academic student drawings from Aix before he went to Paris: a sharp naturalism, a severe and pure line. It's hard to believe that this was the same man who drew the later drawings, portraits, still-lifes, landscapes, the painter of *Baigneuses*. The difference is that in his youthful work Cézanne was still a humble student, deprived of vision, and in the later works he saw synthetically, with his own unique eye, the reality around him.

Auguste Bréal, the painter and author of the book *Cheminement*, an academy friend of Matisse (both were students of Gustave Moreau, with Rouault and Marquet), told me that Matisse came to his "lightning" paintings, sometimes done within a few minutes, often after many months of work on naturalistic, polished canvases — which he didn't show at exhibitions. At his big exhibition in Paris in 1931 I saw two studied copies of Ruysdael and Chardin, studentlike in their precision: an enormous canvas — game, fish, a mortar, a cat. It's hard to think of an approach to painting more in contradiction to his style. I have to say that those canvases of which Bréal spoke with delight struck me as dull *(empatées)*, differing from the originals in their lack of the wonderful discreet vibrancy of color that marks every Ruysdael or Chardin; they also lacked the sonority of Matisse's best canvases — an uneven but great painter.

Speaking of myself, I was long tormented by a duality of approach — analytical on the one hand, rational, growing from the Dutch tradition and to a certain extent from the Pointillists, and on the other hand, the mad, the unpredictable — the true leap into the abyss. In this I saw a lack of unified personality, a kind of psychic dividedness that I tried to overcome artificially, without success. With time I noticed the same phenomenon not only in painters of Matisse's stature, but even in one of the very greatest, in Goya. It's enough to look at Goya's paintings in the Prado. His cold, masterful portraits of great ladies, dignitaries, kings, and cardinals are painted so smoothly, to the degree that we don't feel the angle of the brush, they are classical in composition and in the miraculous control of every detail, in the materiality of the object, the consideration given to local colors, careful in the advance gradation of the values. Next to these portraits, in a badly lit side room, there were hung in 1930 paintings of Goya so entirely different that it was difficult to believe they were painted by the same person. War scenes, wild scenes with witches, painted by "lightning," in exaltation, so that we see every movement of the brush, color contrasts so violent they are almost like Soutine, a disdain for local color and the object's materiality, so that some of the canvases give the impression of almost abstract color arrangements.

With the majority of painters this movement from canvases marked above all by high painterly skill, to visionary canvases, is not as visible, not only on the canvas but even in the work process there is often an inscrutably slow transformation, without a transformative breaking off.

But let's take Cézanne's remark, his cult of the masters: "I feel like a child led by the hand when I look at the Louvre masters," but at the same time: "In the face of nature we should forget about all masters and approach the impression as if we were the first to see nature." This is the same breaking off, expressed differently. A breaking off into a unique, personal vision of the world.

One shouldn't be afraid even to lose oneself in the study of nature, in an apprenticeship to past masters, as if one were an ignoramus or lacked individuality; one should take all of it merely as a point of departure, as a springboard to that further and bolder step into the unknown. The more able the artist is to "absorb" nature and at the same time acquire the experience of objective knowledge of his craft and develop his sensibility and capacity for discrimination, the more power he will command at the moment he leaps.

Translated by Alissa Valles

Aleksander Wat

(1900–1967)

Aleksander Wat was proud of his Jewish lineage, which he could trace back to famous mystics and rabbis. His life could be divided into four main periods. First he was an active and rather noisy avant-garde poet (a Futurist) in Warsaw. Later on he became an editor of a communist magazine and, after that, he worked for a respectable publishing house. World War II changed everything: Wat found himself a prisoner of the immense Gulag Archipelago (after being arrested in Lvov, which between September 1939 and June 1941 was part of the Soviet Union before falling into the hands of the Nazis). After the war he returned to Warsaw but a new calamity ensued—a disease that manifested itself mostly in terrible pain. The postwar period consisted of years of sickness for Wat and many journeys abroad for the sake of his failing health. Eventually he became an exile and, after a stay in California, died in France.

The last stage of Wat's biography was the richest in terms of his literary achievement, although each line written had to be measured against an almost permanent pain. These late poems were filled with wisdom, bitterness, and irony. *My Century*, a philosophical memoir dictated on tape (and spoken to Czesław Miłosz, who initiated this exchange), was published in 1977, ten years after Wat's death, and was greeted as one of the great documents of our time.

My Century combines the insight of an artist who came to the limits of literary experiment with the sagacity of a witness to the horror of totalitarianism.

Diary Without Vowels

Berkeley, November 17, 1964

No one, no one but Ola understands anything, anything at all about my illness or about my difficulty writing. They see how I complicate everything: my thoughts, my life, my fate. And Freudians have propagated the label "flight into illness," so it is applied to me, and no one will see that it's the other way around: I complicate my life to flee my illness, so that in the complexities of my fate, a convoluted tangle, I find the explanation and justification for my physical suffering and for my shameful dependence on my body.

And there is some higher level of justice in the fact that they don't admit to their consciousness the idea of a bungled life as the result of physical pain. . . . For that would mean a capitulation to the body, which a Christian can never allow. So many centuries of Christian spiritualism have made them instinctive spiritualists. And at the same time, nothing is more alien to those goyim then *anima naturaliter christiana*. For the latter would always bow down low before suffering. Dostoevsky, who knew all about this because he was a battlefield, as before him only Pascal and Kierkegaard, on which the inner contradictions of Christianity carried on a relentless struggle — not for nothing did Dostoevsky make Alyosha Karamazov kiss Ivan, bowing low before the holiness of suffering. *Anima naturaliter christiana* is probably a Jewish quality, maybe exclusively Jewish? There's a logic in the fact that Christ was born in a Jewish family. And Dostoevsky himself, isn't he a "judaizing" Russian, isn't compassion (pity!) of Jewish origin. The Greeks pitied, the Greeks identified with the victim of a tragedy, but did they sympathize, did they have compassion? And so it is that a man of such rare goodness, delicacy of feeling and vast understanding, it's Kot Jeleński I mean, when he received my desperate letters, must have nodded his head, both in pity and irritation, understanding nothing, or what's worse, understanding wrongly, while Leopold Labedz whose demands on himself and on me are so high, who is so far from understanding the complexities arising from the cultivation of poetry in our times, only looked on and understood, with his Jewish heart.

It's a puzzling thing — to go on about sickness, which to me is a fascinating theme and the mother of philosophy, something that Novalis understood best of all — it is an astonishing thing to what extent people who are not suffering lack even the most elementary understanding of what constant, chronic physical pain is, pain lasting years, *la maladie-douleur*, pain sickness. Even the pains of Proust, who managed to create an oeuvre precisely out of physical suffering (his suffering didn't cross a certain threshold, didn't disturb his brain functions), even that suffering, which imprisoned him for years in a cork-lined room, even that seems to the reader a beautiful lyrical adventure, a kind of exotic lumbago, seasoned with poetry. But pain puts a mask of ugliness on everything, on all the beauties of the world. People who are knocked out by the slightest indisposition, stomach pains or just a toothache lasting a day or two, reducing the whole world to a bad tooth, even they, like Cyryl, shake their heads mistrustfully and reluctantly when they hear that their friend has suffered from a pain analogous to a toothache for twelve years, with very rare intervals. Perhaps they are distrustful because they don't believe, knowing their own reactions, that a sick man can carry on a conversation, even discuss abstract matters, even with humor, even laughing, and at the same time feel acute pain. They don't understand that in the monotonous terrain of long suffering, a laugh, a joke, a discussion are the poor means that, not being a flight from pain but on the contrary arousing pain, at the same time humble it. In everyone suffering from pain sickness there exists in equal measure and parity a need for sacralization and a need for degradation, for humiliation of one's pain. A need for plain satisfactions: look, I suffer, but I am above my pain; I not only mock it, but humiliate it.

But there have been so many creators of spiritual values with sick, suffering bodies. Truly a countless multitude. But there are not only amazing gradations in suffering; beyond that, so much depends on the kind of pain, on where and how it's located.

When I say to a friend, "At this moment I feel terrible searing pains on the left side of my face," I demand a lot of him. First, the belief that I am really feeling pains at that moment at all. I may only be recalling past pains. Next, that the pains I feel are really terrible. He searches my face for those wordless signs that are usually associated with pain. And the need for the testimony of a scream, a moan, or a facial expression shows how little people trust words. And they trust them so little not only because, hearing only words, they are equally inclined to believe and not to believe in my sincerity when I express in words what I really feel. But also, they believe and don't believe, they don't know whether or not to believe, in my intellectual and moral competence to express accurately and adequately a thing generally as difficult to express as pain. And even if that obstacle is overcome, my friend will still look for signs that he knows from his own experience are also not entirely certain but possess a greater degree of objective credibility than words. And so, passing over the scream or groan — the face in pain and its iconography, of which painters and actors have availed themselves for centuries, those who explored the speech of wordless experience; for example, a furrowed brow and lines on the forehead, up from the base of the nose, parallel to the mouth, the corners turned down, creases near the nostrils cutting deeply, a look of intensity or on the contrary a diffuse look, sunken into itself, absent. If there are no such indications, the basis of credibility is not necessarily destroyed. But it must be sustained by the constant effort of a trusting imagination. Furthermore, when these difficulties are also overcome, when a friend hears that I feel hellish burning pain in the left half of my face, he has to look for a model in himself, in his own experience, he has to measure that personal experience against the meaning of the word "burning" and localize it on his face, when he has never experienced burning pains or facial pains. Whereas he will remember roughly all the bad experiences of his own organism, remembering within the framework of pure imagination (if he has only known contracting stomach pains up to this point, he has to use that material to make a burning pain on his own face: He only becomes aware of "pain in general" in this comparative confrontation) that he knows two fundamentally different kinds of pain: those he could bear so that they didn't form an obstacle to living, didn't destroy an active routine, and those (for example, a bad toothache) that he is convinced he couldn't bear for longer than a certain very short time. Whereas a normal person doesn't know extreme experiences — i.e., severe pains endured for an unlimited term, months, years — that oversteps the boundaries of their recollection. My saying that I have felt hellish pains for about twelve years doesn't find any models of understanding in my friend's mind, and instead of leading to admiration of my "superhuman" endurance, it engenders on the contrary a conviction of my hysteria or hypochondria, of my sickly oversensitivity and self-pity, my indulgence of any old sensations, of my *delectatio morosa* and flight into sickness in difficult life situations. I have constant proofs of the difficult, multiform, and complex intellectual and psychic operations required for a just understanding of my pain: Friends who have heard about my facial pains for years still ask me about my migraines, though I don't know how many times I've already corrected that insensitive mistake, which engenders bitterness in me ("I endure so much, and you're too much of a coward to imagine for one instant the nature of my pains. I ask nothing else of you, only that one sign of friendship: not pity, but sympathy, even if only for a second.") And if that friend offers me active aid to boot, it's even worse — that aid humiliates me, even if the friend didn't intend it to be. Because aid was not offered to my suffering, which would immediately ennoble it (Alyosha's kiss), but to the unfortunate *emmerdeur*, who for base reasons isn't in full control of his own life.

In one of my first poems I wrote of myself as "boring as a boring tired pencil." Then I attributed the "boring" state of tiredness to the pencil. But even in my futuristic-linguistic insolence I wouldn't have allowed myself such an exaggeration as to say: "The pencil feels burning pains." When I demand understanding of my sufferings from my friends, I wish them to do more or less the same — that is, I demand that they imagine, if only on the basis of the nervous, pained quality of the writing, that my pencil is suffering. But of course, the necessary condition here is experience of one's own suffering. But by demanding understanding for my sickness in this way, do I not give evidence of self-pity, which is what X. so delicately suggested, a need to arouse pity? Nothing of the sort, Ola's understanding is more than sufficient proof that only love can cope where intelligence is powerless. But the characteristic feature of incurable and chronic pain-sickness, with which one can live, but to which one can't become accustomed, is that it suffuses the intelligence and the whole social behavior of the sufferer; so when people look at what I do, write, and say, not seeing what in me is modified by sickness, they create in their minds a model of Aleksander Wat that I can't tolerate in my friends, which is humiliating to me. So more and more often I respond only with a wave of the hand. I insult those who are the most concerned about me, and against my nature I wall myself up in misanthropic silence. And in this way my diabolical sickness can torture me all the better, raising up blind walls around me.

But what do laymen matter, when even medicine until recently saw *maladie-douleur* — as the pain specialist Professor Leriche called it — as a symptom of hypochondria, hysteria, oversensitivity, imaginary sickness, delusionary pains? Undoubtedly delusionary pains, like pain in phantom limbs, arise not on the surface of the body and not in specific organs but in the cerebral cortex, probably in the two homunculuses (with huge faces and huge limbs, with short torsos and without brains), which are inscribed on two side plates of the brain and regulate sensation of pain and pleasure stimuli like the dispatcher tables in automated factories. Central pains, produced in the brain, sent by the brain to different parts of the organism. Or, as Leriche claims, there are no pains more penetrating than those delusionary ones, and they are also the hardest to cure. In my case they are incurable because they aren't functional; rather, they arose as a result of a tiny injury in the medulla oblongata, on the very path to the still mysterious thalamus. Doctor Hartwig told me ten years ago: "From this sickness you can escape — only by the window. . . ." I've only ever encountered two persons who suffered constant burning pains: One in Taormina, the owner of two shops in which his family worked; he was always running from one shop to the other, weeping, with his head wrapped in a dirty piece of flannel, with a bandage over the left side of his face. When he spoke of his illness, he burst out crying. The other in Obory, an aristocratic woman, also perpetually weeping, still young, with a mournful face. Their pains were functional and even so, after a few years both of them were already worn to shreds.

And now — my difficulties writing? My general difficulty in writing: I'm not capable of controlling the speed of my thoughts. Either it is so fast that it becomes impossible to fix thoughts, only conversation with people sets a certain tempo, but when I am alone in front of the sheet of paper, when I begin to set my brain to work, I am not able to rein it in — the faster thoughts gallop, the more aggressive my pains become, the more impatient I become, and so I write in an inadequate shorthand. On top of that, no sleep medication will help the excited cerebral cortex, and then begins the nightmare of mental galloping in a void in the night. Not only can I not regulate the tempo, but my thoughts fly in any direction they choose, after the first associative temptations to come along. Or on the contrary — a state of complete mental stasis, somnolence, lethargy, and the sense of barrenness that accompany it, the desert of my own nonentity, and once again pains increased by depression.

It's true, my friends have a point here. It is not just a matter of illness. I always had a bad intellectual disposition in embryo and in a developed form, of the manic-depressive type. But illness turned quantity into quality, my state is not typical for Babinski-Bageotte syndrome, as neurologists call it.

But there is another difficulty in my work, although perhaps it is itself intimately connected with sickness. It so happened that what I have to write about, what I am obliged and able to write about, the central experience of almost forty years of my life, arouses disgust and hatred in me. Communism. A thing so bloody but also trivial, so that when two years ago I embarked on the reading of documents from the Twenty-second Party meeting, I got persistent eczema over my whole body. The words "communism," "Stalin," "Lenin," or "Khrushchev," "class war," etc., etc., themselves are loathsome, criminally vulgar; even millions of tombs and the vast power that grew from them do not lend this thing stature. Even the martyrdom of millions ennobles nothing in it, any more than mutilations suffered randomly in a gang fight do. Common moral hygiene commands one to shy away from this subject matter. But I, a poet for better or worse, and so justified in my existence by sublimation, I have to write about this, because various circumstances have conspired to make this theme the only one required of me and that which allows me to live in emigration. Second, I have to get rid of it, it has been rotting in me for so many years. Third, it is still the greatest mystery to me, our mystery, the mystery of history and I can't stop thinking about it. Fourth, it fills the cloakroom of memory. Fifth, it is against communism that I tested my own worth, my travails with it give better testimony to me than anything else in my life, apart from that there is just the magma of an intellectual existence. Sixth, seventh.

All right, my friends say, just don't play the sage, don't theorize, so much has been theorized already without you trying to add to it, what are your chances, why don't you write instead what you went through, simply an auto-biography, the theory will emerge by itself. But they don't realize that writ-ing an autobiography means reentering and reawakening in myself all the suffering of the Zamarstynów jail, the Lubyanka, the Third Section [the office created by Tsar Nicholas I in 1826 to conduct secret police operation] in Alma Ata. It means to return of my own free will to my prisons. No, I can't deal with that; I don't have the strength for it in my state. Not even to men-tion that to myself I have always be *le moi haïssable*. Sure, for a few years I resisted communism and paid for it richly, but what about my couple of months of cowardice in Lvov? And my juvenile stupidities, my entanglement in the wickedness of communism? An autobiography is a selection, naturally, but I can pass over my "heroism" in silence; on the other hand, I do have to lay bare and do justice to my disgraces. That is not just a question of good taste; perhaps it comes from my advanced age. My autobiography would have to be a trial, with a defense counsel, of course, but with a public prose-cutor as well. I can't permit myself any tricks here. Only that way would my work have meaning and dignity. How to muster the strength for a trial, in my state?

Translated by Alissa Valles

Julian Przyboś

(1901–1970)

Once the leading poet of the Polish avant-garde—both as a practitioner and a theorist—Julian Przyboś remains now in literary purgatory. When Jan Blonski, an outstanding critic, tried years ago to put the name of Czesław Miłosz (at the time banned for political reasons) back on Poland's literary map, he proposed a juxtaposition that was meant to facilitate the trick: he saw Polish poetry as spun between Przyboś and Miłosz. Przyboś stood for a poetry of pure seeing, in which language was supposed to create itself from the freshness of a lyric impulse. And Miłosz underscored the value of the cultural and historical memory and the usefulness of existing rhetorical modes of poetry. As a matter of fact, both poets represent different sides or aspects of late modernism—Przyboś was fascinated by French cathedrals, and Miłosz was sometimes drawn to poetic novelty.

Przyboś was the author of numerous volumes of poetry and criticism. Before the war he was a militant proponent of the so-called Kraków Avant-Garde. He became later, for a while, a diplomat (Communist Poland's ambassador to Switzerland) and an imposing figure in Poland's literary life.

MORE ABOUT THE MANIFESTO

1971

I plowed, I threaded a needle,
I proclaimed my manifesto to the hostile crowd,
I washed plain canvas on the river,
bleached it in a field,
I danced, I rode a galloping horse, marched with bayonets,
bound an infant's blanket,
closed my father's eyes,
harvested with a scythe,
I aimed, fired in battle, hit my mark,
cut a sunflower's fire-maned
head so it would shine
on your body in our night of love,
cut the pages of a book —
and didn't pick up a pen unless it was on
the vector of my doings and all the things
still
to be done.

I didn't spin a line of verse on a page
— and won't spin any —
which was not a graph of growth
(apart from one — the shortest line — of death).

But it is only now that I am near the Whole,
I see
that by transmitting the motion and labor of my body
to my vocal cords and to the drive
of the tongue hinting heavily at them,
I would avoid
a hyperbole that would grow unstoppably without you,
if I were
separate from the lines of words
lighting up

the image of an artistic light satellite I engendered,
projected — at memory's ignition — as if from a launcher,
I wouldn't want
you others (but how other are you?)
to fix your will on the syntax
and rhythm,
your sight on the speed
with which the brightness of my visions runs,
flare after flare
of imagination, that bright constellation of the mind.

It was me running to you
who broke a sound barrier in the Polish language.
You have the right — I gave it to you — to want
writing
to be the making made of what is written.

Poetry fulfills itself when it is the summoning
of others
to the status of inventors.

— Landscape poet, can you extend
the pen's track to the length of sowing
a handful of seeds?
(I asked, and instead of answering,
he turned his typewriter into a poppy seed sower . . .)

I remember in the spring in my home village,
a twig in my mouth, the first words of a poem:
a whisper lengthened and widened and became
the sprouting expanse of a field
sown with spring wheat, which
(I dream I remember)
an accountant will enter tomorrow as a token of day labor
performed by a universal instrument of light:
my obliging afterword.
And yet I wrote that poem — about what? Again, yet again

and interminably about poetry? So
about nothing, or rather: about everything
concerning nothing, or:
about my interminable assaults on Everything?
Until I put down my pen, in order not to end
but to begin again:
to plow . . . to thread the needle . . . to proclaim a manifesto . . .
I proclaim.

Translated by Alissa Valles

Witold Gombrowicz

(1904–1969)

Without Witold Gombrowicz, Polish contemporary literature would have been different. In an intellectual landscape from which a taste of an old-fashioned and slightly parochial patriotism had not quite evaporated, he was—or had to be—a Polish Genet, Sartre, and Céline. Yet he was very much Gombrowicz, president of a one-party state—and the name of this state was "Gombrowicz." He was a wonderful anomaly thrown into a rather traditional literary world.

Gombrowicz's life perfectly matched the eccentricity of his work: he found himself in Argentina in 1939 simply because he was stranded there when World War II broke out. He had lived in Buenos Aires quite modestly, on the brink of misery, for some twenty-odd years, learning Spanish and founding a small literary sect that worshipped Gombrowicz himself. In 1963, then a sick and prematurely old man, Gombrowicz returned to Europe, to Germany and France, but never to Communist Poland, where indeed he would have cut a bizarre figure among the commissars and dissidents.

Gombrowicz's talent was philosophical, satirical, and sometimes lyrical. His fascinating novels and plays at times seem built on a thesis, but his masterpiece—the three volumes of his *Diary*—is built on his existence, his life, his suffering, and his laughter. His influence is enormous within Polish literature as well as on the way people live and talk—at least among the Polish intelligentsia.

Excerpts from *Diary*

II

Monday

After a sixteen-hour, quite bearable (if it weren't for the tangos that were blaring out of the speaker!) bus ride from Buenos Aires — the green hills of Salsipuedes and I among them with Miłosz's book *The Captive Mind* under my arm. Because it poured all day yesterday, I am almost finished with the book. So you were destined for this, this was your lot, your road, my old acquaintances, friends, companions from the Ziemiańska or the Zodiac. I here, you there, that is how it has been described and unmasked. Miłosz tells the history of the bankruptcy of literature in Poland smoothly and I ride his book straight through that streamlined cemetery, just as, two days ago, I rode the bus along the asphalt highway.

Terrifying asphalt. It does not appall me that *tempora mutantur*, it appalls me that *nos mutamur in ills*. I am not aghast at the change in living conditions, the fall of states, the annihilation of cities and other surprise geysers, spurting out of the womb of History, but the fact that a fellow whom I knew as X suddenly becomes Y, changes his personality like a jacket and begins to act, speak, think, and feel contrary to himself fills me full of fear and embarrassment. What a terrible shamelessness! What a ridiculous demise! To become a gramophone, onto which is put a record with the label "His Master's Voice"? What a grotesque fate for these writers!

Writers! We would save ourselves a great many disillusionments if we did not call everyone who can "write," "a writer." I knew those "writers." They were usually persons of rather superficial intelligence and quite narrow horizons who, as far as I can remember, did not become anybody so that today they don't really have much to give up. These cadavers were characterized in their lifetime by the following: it was easy for them to fabricate the moral and ideological face, thereby earning the approbation of the critics and the more serious part of the readership. I did not believe in Jerzy Andrezejewski's Catholicism for even a second, and, after reading a few pages of his novel, I greeted his suffering and spiritualized face in the Café Zodiac with a face so doubtful that the offended author immediately broke off all relations with me.

Both the Catholicism and the sufferings of the book were received with shouts of "hosanna" by the naive, who mistook a reheated hash for rare tenderloin steak. The besotted nationalism of Gałczyński, who was truly talented, was worth as much as the intellectualisms of the Ważyks, or the ideology of the group around *Prosto z Mostu.** In the Warsaw cafés, just as in the cafés all around the world, there was a need for "idea and faith," the result of which was that writers began to believe in this thing or that overnight. As for me, I always considered this child's play; and I even pretended that it amused me although deep inside, I was appalled at this introduction to the future Great Masquerade.

All of this was cheap and no cheaper than, in the majority of cases, the cloying humanity of various women, the poeticality of Tuwim and the Skamandrites, the inventions of the avant-garde, the murkiness of the aesthetic-philosophical rampages of the Peipers, Brauns, and other manifestations of literary life.

Spirit is born of the imitation of spirit and a writer must pretend to be a writer in order finally to become a writer. Prewar literature in Poland was, with few exceptions, a fair imitation of literature, but that is all. Those people knew what a great writer was supposed to be: "authentic," "profound," "constructive" and they then tried to fulfill these requirements yet their game was spoiled by the awareness that it was not their own "profundity" and "loftiness" that was compelling them to write, but the reverse: they were creating the profundity so that they could be writers. That is how this subtle blackmail of values came about and it was no longer clear whether someone was voicing humility only to elevate himself and stand out, or if that someone was voicing the bankruptcy of culture and literature in order to be a good literary figure. The greater the hunger for real and pure value among these beings, so restricted by their own contradictions, the more desperate the feeling of the inevitable and all-demanding kitsch. O those exhausted intelligences, those inflated heights, those subtleties dragged out by the hair, those souls suffering, all this for a readership! There was only one means by which to get out of this hell: to disclose reality, bare the entire mechanism and loyally acknowledge the primacy of the human over the divine. Yet it is

---

* *Seizure of Power.*

exactly this that literature feared, and it wasn't just our literature that feared it. None of the literati would admit it to the world even though this was the only thing that could arm them with a new truth and honesty. This is the reason that prewar Polish literature was becoming more and more of an imitation. Yet the virtuous little nation which took its literature seriously, was very surprised to see that its "top writers," when pressed to the wall by the historical moment, began to change their skin, easily absorbed the new faith, and even began to dance to the tune that was played for them. Writers! The point is precisely that these were writers who would stop at nothing to be writers. They were ready to make the most heroic sacrifices in order to remain writers.

I don't at all claim that I would not have gone the same route if submitted to the same pressures as they, actually it would have been quite likely, but at least I wouldn't have made a fool of myself, like they did, because I was more honest in relation to myself and those absolute values did not issue from my lips as profusely. Then, in the swarming and noisy coffeehouses of Warsaw, it was as if I had a foreboding of the day of confrontation, the revelation and baring, as a result of which I preferred to avoid platitudes. Not everything in bankruptcy in that bankruptcy, however, and today, in Miłosz's book, I am inclined to look for new possibilities rather than signs of an ultimate catastrophe. The following question is what interests me: how far can these grim experiences assure the Eastern writers a superiority over their Western counterparts?

For it is certain that in their fall, they have an advantage in some special way over the West, and in several instances Miłosz underlines the power and wisdom that can result from that type of mendacity, terror, and consistent deformation. Miłosz himself is an illustration of this specific development, because his calm streamlined word, which watches what he describes with such mortal calm, has the flavor of a specific maturity, somewhat different from that which blooms in the West. I would say that in his book Miłosz is fighting on two fronts: the point is not only to condemn the East in the name of Western culture, but also to impose one's own distinct experience and one's own new knowledge of the world — derived from over there — on the West. This almost personal duel between a modern Polish writer and the West, where the stakes are an exhibition of one's own value, power, distinctness, is far more interesting to me than Miłosz's analysis of Communist issues, which, even though it is exceptionally penetrating, cannot introduce elements that are entirely new.

Miłosz himself once said something like this: the difference between a Western and East European intellectual is that the former has not had a good kick in the a ———. In keeping with the thought of this aphorism, our strong point (I include myself in this) would be that we are representatives of a *brutalized culture,* that is, a culture that is close to life. Miłosz himself knows the boundaries of this truth, and it would be pitiful if our prestige were based exclusively on the bruised quarter of our body. A bruised part of the body is not a part of the body in its normal state, and philosophy, literature, and art must also serve people who have not had their teeth knocked out, their eyes blackened, or their jaws broken. Nevertheless, look at Miłosz and see how he tries to adjust his wildness to the demands of Western delicacy.

Body and Spirit. It sometimes happens that bodily comforts intensify the sharpness of the soul and that, behind the still curtains, in the stuffy room of a bourgeois, a severity is born that is completely alien to those who threw themselves at tanks. Therefore, our brutalized culture can be of use only if it can be digested as a new form of real culture that is thought through and organized by our contribution to the universal spirit.

Question: Is Miłosz, is a free Polish literature, capable of even partially fulfilling these demands?

I am writing all of this in my room and I must stop as supper is waiting for me at the rooming house, Las Delicias. Farewell for now, little diary, faithful dog of my soul. Don't howl—your master is leaving, it is true, but he will return.

WEDNESDAY

For a while (and, possibly, because of the monotony of my existence here), I have been overcome by a curiosity which I have never before experienced, a curiosity of such pure intensity, curiosity as to what will happen within the next moment. Right before me, a wall of darkness out of which springs the most direct immediacy, like a terrifying revelation. What will come around the corner? A man? A dog? If it's a dog, then what shape will it have, what pedigree? I sit at the table and in a moment, my soup will arrive, but, what kind of soup? This very basic feeling has not been adequately treated in art. Man — as an instrument transforming the unknown into the known — does not figure in the pantheon of its heroes.

I have finished Miłosz's book.

It is immeasurably instructive, stimulating, and shocking reading for all of us Polish literati.

I think about it almost nonstop when I am alone and I have to say that Miłosz the defender of Western civilization interests me far less than Miłosz the opponent and rival of the West. When he tries to be different from Western writers is when he is most valuable to me. I feel the same thing in him that I find in myself: antipathy and condescension in relation to them, mixed with a bitter powerlessness. Comparing Miłosz with Claudel, for example, with Cocteau or even Valéry, leads to odd conclusions. It would seem that this Polish writer, this pal of Andrzejewski and Gałczyński, this habitué of the Ziemiańska, dispenses a greater dose of realism and is more "modern," and, what's more, more free spiritually, more open to reality and more loyal to it. Furthermore, one has the impression that he is even more isolated and more, that he has cast off the remainder of the illusions that Western seers cling to (Valéry, although he was completely bereft of illusions, did not stop being a man tied to a certain milieu and to a certain social order, while Miłosz has been completely thrown from the saddle). So one could say that a brutalized culture furnishes one with considerable advantages. Yet all of this is as if it were unfinished, unarticulated, and unconsolidated and we lack, perhaps, the final consciousness that lends full distinction and power to our truth. We lack the key to our riddle.

How the indistinctness of our relationship to the West chafes! A Pole, when confronting the East, is a Pole delineated and known in advance. A Pole with his face turned toward the West has a turbid visage, full of unclean angers, disbelief, and secret sore spots.

THURSDAY

It is raining and is still quite cold. Because of this, I spent all day reading *The Brothers Karamazov* in an excellent edition, which includes the author's letters and commentary.

FRIDAY

The mail: R. sent me letters and periodicals, among them the latest issue of *Kultura*. I find out that Miłosz won the Prix Européen for a novel which I have not read: *La prise du pouvoir*.* In that same issue of *Kultura* are Miłosz's comments on *The Marriage* and *Trans-Atlantic*.

SATURDAY

Most of the many letters that I am getting regarding *Trans-Atlantic* are neither an expression of protest — because of the "affront to the most sacred of feelings" — nor a polemic, nor even a commentary. No. Only two issues might concern these readers: How dare I write certain words with capitals in the middle of a sentence? How dare I use the word sh ——?

What am I supposed to think about the intellectual and other levels of a person who does not yet know that a word changes depending on how it is used? That even the word "rose" can become less than sweet-smelling if it appears on the lips of a pretentious aesthete, and that the word "sh ——" can be considered genteel if it is used intentionally by a discipline conscious of its goals?

But, no, they read literally. If a person uses lofty words, that person is noble. If he uses strong words, he is strong; if crude words, he is crude. And this dull literalness reigns on even the highest rungs of society, so how then is one to dream of a Polish literature on a more universal scale?

THURSDAY
(TWO WEEKS LATER, AFTER RETURNING FROM BUENOS AIRES)

I received a letter from Miłosz, who writes the following critique of *Trans-Atlantic*.

> "At the same time I would like to share with you my thoughts about your writing. There are times when I have the feeling that you act like Don Quixote, who lends a certain life to windmills and sheep. From a *Polish* perspective (that is, from the perspective of the terrible thrashing which they got), the 'Poles,' whom you try to free from Polishness, are poor shadows with an unusually low degree of being. In other words, you sometimes act as if that entire horrifyingly effective liquidation there in Poland had not happened, as if Poland had been swept away by a lunar catastrophe and you come along with your revulsion to an immature, provincial Poland from

before 1939. Perhaps this settling of accounts is needed and very necessary, but in my view, this has already been done quite categorically. Many issues have already been settled this way. This is a difficult problem, which is based on the fact that Marxism eliminates certain problems (by the same principle that the blowing up of a city eliminates marital quarrels, concerns about the furniture, etc.).

"There is a nihilistic trap here and we are poised somewhere between the desire to speak to people in Poland, that is, to create a post-Marxist formation (which must digest and engulf Marxism) and the entirely *personal* desire for independent thought (which cannot take the climate over there, in conquered countries, into consideration but which, nonetheless, changes the past as well as the future). When I read your work, I always think of this. . . ."

To which I answered:

"Dear Czesław:

"If I understand you correctly, you have two reservations about Trans-Atlantic: first that I am settling accounts with a pre-1939 Poland, which has vanished into thin air, and that thereby I avoid today's Poland, the real Poland. That my thoughts, like a cat, stray too much along their own paths, that I have my own world, which seems chimerical or outdated.

"Yet, as you correctly observe, you judge this issue from the perspective of the homeland while I cannot see the world in any other way except from my own perspective.

"To introduce a certain amount of order into my feelings, I decided quite a while ago that I would write only about my own reality. I cannot write about Poland as it is today because I do not know it. This 'memoir,' that is, *Trans-Atlantic,* concerns my experiences before 1939 in the face of the Polish catastrophe of that time.

"Can this settling of accounts with Poland be important for today's Poland? You mention *Don Quixote* in your letter and I think to myself that Cervantes wrote *Don Quixote* to settle accounts with the bad knighthood romances of his time, of which not a single tract has survived while Quixote has. From which humbler authors can derive the moral that one can write in a lasting way about things that are nonlasting.

"Even though *Trans-Atlantic* uses pre-1939 Poland, it is aiming at all Polish presents and futures, where the point is victory over national form as such and an elaboration of distance to any kind of 'Polish style,' whatever it may be. Today, Poles in Poland are subjected to a certain 'Polish style,' born there under the pressure of their new collective life. In a hundred years, if we are still a nation, other forms will emanate from among us and my future grandchild will rebel against them just as I am rebelling today.

"I attack Polish form because it is my form, because all of my works desire to be, in a certain sense (certain because this is only one of the sense of my nonsense), a revision of the modern man in relation to form, to form which is not a result of him but which is formed 'between' people. I do not need to tell you that this thought, together with all of its ramifications, is a child of our times, when people have intentionally set out to remake man. It even seems to me that it is the key to understanding today's consciousness.

"Yet even though there is nothing that appalls me more than anachronism, I prefer not to identify too much with the slogans of the present day, which change rapidly. I feel that art should maintain a distance from slogans and look for its own, more personal, paths. In works of art I like the mysterious deviation the best, the deviation that causes that a work, even while adhering to its epoch, nevertheless is the work of a separate individual who lives his own life. . . ."

I include this exchange of letters to let the reader in on the conversations of writers like Miłosz and myself who search for a certain line in writing, each in his own way. I must add a few comments though. My letter to Miłosz would have been a great deal more honest and complete if I had included this truth in it: that I really don't care all that much about these theses, ways, and problems and that I occupy myself with them against my will. Basically, I am *childish*. Is Miłosz, too, *primarily* childish?

WEDNESDAY

Miłosz is a first-rate force. This is a writer with a clearly defined purpose, called to quicken our pulse so that we can keep up with the epoch. He has a magnificent talent, finely tuned to complete his tasks. He possesses something that is worth its weight in gold, something that I would call a "will to reality" and, at the same time, a sensitivity to the crucial points of our crisis. He belongs to those few whose words have meaning (the only thing that can undermine him is haste).

This writer, however, has currently transformed himself into an expert on Poland and Communism. Just as I distinguished between an Eastern Miłosz and a Western one, now perhaps I should also make a distinction between Miłosz the "absolute" writer and Miłosz the writer of the immediate historical moment. It is precisely the Western Miłosz (the one who in the name of the West, judges the East) that is the Miłosz of a lesser, more topical, caliber. One could accuse this Western Miłosz of many things that pertain to that entire section of today's literature that lives off of just one problem: Communism.

The first reproach is: *they exaggerate.* Not in the sense that they magnify the danger, but in the sense that they impute certain demonic traits to that world, some type of extraordinariness, something new and shocking. This approach is simply not reconcilable with maturity, which, in knowing the essence of life, does not allow itself to be surprised by its events. Revolutions, wars, cataclysms — what does this foam mean when compared to the fundamental horror of existence? You say there has been nothing like it before? You forget that in the nearest hospital no lesser atrocities take place. You say that millions are dying? You forget that millions have been dying, incessantly, without a moment's respite, since the beginning of time. You are horrified and dumbfounded by that horror because your imagination has fallen asleep and you forget that we rub up against hell with our every step.

This is important because Communism can be judged effectively only from the perspective of the most severe and profound sense of existence, never from a point of view that is superficial and subdued, never from a bourgeois point of view. You get carried away by the desire (appropriate to artists) to paint the picture in brighter colors, to lend it as much expression as possible. That is why your literature is a magnification of Communism and in your imagination you build a phenomenon that is so powerful and so extraordinary that it doesn't take much more for you to fall to your knees before it.

Therefore, I ask you: Wouldn't it be more in keeping with history and with our knowledge of man and the world if you treated the world from behind the curtain not as a new, incredible, and demonic world but as a devastation and distortion of a normal world? If you maintained the right proportion between the convulsions of a destroyed surface and the unrelenting, powerful, and profound life that continues beneath it?

And the second reproach: by reducing everything to that one antinomy between East and West, you must inevitably conform to patterns that you yourself create. And even more so because there is on way to make the distinction between what is the quest for truth in you and what a desire for psychological mobilization in the battle. I don't mean to say that you cultivate propaganda. I want to say that deep collective instincts, that today dictate to humanity that it should concentrate on just one struggle, are speaking through you. You swim with the current of the mass imagination, which has already created its own language, ideas, images, and myths, and the current is carrying you farther than you would like to go. How much Orwell is there in Miłosz? How much Koestler is there in Orwell? How much of both of them is in the thousands upon thousands of words uttered on that one subject and produced by printing presses day after day, which is not due to the American dollar but is the result of our very nature, which desires a sharply defined world for itself? In you, the boundlessness and richness of life are reduced to a few issues, and you use an oversimplified concept of the world, a concept you well know is provisional.

Why, the value of pure art is exactly in its breaking up of these set patterns.

The third reproach is even more painful. Whom do you wish to serve, the individual or the masses? Communism is something that subordinates man to a human collectivity, from which one should conclude that the best way to fight Communism is to strengthen the individual against the masses. Since it is obvious that politics, the press, and topical literature, calculated for practical effect, desire to create a collective force capable of battling the Soviets, the task before serious art is quite different. Serious art will either remain what it has been for centuries — the voice of the individual, the medium of man in the singular — or it will perish. From this standpoint, one page of Montaigne, a single Verlaine poem, or one sentence by Proust is far more anti-Communist than the accusing choir which you represent. They are free and therefore they are liberating.

And last, the fourth reproach: genuinely ambitious art (these reproaches are directed only at creators with high aspirations, at those who do not deny the name of artists) must be in advance of its time, it must be the art of tomorrow. How is one to reconcile this wonderful task with reality, that is, with today? Artists are proud that recent years have expanded their perception of man. By comparison, more recently deceased authors appear naive. Yet all of these truths and half-truths were given to them just so they could surmount them to discover others lurking beneath. Art must destroy today's ideas in the name of impending ones. But those impending tastes, tomorrow's issues, the awaiting spiritual states, concepts, feelings: how can they be born under a pen that strives only to consolidate today's vision, today's contradictions? The observations that Miłosz published in *Kultura* about my play are a good illustration of this. He saw what was "timely" in *The Marriage*, the despair and the moan that result from the degradation of human dignity and the violent crash of civilization, but he did not notice how far delight and play — which are ready to raise man above his own defeats at a moment's notice — hide behind that facade of today!

Gradually we are becoming sated with today's feelings. Our symphony is getting close to the moment when the baritone rises and sings: brothers, cast off your songs; let other tones resound! The song of the future, however, will not be born under a pen that is excessively tied to the present time.

It would be stupid if I harbored ill feelings toward people who, upon seeing a fire, sound the alarm. Such are not my intentions. Yet I am saying: let each person do what he was called to do and what he is capable of doing. Literature of a high caliber must aim high and concern itself chiefly with not allowing anything to impede its range. If you want a projectile to soar, you must point the barrel upward.

[. . .]

IV

FRIDAY

I write this diary reluctantly. Its dishonest honesty wearies me. For whom am I writing? If I am writing for myself, then why is it being published? If for the reader, why do I pretend that I am talking to myself? Are you talking to yourself so that others will hear you?

How far I am from the certitude and vigor that hum in me when I am, pardon me, "creating." Here, on these pages, I feel as if I were emerging from a blessed night into the hard light of dawn, which fills me with yawning and drags my shortcomings out into the open. The duplicity inherent in keeping a diary makes me timid, so forgive me, oh, forgive me (perhaps these last words are dispensable, perhaps they are already pretentious?).

Yet I realize that one must be oneself at all levels of writing, which is to say, that I ought to be able to express myself not only in a poem or drama, but also in everyday prose — in an article or in a diary — and the flight of art has to find its counterpart in the domain of regular life, just as the shadow of the condor is cast onto the ground. What's more, this passage into an everyday world from an area that is backed into the most remote depths, practically in the underground, is a matter of great importance to me. I want to be a balloon, but one with ballast; an antenna, but one that is grounded. I want to be capable of translating myself into everyday speech, but — *traduttore, traditore.* Here I betray myself, I am beneath myself.

The difficulty consists in the fact that I write about myself not at night, not in isolation, but right in a newspaper in front of people. In these circumstances, I cannot treat myself with the appropriate gravity, I have to be "modest" and then again, I am tormented by that which has tormented me throughout my entire life and which has so greatly influenced my way of being with other people. The necessity of slighting myself in order to be in tune with those who slight me, or who don't know the least little thing about me. I will not submit myself to that "modesty" at any price and I consider it my mortal enemy. Happy Frenchmen who write their diaries with tact, except that I don't believe in the value of their tact, I know that theirs is only a tactful circumvention of the problem, which by its very nature is unsociable.

But I should grab the bull by the horns. From childhood I have been very much initiated into this matter, it grew right along with me so that today I should be pretty comfortable with it. I know and I have said this on many occasions, that every artist has to be pompous because he aspires to be on a pedestal. Yet I have also said that concealing these pretensions is a stylistic flaw, and a sign of a faulty "inner resolution." Openness. One must play with uncovered cards. Writing is nothing more than a battle that the artist wages with others for his own prominence.

Yet if I am incapable of making this thought real here in the diary, what is it worth? Yet somehow I cannot, and something bothers me because there is no artistic form between me and people and our contact becomes too embarrassing. I ought to treat this diary as an instrument of my becoming before you. I ought to strive to have you understand me in some way, in a way that would enable me to have (and let this dangerous word appear) talent.

Let this diary be more modern and more conscious and let it be permeated
by the idea that my talent can arise only in connection with you, that is, that
only you can excite me to talent or, what's more, that only you can create it
in me.

I would like people to see in me that which I suggest to them. I would like
to impose myself on people as a personality in order to be its subject forever
after that. Other diaries should be to this one what the words "I am like this"
are to "I want to be like this." We are used to lifeless words that merely ascer-
tain. A better word is one that brings to life. *Spiritus movens.* If I could only
succeed in summoning the spirit that moves to the first pages of this diary,
I could do a great deal. I could, first of all (and I need this even more because
I am a Polish author), shatter this narrow cage of concepts in which you
would like to imprison me. Far too many people, worthy of a better fate,
have been shackled. I alone should designate the role I am to play.

Furthermore, by suggesting, somewhat in the way of a proposition, certain problems, more or less linked to me, I pull myself into them and they
lead me to other secrets still unknown to me. To travel as far as possible into
the virgin territory of culture, into its still half-wild, and so indecent, places,
while exciting you to extremes, to excite even myself . . . I want to meet you
in that jungle, bind myself to you in a way that is the most difficult and
uncomfortable, for you and for me. Don't I have to distinguish myself from
current European thought? Aren't my enemies the currents and doctrines to
which I am similar? I have to attack them in order to force myself into con-
tradistinction and I have to force you to confirm it. I want to uncover my
present moment and tie myself to you in our todayness.

In this little diary I would like to set out to openly construct a talent for
myself, as openly as Henry fabricates a marriage for himself in the third act.
Why openly? Because I desire to reveal myself, to stop being too easy a riddle for you to solve. By taking you to the backstage of my being, I force
myself to retreat to an even more remote depth.

That is all. If only I could summon the spirit. But I don't feel equal to the
task. Three years ago, unfortunately, I broke with pure art, as my kind of art
was not the kind that could be cultivated casually, on Sundays or holidays. I
began to write this diary for the simple reason of saving myself, in fear of
degradation and an ultimate inundation by the waves of a trivial life, which

are already up to my neck. Yet it turns out that even here I am incapable of total effort. One cannot be nothingness all week and then suddenly expect to exist on Sunday. Journalists and you, honorable counselors and spectators, have no need to fear. You no longer need to feel threatened by any conceit and incomprehension on my part. I am tumbling into publicism along with you and the rest of the world.

[. . .]

FRIDAY

Giedroyc wanted me to reply to Cioran's (a Romanian writer) article, "The Conveniences and Inconveniences of Exile." The answer contains my view of the role of literature in exile.

> Cioran's words reek of a basement coolness and the rot of the grave, but they are too petty. Who is he talking about? Who should one understand to be the "writer in exile"? Adam Mickiewicz wrote books and so does Mr. X, quite correct and readable ones, both are "writers" and, nota bene, writers in exile, but here all parallels end.
>
> Rimbaud? Norwid? Kafka? Słowacki? (There are a variety of exiles.) I believe that none of them would have been too horrified at this category of hell. It is very painful not to have readers and very unpleasant not to be able to publish one's works. It certainly is not sweet being unknown, highly unpleasant to see oneself deprived of the aid of that mechanism that pushes one to the top, that creates publicity and organizes fame, but art is loaded with elements of loneliness and self-sufficiency, it finds its satisfaction and sense of purpose in itself. The homeland? Why, every eminent person because of that very eminence was foreigner even at home. Readers? Why, they never wrote "for" readers anyway, always "against" them. Honors, success, renown, fame: why, they became famous exactly because they valued themselves more than their success.
>
> And that which is a little Kafka, Conrad, or Mickiewicz in even the smaller caliber writer, that which is genuine talent and real superiority or real maturity, will in no measure fit into Cioran's basement. I would also like to remind Cioran that not only émigré but all art remains in the most intimate contact with decay, it is born of decadence, it is a transmutation of illness into health. All art, generally speaking, borders on silliness, defeat, degradation. Is there an artist who is not, as Cioran says, "an ambitious being, aggressive in his defeat, embittered, a conniving conqueror"? Has Cioran ever seen an artist or writer who was not, who did not have to be, a megalomaniac? And art, as Boy once correctly said, is a graveyard: for every

thousand people who were incapable of "coming into existence" and who remained in a sphere of painful insufficiency, barely one or two is capable of really "coming into existence." This dirt, therefore, this venom of unsatisfied ambitions, this tossing and turning in a vacuum, this catastrophe has very little to do with emigration and a lot to do with art. They make up an aspect of every literary café and truly it is a matter of indifference where in the world the writers who are not writers enough in order to really be writers, suffer.

And perhaps it is healthier that they were deprived of doles, applause, all those tiny caresses that the state and society lavished upon them in the good old days in the name of "supporting native creativity." This family playing at greatness and distinction, the sympathetic noise created at one time by the condescendingly smiling press and the half-baked critics, deprived of a feeling for the scale of events, that process of artificially pumping candidates up into a "national writer ". . . didn't all this reek of kitsch? And the result? Nations that at best were capable of producing a few authentic writers nurtured entire hosts of wonders in this incubator, and in this familial warmth, which was a mixture of spinsterish goodness and a cynical disregard for values, all hierarchy disintegrated. Is it surprising then that these hothouse creations, nurtured in the womb of the nation, wilt when out of the womb? Cioran writes about how a writer torn away from his people is lost. If that is the case, this writer never existed in the first place: he was a writer in embryo. Instead, it seems to me that theoretically speaking and bypassing material hardship, the immersing of oneself in the world, that is, emigration, should constitute an incredible stimulus for literature.

For lo and behold the country's elite is kicked out over the border. It can think, feel, and write from the outside. It gains distance. It gains an incredible spiritual freedom. All bonds burst. One can be more of oneself. In the general din all the forms that have existed until now loosen up and one can move toward the future in a more ruthless way.

An exceptional opportunity! The moment everyone has dreamed of! It would seem, therefore, that the stronger individuals, the richer individuals would roar like lions? Then why don't they? Why has the voice of these people faded abroad?

They do not roar because, first of all, they are too free. Art demands style, order, discipline. Cioran correctly underscores the danger of too much isolation, of excessive freedom. Everything to which they were tied and everything that bound them — homeland, ideology, politics, group, program, faith, milieu — everything vanished in the whirlpool of history and only a bubble filled with nothingness remained on the surface. Those thrown out of their little world found themselves facing a world, a boundless world and, consequently, one that was impossible to master. Only a universal culture can come to terms with the world, never parochial cultures, never those who live only on fragments of existence. Only he who knows how to reach deeper, beyond the homeland, only he for whom the homeland is but one of the revelations in an eternal and universal life, will not be incited to anarchy by the loss of his homeland. The loss of a homeland will not disturb the internal order of only those whose homeland is the world. Contemporary history has turned out to be too violent and borderless for literatures too national and specific.

And it is exactly this excess of freedom that inhibits the writer most. Threatened by the enormity of the world and the finality of its affairs, they grasp at the past convulsively; they cling desperately to themselves; they want to remain as they were; they fear even the slightest change in themselves, thinking that everything will then fall apart; and, finally, then cling convulsively to the only hope remaining: the hope of recovering the homeland. Recovering the homeland, however, cannot come to pass without waging a battle, and a battle requires strength and collective strength can be achieved only by giving up one's I. In order to produce this strength, the writer must impose a blind faith, among other deficiencies, on himself and his compatriots and the luxury of objective and free thinking becomes a grievous sin. He does not know how to be a writer without a homeland or in order to regain his homeland, he has to stop being a writer, at least a serious writer.

Though perhaps there is yet another reason for this spiritual paralysis, at least where it is not a matter of intellectuals but artists. I have in mind the very concept of art and the artist, as it has come to be accepted in Western Europe. It does not seem to be that our modern beliers concerning the essence of art, the role of the artist, the relationship of artist to society have tallied with reality. The artistic philosophy of the West derives from the elite in crystallized societies where nothing interferes with conventional language but there is nothing a man thrown outside the limits of convention can do with such a philosophy. The concept of art forged on that side of the curtain by the victorious bureaucracy of the proletariat is even more elitist and more naive. An artist in emigration, however, is forced to exist not only outside of his people, but also outside of the elite. He confronts the spiritually and intellectually inferior sphere far more directly. Nothing isolates him from this contact, he has personally to endure the pressure of a brutal and immature life. He is like a bankrupt count who sees that the manners of the salon are worthless if there is no salon. Sometimes this pushes people in the direction of "democratic" shallowness, into a kindly ordinariness or into a crude "realism" and sometimes it condemns them to isolation. We have to find a way to feel like aristocrats once again (in the deeper sense of the word).

Therefore, if there is talk about the disintegration and decadence of émigré literature, then this notion of the issue would be closest to me because here, at least, we liberate ourselves for a moment from the vicious circle of trivialities and touch the difficulties capable of destroying authentic writers. I do not deny at all that overcoming these problems requires a great determination and boldness of spirit. It is not easy to be an émigré writer, which means almost total isolation. Why should it be surprising, therefore, that overcome by our own weakness and the enormity of the tasks, we bury our heads in the sand and, organizing parodies of the past for ourselves, we flee the big world to live in our little one?

Yet sooner or later our thought must work its way out of the impasse. Our problems will find people to solve them. At some point, it is no longer a matter of creativity itself, but the recovery of the capacity to create. We have to produce that portion of freedom, boldness, ruthlessness, and even, I would say, irresponsibility, without which creation is impossible. We have to accustom ourselves to a new scale of existence. We will have to treat our most cherished feelings unceremoniously, with sangfroid in order to attain other values. The minute we begin to shape the world in the place where we happen to be and with the means at our disposal, the enormity of the task will shrink, the boundlessness will become delineated, and the turbulent waters of chaos will begin to recede.

[. . .]

SUNDAY

Today, years later, when I am a lot calmer, less at the mercy and the lack of mercy of judgments, I think about the basic assumptions of *Ferdydurke* regarding criticism and I can endorse them without reservation. There are enough innocent works that enter life looking as if they did not know that they would be raped by a thousand idiotic assessments! Enough authors who pretend that this rape, perpetrated on them with superficial judgments, any kind at all, is something that is not capable of affecting them and should not be noticed. A work, even if it is born of the purest contemplation, should be written in such a way as to assure the author an advantage in his game with people. A style that cannot defend itself before human judgment, that surrenders its creator to the ill will of any old imbecile, does not fulfill its most important assignment. Yet defense against these opinions is possible only when we manage a little humility and admit how important they really are to us, even if they do come from an idiot. That is why the defenselessness of art in the face of human judgment is the sad consequence of its pride: ah, I am higher than that, I take into account only the opinions of the wise! This fiction is absurd and the truth, the difficult and tragic truth is that the idiot's opinion is also significant. It also creates us, shapes us from inside out, and has far-reaching practical and vital consequences.

Criticism, however, has yet another aspect. It can be seen from the author's side but it can also be seen from the side of the public and then it takes on even gaudier tones of scandal, mendacity, and deception. How do these things look? The public desires to be informed by the press about books that appear. This is the source of journalistic criticism, manned by people having contact with literature. Yet if these people really had something to do in the field of art, if they really were rooted in it, they certainly would not stop at these articles. So, no, these are practically always second- and third-rate literary figures, persons who always maintain merely a loose, rather social, relation with the world of the spirit, persons who are not on the level of the concerns that they write about. This then is the source of the greatest difficulty, which cannot be avoided and from which arises the entire scandal that comprises criticism and its immorality. The question is the following: How can an inferior man criticize a superior man, how can he assess his personality and arrive at the value of his work? How can this take place without becoming absurd?

Never have the critics, at least the Polish ones, ever devoted even a single minute of time to this delicate matter. Mr. X, however, in judging a man of Norwid's class, for example, puts himself in a suicidal, impossible position because in order to judge Norwid, he must be superior to Norwid but he is not. This basic falseness draws out an infinite chain of additional lies, and criticism becomes the living contradiction of all of its loftiest aspirations.

So they want to be judges of art? First they must attain it. They are in its antechamber and they lack access to the spiritual states from which art derives. They know nothing of its intensity.

So they want to be methodical, professional, objective, just? But they themselves are a triumph of dilettantism, expressing themselves on subjects that they are incapable of mastering. They are an example of the most unlawful usurpation.

Guardians of morality? Morality is based on a hierarchy of values and they themselves sneer at hierarchy. The very fact of their existence is in its essence immoral: there is nothing that they have exhibited and they have no proof that they have a right to this role except that the editor allows them to write. Giving themselves up to immoral work, which consists of articulating cheap, easy, hurried judgments without basis, they want to judge the morality of people who put their life into art.

So they want to judge style? But they themselves are a parody of style, the personification of pretentiousness. They are bad stylists to the degree that they are not offended by the incurable dissonance of that accurse "higher" and "lower." Even omitting the fact that they write quickly and sloppily, this is the dirt of the cheapest publicism. . . .

Teachers, educators, spiritual leaders? In reality, they taught the Polish reader this truth about literature: that it is something like a school essay, written in order that the teacher could give it a grade; that creativity is not a play of forces, which do not allow themselves to be completely controlled, not a burst of energy or the work of a spirit that is creating itself but merely an annual literary "production," along with the inseparable reviews, contests, awards, and feuilletons. These are masters of trivialization, artists who transform a keen life into a boring pulp, where everything is more or less equally mediocre and unimportant.

A surplus of parasites produces such fatal effects. To write about literature is easier than writing literature: that's the whole point. If I were in their place, therefore, I would reflect very deeply on how to elude this disgrace whose name is: oversimplification. Their advantages are purely technical. Their voice resounds powerfully not because it is powerful but because they are allowed to speak through the megaphone of the press.

What is the way out of this?

Cast off in fury and pride all the artificial advantages that your situation assures you. Because literary criticism is not the judging of one man by another (who gave *you* this right?) but the meeting of two personalities on absolutely equal terms.

Therefore: do not judge. Simply describe your reactions. Never write about the author or the work, only about yourself in confrontation with the work or the author. You are allowed to write about yourself.

In writing about yourself, however, write so that your person takes on weight, meaning, and life, so that it becomes your decisive argument. Do not write as a pseudoscientist but as an artist. Criticism must be as tense and vibrant as that which it touches. Otherwise it becomes gas escaping from a balloon, a sloppy butchering with a dull knife, decay, an anatomy, a grave.

And if you don't feel like doing this or cannot do this, leave it alone.

(I wrote this after finding out that the Association of Polish Writers in Exile, which considers criticism especially important to writing, has established an award of twenty-five pounds for the best work of criticism. Even though all the awards go on somewhere beyond me, even though this is a dance to which I have not been invited . . . hmm, who knows, maybe this time? I submit the following "critical work" for the prize and highly recommend it to the Committee.)

SATURDAY

To persons who are interested in my writing technique, I offer the following recipe:

Enter the realm of dreams.

After which begin writing the first story that comes to mind and write about twenty pages. Then read it.

On these twenty pages, there may be one scene, a few sentences, a metaphor, which will seem exciting to you. Then write everything all over again, attempting this time to make the exciting elements the scaffolding and write, not taking reality into consideration, and striving only to satisfy the needs of your imagination.

During this second editing your imagination will head in a specific direction and you will arrive at new associations, which will clearly delineate your field of action. Then write an additional twenty pages, constantly heading along the same line of association, always seeking an exciting, creative, mysterious, revealing element. Then write everything all over again. By doing this you will barely notice the moment when a whole series of key scenes, metaphors, symbols (like the "walking," the "empty pistol," or "stallion" in *Trans-Atlantic* or the "parts of the body" in *Ferdydurke*) create themselves and you have arrived at the appropriate code. Everything will begin to take on flesh under your fingers by the power of its own logic: scenes, characters, concepts, images will demand fruition and that which you have already created will dictate the rest to you.

The whole trick, though, is that while surrendering yourself passively to the work and letting it create itself, you do not, even for a moment, stop controlling it. Your rule in this matter is to be: I do not know where the work will lead me, but wherever it leads me, I have to express myself and satisfy myself. When beginning *Trans-Atlantic,* I hadn't the slightest idea that it would lead me to Poland, yet when it happened, I tried not to lie, or, to lie as little as possible, and to exploit the situation to release energy and participate with relish. All the problems that a work being born and blindly creating itself suggest to you — problems of ethics, style, form, intellect — must be solved with the full participation of your most alert consciousness and with maximum realism (as all of this is a game of compensation: the crazier, more fantastic, inventive, unpredictable, irresponsible you are, the more sober, controlled, and responsible you must be).

In the end a battle arises between you and the work, the same as that between a driver and the horses which are carrying him off. I cannot control the horses, but I must take care not to overturn the wagon on any of the sharp curves of the course. Where I will end up, I don't know, but I must get there in one piece. Moreover, I must, when I get the chance, recall the delicious terror of the ride.

Finally: out of the struggle between the inner logic of the work and my person (for it is not yet clear: is the work a mere pretext for expressing myself or am I a pretext for the work), out of this wrestling is born a third thing, something indirect, something that seems not to have been written by me, yet it is mine, something that is neither pure form nor my direct expression, but a deformation born in an intermediary sphere; between me and the world. This strange creation, this bastard, I put in an envelope and mail to a publisher.

After which you read in the press: "Gombrowicz wrote *Trans-Atlantic* in order to inform . . ." "The thesis of the drama *The Marriage* is . . ." "In *Ferdydurke,* Gombrowicz wants to say . . ."

[. . .]

FRIDAY

Yet somehow I have made it. . . . This is almost like fame. At any rate, respect. It would seem, Gombrowicz, that you have triumphed on this home front and can now intoxicate yourself with the sight of those confounded faces . . . which considered you a clown not too long ago. Revenge is the delight of the gods! That hussy can no longer act brazenly toward you. That cretin had to back down from his opinion. I am walking in glory. But this glory . . . hmm . . . no, dullness cannot be conquered! It is invincible!

Yesterday I met Mrs. X., whose ears had picked up news of my many triumphs. After greeting me she looked at me with a certain approval and said:

— "Well, well . . . Congratulations . . . you have gotten serious!"

Accursed woman! So you still have not come to the conclusion that I was serious when you considered me a fop. You think I have gotten serious only since my triumphs!

She said: You have an easy life. I said: Why do you think that I have an easy life? She said: You have talent! You can write whatever you feel like writing and you have recognition and various daily amenities.

I said: But do you realize what it costs in effort to write? She said: When one has talent, everything comes easy. I said: Why "talent" is an empty word, in order to write one has to *be* someone, one must work on oneself unstintingly, even fight with oneself, it's a matter of development. . . . She said: Tsk, tsk, why should you work if you have talent. If I had the talent, I would write, too.

You write? Everybody is writing nowadays. I myself have written a novel. I: Really? She: Yes, and I even got some pretty good reviews. I: Congratulations! She: Oh, I'm not saying this to fish for compliments, I merely wanted to emphasize that everybody is writing nowadays. It's something that everybody can do.

[. . .]

Translated by Lillian Vallee

Czesław Miłosz

(1911–2004)

A witness or a prophet? Czesław Miłosz saw himself as a poet who only happened to wander in long corridors of history; poetry came first and went last—he was among the most remarkable poets still creative in old age. And yet he witnessed more of the dark side of history than did the majority of his contemporaries. Born as the son of an engineer who worked for the Russian government, Miłosz was a student and a young poet in between-the-wars Poland, a Resistance member (though never a combatant) under the Nazi occupation, a middle-rank diplomat in the postwar People's Republic administration, an exile in Paris, a U.S. university professor and citizen, and finally a world-famous poet who returned to Poland (Kraków) during his final years.

Poetry was for Miłosz the highest vocation—and he never separated it from thought and philosophy. He was a religious person, a thinker with a great gift for putting words together. A long series of his books of poetry was accompanied by a long series of his collections of essays: what couldn't become a poem was turned into an essay. His writing was an endless meditation on the meaning of life, the quest for God, the place of justice in human society. He gave himself the right—something only great poets can afford—to attack the most central themes.

Miłosz was passionately interested in other literatures and cultures; he translated poetry from several languages. Because he lived and taught in the

United States for many decades—though he never tried to write poetry in
English—he was regarded by many as an American poet and man of letters.
He was a teacher and a friend to many of his younger acquaintances. Miłosz
was of those few writers who not only outlived the monsters of the twentieth
century, but also succeeded in defeating them and in keeping the serenity of a
great mind.

Ars Poetica?

Berkeley, 1968

I have always aspired to a more spacious form
that would be free from the claims of poetry or prose
and would let us understand each other without exposing
the author or reader to sublime agonies.

In the very essence of poetry there is something indecent:
a thing is brought forth which we didn't know we had in us,
so we blink our eyes, as if a tiger had sprung out
and stood in the light, lashing his tail.

That's why poetry is rightly said to be dictated by a daimonion,
though it's an exaggeration to maintain that he must be an angel.
It's hard to guess where that pride of poets comes from,
when so often they're put to shame by the disclosure of their frailty.

What reasonable man would like to be a city of demons,
who behave as if they were at home, speak in many tongues,
and who, not satisfied with stealing his lips or hand,
work at changing his destiny for their convenience?

It's true that what is morbid is highly valued today,
and so you may think that I am only joking
or that I've devised just one more means
of praising Art with the help of irony.

There was a time when only wise books were read,
helping us to bear our pain and misery.
This, after all, is not quite the same
as leafing through a thousand works fresh from psychiatric clinics.

And yet the world is different from what it seems to be
and we are other than how we see ourselves in our ravings.
People therefore preserve silent integrity,
thus earning the respect of their relatives and neighbors.

The purpose of poetry is to remind us
how difficult it is to remain just one person,
for our house is open, there are no keys in the doors,
and invisible guests come in and out at will.

What I'm saying here is not, I agree, poetry,
as poems should be written rarely and reluctantly,
under unbearable duress and only with the hope
that good spirits, not evil ones, choose us for their instrument.

Translated by Czesław Miłosz and Lillian Vallee

ELEGY FOR N. N.

BERKELEY, 1962

Tell me if it is too far for you.
You could have run over the small waves of the Baltic
and past the fields of Denmark, past a beech wood
could have turned toward the ocean, and there, very soon
Labrador, white at this season.
And if you, who dreamed about a lonely island,
were frightened of cities and of lights flashing along the highway
you had a path straight through the wilderness
over blue-black, melting waters, with tracks of deer and caribou
as far as the Sierras and abandoned gold mines.
The Sacramento River could have led you

between hills overgrown with prickly oaks.
Then just a eucalyptus grove, and you had found me.

True, when the manzanita is in bloom
and the bay is clear on spring mornings
I think reluctantly of the house between the lakes
and of nets drawn in beneath the Lithuanian sky.
The bath cabin where you used to leave your dress
has changed forever into an abstract crystal.
Honey-like darkness is there, near the veranda,
and comic young owls, and the scent of leather.

How could one live at that time, I really can't say.
Styles and dresses flicker, indistinct,
not self-sufficient, tending toward a finale.
Does it matter that we long for things as they are in themselves?
The knowledge of fiery years has scorched the horses standing at
     the forge,
the little columns in the marketplace,
the wooden stairs and the wig of Mama Fliegeltaub.

We learned so much, this you know well:
how, gradually, what could not be taken away
is taken. People, countrysides.
And the heart does not die when one thinks it should,
we smile, there is tea and bread on the table.
And only remorse that we did not love
the poor ashes in Sachsenhausen
with absolute love, beyond human power.

You got used to new, wet winters,
to a villa where the blood of the German owner
was washed from the wall, and he never returned.
I too accepted but what was possible, cities and countries.
One cannot step twice into the same lake
on rotting alder leaves,
breaking a narrow sunstreak.

Guilt, yours and mine? Not a great guilt.
Secrets, yours and mine? Not great secrets.
Not when they bind the jaw with a kerchief, put a little cross
      between the fingers,
and somewhere a dog barks, and the first star flares up.

No, it was not because it was too far
you failed to visit me that day or night.
From year to year it grows in us until it takes hold,
I understood it as you did: indifference.

Translated by Czesław Miłosz and Laurence Davis

"Elegy for N. N." was written in 1962, but for a long time it remained in manuscript, as I hesitated whether to publish it at all. The poem seemed to me shamelessly autobiographical, and in fact, it tells quite faithfully a personal story. This is good, for poetry should capture as much reality as possible, but a degree of a necessary artistic transformation is a delicate point. Fortunately, the person of whom I speak has not been named; nevertheless, the situation is as melodramatic as only life is: I live in Berkeley, I learn through a letter from Poland that a woman with whom I had once a loving relationship died recently. There are several details significant for those who read the poem in the original. The house by a lake is "beneath the Lithuanian sky," which is enough to invoke the exodus of populations at the end of World War II, when Lithuania found itself within the borders of the Soviet Union. "The horses standing at the forge," "the little columns in the marketplace," "the wig of Mama Fliegeltaub" mean that in the neighborhood there was a little town and that many Jews lived there before 1939. They were doomed once Hitler's army entered that area.

A reference to somebody dear to the heroine of the poem (a husband? a brother? a son?) who became "the poor ashes in Sachsenhausen" presupposes a knowledge of some historical facts: Oranienburg-Sachsenhausen was a large German concentration camp located near Berlin. As the Nazis placed the Poles on their list of "inferior races" close to the Jews, many were

The comments following the poem were written in English by Czesław Miłosz.

deported there, with a poor chance of surviving. By saying, "You got used to new, wet winters," I clearly state that my heroine moved after the war from her province to the territories situated to the West, formerly German, which were offered by Stalin to Poland as a compensation for the territories he had taken from Poland in the East.

Thus, the poem moves on the margin of big events in the history of the twentieth century. For an American reader that is no more than the history of East Central Europe. For me, it is simply the history of our planet — and not because I am a Polish poet, but because quite early, already at the time of World War II, consequences of what occurred in that part of the world could be foreseen. But, of course, when writing the poem I did not try to speak of history or to convey any message. I was following a true biography, though now I notice that the poem calls for copious historical footnotes.

There are two houses in the poem. One, by a lake; another, probably on the shore of the Baltic Sea ("wet winters"), a villa whose German owner has been killed, obviously in 1945, when the Soviet army overran that area in its march on Berlin. I ask myself whether I should now provide more information on those houses. The poem does not tell anything about how I became acquainted with them, whether I visited or lived there, etc. Images connected with those places are so vivid in my mind, I have so much to say on the subject, that my memory at once starts to spin a narrative amounting to a novel. Yet even though I have written two novels in my life, I have never been able to rid myself of uneasiness about that literary genre. After all, a novelist exploits most intimate details from his or her life in order to prepare a concoction in which truth and invention are indistinguishable. A great master of such brazen operations was Dostoevsky. For instance, in *Crime and Punishment* he took his recently dead wife, Masha, for a model to depict crazy Mrs. Marmeladova, and even worse, in *The Idiot* he made comic General Ivolgin tell a tall tale on the burial of his own leg and on an inscription he placed on its tomb: the inscription, as we know today, was identical with that on the tomb of Dostoevsky's mother. To be able to sacrifice everything, even what one considers the most sacred, for the sake of an artistic composition seems to be a mark of the born novelist. But a poem does not aspire to a gossipy reconstruction of individual lives. Every poem is to a large extent circumstantial, and some familiarity on the part of the reader with circumstances behind the scene may help, provided that certain limits are preserved, so that enough of a *chiaroscuro,* of a mysteriousness, remains.

Information on the house by a lake, contained in the poem itself, must, I feel, suffice. It does not satisfy my craving for reality, yet I am aware of obstacles on the road toward capturing it. Social, political, psychological elements tempt us and tend to dilute that sort of conciseness which distinguishes poetry from prose. My commentary on the new home of my heroine would be even more prosaic. In 1945 I myself visited the "Western Territories" of Poland and to my surprise became an owner of a house previously belonging to a German: to explain why it was easy then to acquire a property — especially if you were a writer, a member of the Writers' Union — would need a whole treatise; as well as why property was practically worthless.

The poem does not explain what sort of relationship existed between N. N. and me. Love affairs between men and women are of an infinite variety, but stylistic means of expression at our disposal prove their inadequacy especially in that domain. The language tends to reduce individual cases to a common denominator proper to a given epoch. Lyrics of the sixteenth century sing of love that is not like ours, madrigals of the eighteenth century are imbued with a sensibility at which we look from a remote perspective. Similarly, love motives in the poetry of our time will be alien to the sensibility of the future. We may even suspect that a complex interplay of the mind and the flesh, making for a human sexuality so different from that of animals, constantly undergoes transformations that go together with transformations of the *Zeitgeist.* Of course, every poet is guided by Eros, who according to Plato is an intermediary between gods and men. Yet, considering the intricacies of our century, it is difficult today to write love lyrics. I have written a number of strongly erotic poems but very few addressed to a given woman. And "Elegy for N. N." is, for better or worse, an example of a rather reticent approach. It happens, though, that now, returning to the poem after many years, I discover its value as a memorial. I have brought her to life in a way and now again I feel her presence.

I discover also that this is a sad poem. Think how many dead are in it: N. N. herself; Mama Fliegeltaub, who was the owner of the only inn in the town and who stands for its whole Jewish population — as far as I know the Germans did not even care to deport them but executed them on the spot; a person close to N. N., who died in Sachsenhausen; a German owner of the villa. And all that just because I gave account of facts. But the saddest is the ending and I am not sure whether I approve of it. Probably not, which would mean that I have changed since the time the poem was written. Indifference and a feeling of distance from the world of the living have been ascribed to the shadows of the underworld, inhabitants of Hades. Upon my arrival in Berkeley in 1960 directly from Europe, I was for a long time visited by a thought that the distance separating me from the places of my childhood and youth had something eerie in it, that perhaps I found myself, if not in Hades, at least upon some unearthly fields among lotus-eaters; in other words, that I started to lead a sort of after-life. This found its reflection in the poem's last stanza. Which is invalidated by the rest of the poem. For N. N. visited me, after all. And by writing about her, I proved that I was not indifferent.

THE SAND IN THE HOURGLASS

1974

The contemplation of time is the key to human life. It is a mystery that cannot be reduced to anything, and to which no science has access. Humility is inescapable when we know that we are not certain how we shall behave in the future. We achieve stability only by disowning our I, which is subject to time and changes.

Two things cannot be reduced to any rationalizing: time and beauty. One must begin from them.

— SIMONE WEIL, *SELECTED WRITINGS*

Mystery deserves respect. If man were unaware of the ephemeral nature of his life and of all human things, he would not be man. Beauty, whose very essence is both impermanence and the power of the moment confronting the passage of time, would also be beyond his reach. The words of Ecclesiastes are a model for all lyric poetry, for he who speaks through them both affirms that he must die like all other men and rises above his vulnerability to destruction through the rhythm of language. In just the same way, line and color deliver us from our I, and regardless of the filth that may have nourished the creative act, they are transposed into the not-I.

Continual meditation on time is impossible because it would paralyze our actions, whispering that each of them will be in vain. People must aspire, love, hate, establish families, earn a living, struggle. Their days must be subordinated to the discipline imposed by immediate goals. The artistic temperament is characterized by a sensitivity to the current of time itself with its mesmerizing effect, as when a snake mesmerizes a rabbit. One cannot refute the reasoning of those who have seen in art and in religious contemplation a distancing from Will, the will to life, an ascent above the circle of birth and death. That is why people can be divided into two enduring types: the people of Will and people of Meditation, which does not mean that these types exist in a pure, unalloyed state, or that they do not at times come into conflict with each other within a single corporeal shell.

When I was a child, no one initiated me into the dread mystery of ephemerality; I stumbled upon it myself, receiving it, as it were, as a gift from nature. The way I read a certain book for young readers is worth mentioning. It was Fenimore Cooper. It is virtually impossible to read Cooper in English today because of his prolixity. But if I remember the book correctly, it was an abridged edition, a selection from all the volumes, perhaps a translation of a French or Russian abridgment. In the first part, the hero, Natty Bumppo, appeared as a young man, the Pathfinder, the Deerslayer; in the last, as an old man named Leatherstocking. My experience of this book was so piercing, so sweetly painful, that is has remained with me to this day, as if it were just yesterday that I was in that hero's company. At that time it was naked, beyond words; now I am able to evaluate its by no means paltry dimensions and to name it. The Pathfinder traveled — in space, because in his flight from civilization he kept moving farther and farther West, to the wilderness where only Indians lived; in time, because he changed from a vigorous, carefree youth into a mature man, and finally into an old man. That was when he had his encounter with a civilization that was ruled by a different time. The region where he had spent his youth was by now densely populated; his Indians friends had perished in battles or died; for the new generations of colonists his authentic forest fatherland was only a legend and he himself was an eccentric relic with his old-fashioned, long harquebus. Completely alone, no longer sharing a common language with anyone, once again he walked away, into ter-

ritory that meant exile, because it was no longer forest but wilderness —
the empty, boundless prairie.

I read Cooper, then, as a symbolic parable about human fate. A young boy,
I empathized with the old trapper for whom everything was already in his
past. And who knows, perhaps it was Cooper speaking in a poem that I
wrote later on as a twenty-three-year-old:

> The gale combs the gray hair
> With its fingers and at last repeats
> Authentic words for those who stare
> into memory's abyss, open.

By the way, just as a single grain helps to crystallize a solution, so one image
in Cooper could provide the germ for my reveries about ordering space. Let
us imagine a lake, surrounded on all sides by virgin forest, and in the center
of the watery surface a sort of ark at anchor, a floating house. When the
Pathfinder was a young man, the colonists had not yet made their way to
Lake Otsego in the northern part of New York State. In the ark, unfriendly
to other people and fenced off by the water from the rampaging Indians of
the primeval forest, lived a retired pirate and his two daughters. Was that not
the model of a completely secure state for a child's imagination?

Thus, Cooper, the Romantic American, spoke to me earlier than the
Polish Romantics. When I made their acquaintance later on, I was not particularly sensitive to Gustaw's madness in love, but I was very sensitive to his
grief over what had vanished — when he visited his childhood home and saw
"ruins, emptiness, devastation." I was thoroughly captivated by Słowacki's
"The Hour of Thought," with its heartrending tone heightened by a still
classical restraint, a tone of remembrances accompanied by tears that, as I
learned much later, Edgar Allan Poe considered closest to the very essence
of poetry. "The Hour of Thought," unlike any other work, mythologized the
streets on which I walked — St. John's, Dominican Street, and also the park
grounds of the Jaszuny estate, twenty kilometers away, where Słowacki and
Ludwika Śniadecka used to go out riding together.

"The sorrow of ephemerality" can also be found in the ancient Chinese
poets, and in a poem that had a particular influence on the Romanticism of
the Slavic countries — Thomas Gray's "Elegy Written in a Country Church-

yard." As one who has been addicted since childhood to grief over transitoriness, I could not help contemplating (exactly when this began, it would be hard for me to say) the moral flaw inherent in the aesthetic temperament. If we treat what is actually happening to us or around us as already in the past, as material given to us only so we can transfer it at this very moment into the past and observe it as if it were already a memory, then such an immense distance arises in our response to the "now" that even in the most hellish circumstances (such as there has been no lack of in our era) the spectator in us preserves his coldness and impassivity; and this is indisputably inhuman. Perhaps not only coldness and impassivity, for the spectator does not lack an inclination toward sadism. After all, the aesthetic attitude is not the exclusive privilege (some privilege!) of artists. Every highly aroused and acute consciousness flees toward similar solutions and, by splitting into subject (I observing) and object (I being observed), somehow relents toward the object and even derives satisfaction from its improper behavior, as in the case of dandyism, buffoonery, and mental cruelty.

Meditation on ephemerality has always been man's companion and will never leave him; however, its tonality changes and the *Danse Macabre* of the late Middle Ages, for example, is fundamentally different from the Renaissance prescriptions about profiting from the moment because youth lasts for such a short time and life is brief. The *carpe diem* in Kochanowski's Horatian poems (translations and imitations) always struck me as rather insipid rhetoric, although I understand that, just as in the dance of death, the point here was to emphasize a truism: you are neither the first nor the last to whom this has happened.

The attitude toward passing time, even if we disposed of no other data about specific historical periods, would suffice to suggest a diagnosis. When I was reading Cooper, Friedrich Nietzsche's predictions had already been fulfilled literally, and since that time I have either had to submit to or oppose the workings of "European nihilism." Nihilistic time, to judge by contemporary art and literature, is completely devoid of values; neither its specific moments nor their duration makes any sense. It manifests itself as only a destructive, absurd force; Horace can no longer be of help, because even the pagan respect for the Great Rhythm has been lost. This also accounts for the "fainting" attitude (it was, it passed, it's gone) or the vindictive attitude (the accursed absurdity of being) toward the passing of time. Nietzsche was not the only one to notice the harbingers of this devaluing of time (and also of human life); the Russian writers who raged against Western Europe sensed it, too.

> *The perfect nihilist* — The nihilist's eye idealizes in the direction of ugliness and is unfaithful to his memories; it allows them to drop, lose their leaves; it does not guard them against the corpselike pallor that weakness pours out over what is distant and gone. And what he does not do for himself, he also does not do for the whole past of mankind: he lets it drop.
>
> — NIETZSCHE, note 21 from *The Will to Power,* 1887
> [Translated by Walter Kaufmann and R. J. Hollingdale]

Mnemosyne was the mother of the Muses. Her role demands a new rethinking under the conditions of "European nihilism." In the past, the poet would address a beautiful girl and prophesy that one day, as an old woman doing her spinning of an evening, she will rejoice: "Ronsard praised me when I was beautiful." That is, her beauty was something objective and found its reflection, as in a mirror, in the poems of Ronsard, with the difference that the image in the mirror cannot be retained, while poetry defies the action of time. That was the foundation of all representational art, whether it represented a human figure or a landscape. Memory may be unfaithful, but it finds support in the lines and the color that belong to the things of this world and that supply us with clues as to when memory is being faithful and when it is mistaken. If we wish to know what has happened, let us consider for a moment the decline of representational painting, but let us also analyze our impressions when we watch a film from fifty years ago. Film stars who were once famous for their beauty look pitiful, all decked out in their comical rags and their comical gestures; they are imprisoned in a style, in their era's mannerisms, so that it is hard to understand how they were enchanting at one time, although it is not hard to understand that they did enchant people who, like them, were also imprisoned. Film, then, hands us a nasty, distorting mirror and confirms what sociology and psychology have taught us. It is possible, in fact, that film, because it is a segment of unfolding time, is hostile to beauty, which must be motionless (movement in poetry, in music, is of a different order and, so to speak, suffers from its inability to freeze).

Because of what we have been taught, memory is assumed to be deceitful and has acquired the consistency of dreams. Since everything that one is is subject to ceaseless transformations (and because the dark domain within us demands a past that has been censored in one way or another, and because, seized by the Spirit of Time, we project its measurements into the past), it is difficult to believe in the truthfulness of memory. And yet Nietzsche distinguished between the eye that is faithful to memories and the unfaithful eye, calling the latter the eye of the perfect nihilist, and since he uncovered nihilism in himself, no doubt he knew what he was talking about. If his formulation contains a condemnation of modern psychologizing, which, by the way, did not being with Freud, then of course I am on Nietzsche's side.

Those who pay tribute to Mnemosyne as the mother of the Muses find themselves in a peculiar trap. They tell stories about how, for example, many years ago they encountered a lion, but then they must hasten to place this event in parentheses, making us understand that to a certain extent it was a lion but to a certain extent it wasn't, because it exists only in their treacherous minds. That is why reality "faints" every so often beneath their pens, and though color is more or less preserved, the lines dissolve like the outline of a clouds reflected in waves (not for nothing did Impressionism announce the end of representational painting). In these conditions, Proust's undertaking, his desire to rescue time past, was heroic and hopeless. His work recalls those marvelous, colorful Oriental carpets: the paintings of Bonnard and Vuillard, woven out of fragments of "psychological time." And like those paintings, it was already passé the moment it was conceived. For it had already been proclaimed that memory deceives us if it does not "idealize in the direction of ugliness." In some museum of the future, Proust's volumes will be placed side by side with Beckett's *Krapp's Last Tape*, in which the narrator, an old man, listens to tapes of himself recorded in the distant past. He replies to the ludicrous nothingness of his own life with mocking snorts and grunts.

It is not for me to write the history of European culture; others will take this task upon themselves. For me, the problem is highly personal, because in my poems and prose my support has been the remembered detail. Not an "impression" and not an "experience"; these are so multi-layered and so difficult to translate into language that various methods have been discovered in the attempt to grasp them: speech that imitates the "stream of consciousness" even to the point of eliminating punctuation marks, of becoming verbal magma, mere babbling. The remembered detail, for example, the grain of the wood of a door handle polished by the touch of many hands deserved, in my opinion, to be separated from the chaos of impressions and experiences, to be cleansed in some way, so that all that remained would be the eye disinterestedly contemplating the given object. I know how easy it is to find fault with my insistence on making distinctions; all one would have to do is introduce a couple of concepts from a handbook of psychology, but I have no interest in them, since making distinctions at least brings us closer to the essential line of division and practice confirms it.

I had an amusing and instructive adventure after the appearance of my book *Native Realm* in English translation. Its introductory chapter includes a not very flattering opinion that all autobiographical writings, because they attempt to break through the so-called layers of consciousness; since this is a vain undertaking, time past is falsified in them — that is also why I prefer a selection that has been organized ahead of time, rather than a spontaneous selection. I was told about someone who exclaimed after reading this, "Why should I read any further if the author himself admits that he is not going to tell the truth!" This innocent intellectual believed in the "truth" of various devices which are reputed to open up the contents of memory, although if he were consistent he would have had to come to the conclusion that in that case only grunting, disjointed syllables, groans, as in *Krapp's Last Tape*, do not seem "artificial" and can be taken for sincerity.

What did Nietzsche have in mind when he foresaw that a "corpselike pallor" would veil the things of the past? Another of his aphorisms from the same year (1887) clarifies this: "An extreme form of nihilism would be the view that *any sort* of conviction, any sort of accepting-something-as-true, is of necessity false, because there simply is no *true world*." Approximately ten years earlier Dostoevsky wrote his "Dream of a Ridiculous Man"; the hero-narrator in that story decides to shoot himself, under the impression that since the world exists only in his head, it will cease to exist with his death.

This question cannot easily be sidestepped: What kind of existence can be ascribed to a sunrise, for example, somewhere beside the Mediterranean Sea on a particular morning in May in the year 1215, shall we say, and also to the flowers opening at that moment, the seagull flying fast, the arm of a woman drawing water from a well? Could it be, because no one sees this any longer, that it has no existence? But all the fantastic richness of the works of the human mind and human hand that European civilization has bequeathed to us, so immense that it seems to be beyond our ability to comprehend it, was made possible only because exactly the opposite answer was given. The world, the absolutely authentic world, has endured in each of its moments, independently of the consciousness of a particular subject on his journey from birth to death. Yet something that is seen by no one does not exist. This supposition has been tacitly accepted, albeit with a fundamental emendation: one supreme subject, God — who is the most subjective of subjects because although unseen Himself, He sees — has been embracing with his vision all the moments of time which lie spread out before him like a deck of cards, for they are simultaneous, beyond any "was, is, will be." The physics that would be born eventually (Einstein's) offered as yet no help; however, religion had successfully maintained its intuitive conviction about the relativity of time and space, which did not exist before the Act of Creation. The scientific conceptualization of time and space as absolute, along with its nihilistic consequences in the humanities, is a late acquisition, a part of the scientific-technical revolution or, rather, one phase of that revolution, for it shared the fate of Newtonian physics. Evidently, the particular fields of human thought are subject to a law of unequal development because we still have to wait for an understanding of what is a new phase.

Thanks to religion, over the course of many centuries the authentic world, grounded in the sight of God, offered models for the artist who hoped to approach them not so much imitation as by analogy. Memory played an important, but a rather secondary, role in this, for it was understood that "idealization," that is, the extraction of that which is quintessential for a particular given thing, is inevitable. In the civilization that we call Christian, visionaries responded quite unfavorably to Mnemosyne, calling her "the mother of the fallen natural Muses." And they were right, it seems, because when she found herself alone, confronting a world deprived of values, she turned out to be an unreliable guide.

One recognizes the taste of a cake while eating it. At this moment, after all, as I am putting these words on paper, I am making a choice, resisting memory's various temptations. For example, memory is offering me my university studies — the "argument about the existence of the world" that was threshed out in the lecture halls, and at the same time the argument about the grounding of values — and is even expressing annoyance with me for conflating two orders of reasoning. No doubt it is better to know that this labyrinth of concepts has been erected, but it is a barren labyrinth, for there is no place in it for our own sense of anguish. If in our moments of happiness, mastery, ecstasy, we say Yes to heaven and to earth, and all we need is misfortune, sickness, the decline of physical powers to start screaming No, this means that all our judgments can be refuted tomorrow and that it is easy to mistake our life for the world. It is not obvious, however, why weakness — whether of a particular person or of an entire historical era — should be privileged and why the old nihilist from Beckett's *Krapp's Last Tape* should be closer to the truth than he himself was when he was twenty years old.

The contemplation of time is the key to human life — but one can only circle around that key, one cannot touch it. One thing is certain: not every contemplation of time is equally good; however, since it cannot be expressed in words, we can recognize its quality by the use a given individual has made of it.

"I am suffering." It is better to say this than to say, "The landscape is ugly."
— SIMONE WEIL, *Selected Writings*

Translated by Madeline G. Levine

REALITY

1974

You shall forget these things, toiling in the household,
You shall remember them, droning by the fire,
When age and forgetfulness sweeten memory
Only like a dream that has often been told
And often been changed in the telling. They will seem unreal.
Human kind cannot bear very much reality.
— T. S. ELIOT, *MURDER IN THE CATHEDRAL*

There goes a fascist. Kill the fascist. Crash! Crash!
Also a communist. Kill the communist. Bash! Bash!
O reality! Holy mother!
For you killing spiders is as little a bother.
— к. i. GAŁCZYŃSKI. Quoted from memory. It probably
    comes from Solomon's Ball (a prewar edition)

The sound of this word is hideous; it is a literal translation of the French *réalité*, interchangeable at times with the nature of things (*la réalité des choses*). French distinguishes between *la réalité* and *la réel*; Polish lacks this distinction but needs it. Reality. *Wirklichkeit*. Russian has both *desitvitel'nost'*, derived from the word for taking action, not from the word for thing (as in Polish: *rzecz* [thing], *rzeczywistość* [reality]) and *realnost'*.

What does this word mean? Why does everyone pay homage to *things*? In common parlance this word refers to all things that act according to their own laws and in such a way that, if we should find ourselves on the track along which they are moving, we would be killed. For we are fragile beings and an avalanche tumbling down from the mountains, a hurricane, bacteria, viruses, chemical changes in the cells of our bodies can destroy us. However, we have learned to resist the forces of nature, and although for a significant portion of mankind drought, floods, and soil erosion are still a danger, what is left to us from among the elemental disasters are mainly aging and such diseases as have not yet been conquered by science. The thing which is most threatening to us is another man, either because he is armed and we are unarmed or poorly armed, or because (and it's all the same in the end) he has the power to deny us money, that is, nourishment. The foundation of human society is still the death penalty, whether it be death from a bullet, or in prison, or from hunger, and the humanitarian choruses will have no effect on this.

For us, then, reality is social above all; that is, it is such that people-things follow orders dictated to them by other people, who appear to be masters of their own and others' fates, but who in fact have been transformed into things by the so-called necessities of life. We have not made much progress in understanding how all of this dovetails, and the scientist who studies viruses or send rockets to other planets may react to self-appointed specialists in the social sciences with a sense of well-founded superiority.

I started paying attention to this nature of things early on, convinced that a poet who refuses to recognize its weight is living in a fool's paradise. While trying to cope with it, I also managed to collect many experiences as early as the years 1930–39; that is, in a period that is virtually unknown today. Unfortunately, if a reader should wish to find out what that period was like in Poland and Europe, I would be unable to point to any sources, because neither literature nor history has achieved even a passably accurate picture. Social reality is distinguished by the fact that it is opaque, treacherous, that with its myriad guises it deludes everyone who is entangled in it. In those days there were additional reasons for befuddlement, as happens when a man has received a powerful blow to the head. Let us consider that this was going on only a few years after World War I and that although people talked a lot of nonsense, they seemed to be doing so in order to avoid thinking about what reality signified. When I was a student, I got to know a modest clerk from Poznań who was utterly absorbed in the by no means so distant past. For he had fought at Verdun as a soldier in the German infantry and had written a book about this for which he was vainly seeking a publisher. I read the typed manuscript. This report of a sojourn in the fifth or sixth circle of hell was probably more detailed and thus more horrifying than Remarque's widely acclaimed novel *All Quiet on the Western Front*. The older members of my family had in their past the years of war spent in the tsarist army, and even my beautiful cousin Ela, whose portrait painted by Janowski, is one of the loveliest examples of Polish painting from around 1914, was a *sestritsa* [a Russian military nurse] at the time. For a vast number of the inhabitants of our country reality still meant tsarist Russia or Habsburg Galicia, and above all the world war and the 1920 campaign — perhaps even more than independent Poland itself. How well was it understood that the year 1914 was the manifestation of all of Europe's defects and of her end, that the longed-for war of nations had brought Poland to life as a posthumous creation? Pride in "one's own rubbish heap regained" counseled putting on a face that suggested nothing was wrong, but various subterranean currents were at work undermining the supports of official thinking. And just when virtually every grown man was struggling with some Verdun of his own, there came a new blow to the head: the 1929 crash on the New York Stock Exchange, mass unemployment, and Hitlerism, orchestrated by the

German combatants of World War I. Soon afterward, a poet who had been one of Piłsudski's Legionnaires of 1914 wrote, "Mother, hand me my boots, / The ones from twenty years ago." The boots may not have had time to grow old but the "acceleration of history" made a few changes in the world around Poland.

When someone assures us after many years that he had a clear awareness of standing "face to face with the end," we should not believe him, because almost no one had such a clear awareness. Among writers, perhaps only Zdziechowski and Stanisław Ignacy Witkiewicz did. As one of the creators of "Catastrophism" I could, in fact, present written evidence on my own behalf, but it would be evidence of only an intuitive, poetic recognition.

Let me briefly explain where catastrophism came from. First, a rather general background, not just the Polish one. The social reality of the nineteenth century weighed upon people in literature and art, so they considered protesting against it the chief aim of their activity, although they reached out for various solutions. However, even the most abstract aesthetic theories had as their foundation a rebellion against the swirling vortex of the oppressors and the oppressed; the artist, as the only free man, had to be set against this vortex. By taking refuge in bohemian circles from the morality of the hated bourgeoisie and concluding numerous alliances with social dreamers, the writer or the artist bore witness to his heritage: the centuries-long yearning for the Second Coming. Secularization was proceeding apace, however, and if Jesus was still the central figure in utopian socialism, this Jesus figured only as an ethical ideal and a reformer. Soon it would be openly announced that Man-God and not God-Man would restore fallen nature.

In my mind, contrary to what I know about frivolous Paris in *La Belle Epoque*, the beginning of my century has a gloomy color and a shape that is, if I may say so, Russo-Anglo-Saxon. The year 1905. The Russian "stormy petrels." The American writers of the class struggle: Upton Sinclair's *The Jungle* (1906), Jack London's *The Iron Heel* (1907). And considering what I know about New York, I do not think that the picture Gorky painted in *The City of the Yellow Devil* (1906) was an exaggeration. Furthermore, a gloomy reality does not appear only in revolutionary writers. It is also present in Joseph Conrad's *The Heart of Darkness* (1902), the novel that Thomas Mann called the beginning of twentieth-century literature, and in *The Secret Agent* (1907). What symbolic titles! Let us recite them: the jungle, the iron heel, the city of the yellow devil, the heart of darkness, the secret agent. Since such grim forces as were described therein had led to the slaughter of the First World War, one can hardly be surprised that writers from various countries, raised on legends that remained in the wake of the American Revolution and the French Revolution, enthusiastically welcomed the Russian Revolution as (the final?) destruction of the Bastille.

Regardless of its specific circumstances as a country that had gained and defended its independence, Poland belonged to a system of linked vessels; for example, the left-wing wave in America and Germany was swelling in Poland precisely during the years from 1930 to 1933. I shall leave aside the question of so-called convictions, because they are not the issue here, although among the literati only a very few had any "convictions." A more important issue is their grasp of reality. I was filled with distaste during the rather short time that I produced social poetry. Because it is obvious that in these various collective movements, whose participants beat the drum for each other, the poet betrays himself, out of pride, out of a need for recognition. They will walk right past a good poem and not notice it, but give them a "theme" and they'll respond immediately with shouts and bravos. Already at that time a riddle had appeared that became more and more painful the further along we moved into the twentieth century. If man is dehumanized and diminished by social reality, is not his diminution confirmed by taking him only and solely as a small part of that social reality? Whence the dullness of all those works about "wrongs" that are, after all, so noble in their intent? Many clamorous poems and not a few pages of comparable prose were written in Poland and elsewhere at that time, but none of this appears to have lasted. "Catastrophism" was an attempt at restoring measure. A literary argument, the catastrophist poets' opposition to such literary schools as Skamander or the Avant-Garde, explains less in this context than their renunciation of "social poetry"; their accusations, which were never formulated as a theory, would have sounded like this: You are preoccupied with reality but it is completely unreal, for you keep on about your provincial world while everything is happening on a planetary scale, the Apocalypse is imminent, and while you strive to reduce man to *homo oeconomicus*, there is a hidden content in the historical Apocalypse that we cannot comprehend. Perhaps a poem such as Jerzy Zagórski's "Ode on the Fall of the Pound" still belonged to social poetry, but there was more to it than just a prediction of the collapse of the British Empire. The same poet's "The Coming of the Enemy" is a surrealistic fairy tale about the advent of the Antichrist; the action takes place on the plains of Eurasia, near the Arctic Ocean, and in the Caucasus.

After 1939, the young poets of underground Warsaw could not remain indifferent to such accurate forebodings by their predecessors. Nevertheless, prewar catastrophism was a threat to these young people, because it was international in its intellectual references and they wanted to enclose themselves in the national dimension whatever the cost. Similarly, when they encountered another catastrophism, Witkiewicz's, what they borrowed from him was chiefly his grotesque, from his plays, whereas we, judging by my own response at least, were influenced primarily by the historiosophical premises of his novels. We were not, however, as pessimistic as the desperately clowning and suicidally earnest Witkiewicz. Who knows if a totally pessimistic poetry is even possible or, if poetry is to be at all valuable, whether it does not always have to be hopeful? In the poetry of the catastrophist, every so often a note of irony toward the fate that befell them can be heard, but there is also a yearning for harmony, for beauty, which ought to be the lot of a saved man.

And what about today, when those dire prophecies and their fulfillment (or, rather, partial fulfillment) are in the past? Our planetary reality has split in two into the so-called West and the so-called East, and I have drunk from both the one and the other poisoned well. I have also become convinced that the puzzle of the thirties still cries out for a solution.

Did the nineteenth century lie when it dreamed its dream of itself? That can't be ruled out. But at least its great metropolis, in which Macbeth's witches stirred their brew, speaks to us from the pages of Balzac, Dickens, Dostoevsky; it is the stage for a human comedy like the *cité infernale* of Baudelaire's poems; it looks at us with the faces of the corrupt judges and venal journalists of Daumier's prints, and with the face of the prostitute from Manet's *Olympia*. There was something then that could be called the will of realism. That will was still in evidence at the beginning of our century, but not for long. Its disappearance from literature and art is more or less contemporaneous with the widespread dissemination of the newsreel and the documentary, which is why people have sought to lay the blame for this on emulation of these new, vicarious means of expression. But the true causes probably lie much deeper. Man is either a *supported* being or he dissolves into mist, into a mirage. For the nineteenth century the impetus given by Christianity still sufficed to support man; that is, to understand individual fate as meaningful. The advocates of Man as the Masses, industriously patching together their social literature during the thirties, fooled themselves into believing that Nietzsche's laughter had nothing to do with them. For no matter what our anger may be like and no matter how strong our sympathy for the fate of the oppressed, we will have a difficult time achieving that minimum of attention without which literature is only paper if we remain convinced that man, whom we are concerned about, is interchangeable, is but a bubble on the current of "processes." It is not for nothing that dread of the future rules the work of Dostoevsky, the second prophet of "nihilism." Dostoevsky was not a psychologist; he was, as he has rightly been called, a pneumatologist, and there is a great difference between the two. *Pneuma*, the spirit, is not the same as that instrument for inscribing impressions that once was called the soul, and the struggle for the salvation of *homo pneumatikos*, despite the temptations of *homo psychikos*, is worth the highest stakes. Dostoevsky considered himself an authentic realist, and he was one, he could still be one, and that is the reason why.

Having lived for a long time in France and in America, I have been astounded by my observation that the tough and predatory reality that surrounds me *does not exist* in the literature of these countries. Not that it would be worthwhile to offer some formulas, because they would turn out to be impossible. Many a formula has been applied by writers who swear that they will faithfully describe only what has truly taken place, will stick to the "facts," and every time the result was, at best, naturalism. But naturalism is total unreality — in disguise. Bundles of reflexes torment bundles of reflexes, bundles of reflexes copulate with bundles of reflexes, bundles of reflexes murder bundles of reflexes. A world not of people but of flies. And if man is only a fly, then why be so upset about his unhappiness? Only a hero, in whose existence both the author and the reader believe, can be a measure of reality. Such nineteenth-century heroes as Rastignac, Raskolnikov, Ivan Karamazov, Fabrizio del Dongo from *The Charterhouse of Parma* still *exist* to this day. The heroes that Western authors have managed to create in the last few decades are striking. The preeminent hero is, without a doubt, the youthful comic-book detective Tintin; far behind him comes another detective, a grown man, Simenon's Maigret. That's the situation in the Francophone countries. On the other hand, in the English-speaking countries, only one character seems to have truly captivated readers. It is Frodo Baggins, the hero of Tolkien's *The Lord of the Rings*, a rich allegorical novel about the struggle between the forces of light and the forces of darkness, similar, in fact, in its narrative strategy, to Sienkiewicz's *Trilogy*. Only, the young Frodo is not even a human child; he is a fantastic creation, a *hobbit,* an elf, the Englishman's daydream of himself, who lives in snug dens, drinks tea in the afternoon, and is capable of heroic deeds — but only if they are absolutely necessary.

Reality, if it is to be captured, demands a hero, but it also demands an organizing idea. This idea does not have to reside within the writer's head, because it permeates his epoch. The nineteenth century still lived with the great hope of the rebirth of man. It was no accident that I referred to utopian socialism, whose significance was enormous. Today's ideas of social justice promise everything that anyone might want, but not that the oppressed will be liberated from the power of people-things; they are therefore insufficiently exciting and their semi-paralysis turns descriptions sour while they are still in embryonic form, since they are inseparable from a sense of direction, of striving. An unseen law of phenomena turns out to be more powerful here than the wishes of numerous Western adherents of revolution, whose sense of reality appears to be on the wane, since they are unable to gain even as much recognition as their predecessors in the thirties.

> There is in all these works a certain atmosphere of universal doom; especially in *Ulysses*, with its mocking *odi-et-amo* hodgepodge of the European tradition, with its blatant and painful cynicism, and its uninterpretable symbolism — for even the most painstaking analysis can hardly emerge with anything more than an appreciation of the multiple enmeshment of the motifs but with nothing of the purpose and meaning of the work itself. And most of the other novels which employ multiple reflection of consciousness also leave the reader with an impression of hopelessness. There is often

something confusing, something hazy about them, something hostile to the
reality which they represent. We not infrequently find a turning away from
the practical will to live, or delight in portraying it under its most brutal
forms. There is hatred of culture and civilization, brought out by means of
subtle stylistic devices which culture and civilization have developed, and
often a radical and fanatical urge to destroy. Common to almost all of these
novels is haziness, vague indefinability of meaning: precisely the kind of
uninterpretable symbolism which is also to be encountered in other forms
of art of the same period.

— ERICH AUERBACH, *Mimesis* [Translated by Willard R. Trask]

Auerbach's book about *mimesis* or the reflection of reality in European literature, beginning with the Greeks, was written in 1942–45 in Istanbul, where
the author, an émigré from Germany, happened to be living. His above-
quoted observations refer to the years before World War II. Since they are
just as apt a characterization of postwar literature up till the present (except
that the features he notices have become even more obvious), we should not
take his judgments lightly, nor those of writers like him when they place the
twentieth century under the sign of a destructive movement that demon-
strates its own continuity.

We are born only once on this earth, and only one and no other historical time is given to us. If we recognize that it is our lot to live in a decadent
era, we are faced with the problem of choosing our tactics. Since man is not
an animal and is in touch with the entire past of his species, and since the
past, to the extent that forgotten civilizations are being rediscovered, is
becoming ever more accessible, we cannot but be depressed by the thought
that instead of trying to equal the greatest human achievements, we yield to
inferior philosophies only because they are contemporary. It is very difficult
to find appropriate tactics for resistance, and our development, if it is to be
worthy of that name, must be founded, I believe, on advancing from unconscious tactics to conscious tactics. Unfortunately, the individual, because he
absorbs the same things as everyone around him, is weak and is continually
considering whether it is not he who is mistaken.

It would be an exaggeration to insist that man can change radically. The
germ of energy which is his alone — let's call it predestination — will remain
the same in evil and in good, in truth and in error; he also has certain set limits; his own ability to interpret things properly. The fundamental constructs

in his life are repetitive, but they can assume a new shape. I did not stop being a "catastrophist" after the Second World War, in the sense that losing one's sense of reality still seems to me to be deserving of punishment. But I have chosen my guides more and more consciously, and not from among the representatives of contemporary *belles letters*, which are infected with the loss of a sense of reality. I also consciously kept apart from that plaintive whimpering that is practically synonymous with the written word these days. Having crossed a certain boundary, inside which, unfortunately, the nature of things is our mistress, one begins to treat such whimperings — and also the entire theater of the absurd, along with the attempts at traditional "realism" that are doomed to failure — as belonging to the past. A pessimistic appraisal of the powerlessness of contemporary forces, and of the literature and art that unconsciously submit to these forces, is not synonymous with a lack of faith in individual achievements or with doubts about an eventual victory of the human race over "reality." After all, consciousness, in the clutches of the epoch, is always incomplete, and as it grows older we shall at best be able to describe clearly what it is that we do not want. And that is how it ought to be, for our zealousness has its source in our nay-saying to what the age obligingly places before us.

"What is truth?" asked Pilate. "What is reality?" people ask. Such a question one should refuse to answer.

Translated by Madeline G. Levine

Adolf Rudnicki

(1912–1990)

Adolf Rudnicki was born in Warsaw and died in Warsaw, although he lived for some time in France as well. He was one of the many Polish writers deeply marked by the Holocaust. Of Jewish origin, he took part in the September 1939 military campaign, was taken prisoner by the Nazis, and later escaped. He spent some time in Lvov, then occupied by the Soviets. He returned to Warsaw and in 1944 participated in the Warsaw Uprising.

An active, visible, and prolific writer, Rudnicki developed a personal style of lyric realism. He made his debut before the war with a series of long short stories. Short story and essay remained his favorite literary forms. For a long time he kept a literary diary (*Niebieskie kartki*, or Blue Pages), in which he roamed freely between the most different themes, from soccer to Dostoyevsky's importance. Yet it's certainly for his numerous elegies for Holocaust victims—written in prose—that Rudnicki will be remembered because of their stunning, sentimental lyricism.

Interestingly, the partner in the conversation in the piece below is the poet Czesław Miłosz.

THE FINE ART OF WRITING

I

Every year on National Independence Day there used to be a military parade here. From the four corners of the country, regiments sent their choice representatives; they arrived in the capital dead beat, but just before the parade began, a sudden nervousness brought back their luster. And from then on, · everything went like clockwork and the choice units returned to their home garrisons in the best of spirits — almost happy. Once on Independence Day crowds stood here and admired the fine looks and might of our "military arm" — today cabbage was growing there. We were looking out over Mokotów Field.

From the very first warm days the inhabitants of the southwestern part of the city had come here with shovels, hoes, and rakes and had been poking in the earth. On every open patch of Warsaw you could observe the same thing. All of a sudden you could tell to what extent Poles were a nation of farmers, a people in love with the earth. The road, smooth as jelly, cut through the elaborately partitioned plots like a fool's map of the world, a river in a child's drawing. It was early June 1944 — the greenery had already faded, it had lost the power to rouse emotion it had had in May and was covered by dust and neglect — the Eastern front had frozen and it seemed it would never thaw. The Second World War was a war of leaps and jumps. But from the turning point of Stalingrad the ones that awakened our hopes were terribly brief compared with the long, dead intervals that followed. Posterity's gaze will never linger on those intervals void of emotion which for us were not void of emotion. When the front came to a standstill, we were touching the lower depths. Posterity's gaze won't find us there; it will pass us by as if it were a love whose requital we found out about when it was already too late.

In front of us were the SS barracks, behind us the Luftwaffe. Both were guarded like wild animals in cages. The Germans didn't only keep us under guard, they kept themselves as well. Themselves above all. They had divided up the Saski Garden, which was accessible only to them, as if it were a zoo. In every compartment, in every pen, a different kind of soldier sat. If they could have, they would have sectioned off the sky. That master race was marked by a mania for division — a people of chemists, not writers. Chemistry may be based on separation, but the human art of writing depends on the mystery of connection — it is a synthetic capacity.

For two hours we had been strolling on the pavement framing Mokotó Field, quite a long walk, in order not to see the barracks and the Luftwaffe. Amid cabbage and potatoes the residents of Mokotó and Ochota were busily working; their movements displayed the amateur's graceful awkwardness, often found in city dwellers working in the fields. We had been talking for two hours — the writer Czesław and I.

II

What can two writers talk about with unwaning passion not just for two hours but for two days, two weeks, two months, two years, and still not be done? About literature. About what literature can two Polish writers talk with unwaning passion? About Polish literature, which for them is the literature of Tadek and Władek, Staszek and Jasiek, with all the personal and impersonal consequences that follow. In what spirit can two Polish writers talk about Polish literature, in order to derive true pleasure from the conversation? Needless to say, in an absolutely negative spirit.

Oh, we didn't leave a dry thread on anyone. Nobody suited us. Nothing suited us. No one found favor in our eyes. We demolished others with the same passion as we demolished ourselves. But when we demolished ourselves, our hearts were suddenly moved and with a slight pain we became aware of what we were doing, what sort of nonsense we were really talking.

That demented negation imbued us with mutual affection, bound us to each other, tightly, warmly — me and the writer Czesław! I don't think we ever loved each other as much, Czesław and I, as we did then under the evening sky of Mokotó Field, trampling on the mortal remains of Polish literature. If we had tried to trample on the cabbage in the plots, the residents of Ochota and Mokotó would have broken our arms and legs.

III

Don't condemn us too severely. We had Auschwitz ahead of us, Treblinka, Majdanek, Wawer, the Pawiak jail behind us; we had Goethe in our hearts but Himmler ruling over us; the Germans shouted *die Kultur, die europäische*

Kultur, at the gate of the world's slaughterhouse you could read the motto *die Kultur und die Kunst*, cannibals defended *die Kultur* — suddenly it turned out the world had no higher legitimation, no higher raison d'être than *die Kultur und die Kunst*.

We who loved art felt cheated. Respect for human beings, humility before the wealth of a person's inner life — that's what it taught us. And what were we looking at? At a world in which soap was made from people, mattresses were stuffed with girls' hair, a world that was beyond any comparison. Up to this point art had not told us about a world like the one that surrounded us every day. We felt cheated.

Art didn't fulfill its tasks. Because it hadn't fulfilled them — we told each other — it was complicit, partly responsible for the crematorium ovens, the soap made from people, the children burned alive. We had the absolute conviction that art had sailed in the wrong direction. It ought — we said — to look different, but entirely different; it should have a completely different point of departure and be fed by completely different sources; it should be unified, moral, and serve the truth, which seemed to us — as it always does to people in the face of death — simple and tangible. We didn't want a world with the Louvre next to Auschwitz. Art had to be deprived of its multiple meanings, made into a friend of man and prevented once and for all from finding itself on the lips of executioners. We told ourselves that the art up to this time had to be destroyed, its beauty torn out and tied to the truth. We didn't want any beauty without truth.

IV

We were fighting for our right to live, for a place on the earth, for dignity, bread, and the honor of our women, and everyone wanted a word for their battle, which for a human being should be like a flower in the earth. In a time of peace the meaning and weight of the word is not grasped. It is not understood as clearly that people and events in order not to fade have to be made enduring by art. Life came to a head and was extinguished before our eyes, place names, repeated a hundred times in the course of a month, after two months had passed, started to sound foreign again. Human responses increasingly became illegible in their complexity.

People died in torture chambers, perished in myriad ways. Their mute testament, their last hope was that a word would be devoted to them. A tortured prisoner, dying without seeing his comrades, believed that there was a heart alive among the people, that the people had eyes to see him. Without faith in those eyes, those ears, that heart, there might not have been any heroism. It was the faith of both those on the street carrying a grenade for a reprisal and those who died slowly and soberly of hunger in camps. In the days of the worst national and personal defeat one understood clearly the meaning of conscience, a writer's conscience.

There's an old legend according to which the sins of each generation are so great that God time and time again wants to end the world. He is kept from this by the Just, of whom there are two or three in every generation. It is due to them that life doesn't perish, those two or three just people whom no one knows. There haven't been prophets for a long time. But I beg you, please show me the writer in whom this legend doesn't awaken a hidden, trembling, insane, joyful, single hope! . . .

V

What do writers say today, now they can give expression to their recent shocks and hopes and reap the benefit of the secrets they heard whispered throughout the war? Writers say that they have changed. Perhaps. The absence of books is a stout bulwark for those worthy confessions, whose force the first publications will probably undermine. For the time being there are arguments about the question of what literature should be between two camps, of which one is called traditional and the other revolutionary.

From the traditionalists we don't expect art like the kind that should in fact flow from correctly received tradition, because correctly received tradition cannot *not* be revolutionary. To be on good terms with tradition is to have it well digested, not oppressive like a heavy meal just eaten. To be on good terms with tradition is to have one's feet firmly on the ground but one's head in the clouds, exposed to storms and mad fits, without which there is no art at all, it is to maintain the sense of a boundary but also have the courage to break it. Shoddy traditionalists have their virtues, but we won't go there to find them, because it wasn't they who worked on them. In literature as in commerce, secondhand is just secondhand.

And the revolutionaries? They are struggling, as revolutionaries always do. They aren't very good speakers, they speak badly, they poke their fidgety hands in other's sensitive insides — what else is art? — they barge in with prescriptions for the impossible, commit hundreds of idiocies, as pioneers often do. But in what they say there is, as in the prophets' anger, the fear of a night passed, the trembling of a voice warning the crucified world: Never, never again this bifurcation! Never again only beauty without truth! You have no right to beauty as long as there exists any chance that what happened will be repeated!!!

Even if they are bad speakers, even if they speak clumsily and make a thousand mistakes, even if they're wrong — since it may be that art and its meaning lies in the word itself, which is broken off again and again, as a result of which the longings that accompany art don't flow into it, because how can it be blamed if the world doesn't have a higher legitimation? — even if, I repeat, they are wrong, how can we not listen to them, how can we not love them, we who saw the Apocalypse and know the only meaning the world has is in not repeating it! [. . .]

Translated by Alissa Valles

Gustaw Herling

(1919–2000)

After a brief but extremely painful stay in a Soviet camp, Gustaw Herling joined the Polish army formed in the U.S.S.R. when Hitler's June 1941 invasion of Russia changed overnight the alliances of World War II. After the war he remained in the West, embarking on the difficult path of a young exile writer. His second wife, the daughter of Benedetto Croce, the famous philosopher and dissident in fascist Italy, offered Herling a home in Naples. A paradox in his writing was the strong tension between the overwhelming beauty of his Italian surroundings and the ugliness of his experiences with Soviet and Nazi totalitarianism, which he had seen in the trenches and through the fate of his family and friends who had stayed in Poland.

Herling admired the writers Franz Kafka and George Orwell, and saw his own task as trying to describe and understand the evils of the twentieth century. At the same time he—like another of his heroes, Stendhal—was fascinated by Italian chronicles and by the marvel of Italian art. His early book, *A World Apart*, was a masterful, understated, quiet depiction of the horror of the Gulag Archipelago. Later Herling meandered in his writing, moving back and forth from short stories (or long short stories) to a writer's diary in which Italy and its history merged with Herling's reflections on literature and politics.

When Poland became a free country (after 1989), Herling received belated but important recognition, providing one of the joys of his literary life. Herling was among those exiled writers who were enthusiastically greeted by the Polish readers in the nineties.

DIARY ENTRIES
EXCERPTED FROM *VOLCANO AND MIRACLE*

DRAGONEA, AUGUST 11, 1974
[PAVESE AND THE BUSINESS OF LIFE]

I tried to explain to C., the Piedmontese woman poet, once an acquaintance and still an enthusiastic admirer of Cesare Pavese, why I do not like his diary *Il mestiere di vivere*.

"In general I do not like diaries that are too personal. They almost always force the author to play the game in such a way that the future reader gradually, step by step, gets the upper hand. Does this make me look all right? And this? Should I groan aloud? Should I muffle the sigh? Will it be grasped? Should I commit myself more deeply? If 'a' is said, does 'b' have to follow? What impression do I make in that situation? There is a part of man, as there should be, which no one, except for God, has the possibility or the right to enter. Paradoxically a good diary, or in any case one that is worth reading, is one in which the author only rarely pokes his antennae out of the shell — and then draws them back at once. When he crawls all the way out of the shell, he is completely defenseless and uttered by others. The utmost sincerity in literature is conceivable only with the license of third-person narrative or a conventional first person. In a diary this is equivalent to accepting a prompter or believing an actor sincere. This is why I assign diaries special status on the periphery of literature. The only exception is when the diary consciously and from the outset accepts the rules of the game and plays them as the theme. Then it turns into a duel between the writer and the others: against distortion from outside and on behalf of one's own 'nakedness' or 'authenticity,' which in any case is never fully displayed: one, because it is only dimly known and two, because it fears being named. This was not the case with Pavese. His diary is literary in the most dangerous sense of the word: in the sense that he is bound to his 'persona,' which is put on public view, and his life is dominated by literature. Pavese was a victim of this domination, and he paid for it with his life. The title of his diary is deceptive and misleading and expresses a longing rather than a reality. It is not 'the business of living' but 'the business of writing.' "

I knew that I was overdoing it, that I was provocatively "over-stating" the case, but there was a grain of very real truth. I am irritated by the Pavese myth in Italy, a country of incorrigible literati and the cult of fine writing, the *bélla pagina*, the beautiful page. I sniff ambiguity, sterile anxious writers feeding on someone else's tragedy, trying on the brave bloodstained feathers of a man who ultimately did not waver in his desperate attempt to get free of the snares that trapped him.

We were walking along the path in the direction of Molina, the heat was scorching, on the horizon the valley was ringed with fires. C. listened in silence, or perhaps she was not listening at all, because she simply recalled in a plaintive little voice that "it was August when it happened."

Yes, August 1950. The forty-two-year-old Pavese was at the peak of success: praised, feted, awarded prizes, translated, and dubbed the "restorer" of Italian literature. A volume of poems, several collections of well-wrought stories, and an enormous effort to familiarize Italy with American literature (his translation of *Moby Dick* is a masterpiece). Life was writing, sailing an ocean of paper in pursuit of the white whale. And then came that sultry August day in a deserted Turin, when the air was motionless, the paper Captain Ahab's spyglass was sucked into the empty whiteness on the horizon. He rented a room in the Albergo Roma across from Porta Nuova, drank down a horse's dose of sleeping pills with a glass of water, and stretched out comfortably on the bed without undressing. On the night table they found his little volume of poems *Dialoghi con Leucò* with an inscription on the title page: "I forgive everyone and ask everyone to forgive me. All right? Don't gossip too much." A few days earlier he had said farewell to his diary with words that his admirers today still repeat as if it were a password: "*Tutto fa schifo . . . Non scriverò più*" ("Everything stinks . . . I will no longer write"). With a curse and the declaration that "I will no longer write" is how the "business called living" ends.

A letter survives that was sent to friends a week before his suicide: "I am like Laocoön. I adorn myself artistically with garlands of snakes and ask for admiration, but every now and then, I realize the state I am in and I shake off the snakes, I tear them away and they writhe and bite. The game has been going on for twenty years. I begin to have enough of it."

Poor C. will probably never understand it, this rebellion of a life in the grip of greedy overbearing literature. For her it would be a sign of cruelty to conclude a quarter century later that Pavese's death in the Turin hotel will outlive his books, including the diary.

[. . .]

APRIL 8, 1976
[HOFMANNSTHAL AND LITERARY SILENCE]

Dear friend, it cannot be simple coincidence. The day I left Maisons-Laffitte, when I was saying good-bye to Józef Czapski in his small picture-crammed room, he suddenly took a worn little book off the shelf. It was Hugo von Hofmannsthal's *Letter of Lord Chandos.* "I have been reading it often lately," he said. Today I received your note from Kraków with the concluding passage of the *Letter* and your remark in the same spirit as Czapski's admission. And again today, while I was looking at the latest arrivals in the bookstore, I found the *Letter* with an introduction by Claudio Magris, an intelligent Italian scholar of German. So Hofmannsthal's text, written on the threshold of this century (1901), has rather unexpectedly come back to life. As soon as it was published it created something of a sensation, and then it gathered a layer of dust. What is the meaning of this revival? And is it really so unexpected?

A young English aristocrat, a highly esteemed writer, announces in the *Letter* sent to Francis Bacon in 1603 that he has decided to put away his pen forever and "completely abandon literary activity." The fragment you cite in your note reads: "[never] shall I write [another] book whether in English or in Latin . . . because the language in which I might be able not only to write but to think is neither Latin nor English, neither Italian nor Spanish, but a language none of whose words is known to me, a language in which inani-

---

*"The Letter of Lord Chandos," translated by Tania and James Stern, in Hugo von Hofmannsthal's *Selected Prose* (London: Routledge & Kegan Paul, 1952).

mate things speak to me and wherein I may one day have to justify myself before an unknown judge."

Let us consider briefly the premises for this decision. Lord Chandos realizes that the distance from which he observes human beings and their actions has been frightfully reduced, and now he sees the surrounding world as close up as he had once looked at his little finger through a magnifying glass, like a vast field full of holes and furrows. He is no longer able to grasp things with the "simplifying eye of habit." "Everything disintegrated into parts, those parts again into parts; no longer would anything let itself be encompassed by one idea." One by one, words floated around him and turned into eyes. These eyes obstinately stared at him. And he stared back, but this made his head spin. They were like whirlpools, reeling around incessantly, sucking him down and submerging him, and beyond the words he fell into the void. It is not this way with the whirlpools of inanimate objects. They also carry one away, but, unlike the whirlpools of language, they do not lead to the void. On the contrary, in a certain sense they allow recognition of the self and give breathing space in the deepest recesses of a placated world. And then comes the conclusion which you evidently consider your own: a farewell to literature and an attempt to establish a secret alliance with reality without the mediation of words.

Mockery would be easy: this literary manifesto of silence and the rejection of the mediating functions of language had to be expressed in words, after all. It was not by silence that Lord Chandos informed the illustrious Bacon of his renunciation but by a masterpiece of epistolary eloquence; and Hofmannsthal's writing did not come to an end with the publication of the *Letter.*

It did not come to an end, and yet the *Letter* was something more than the personal testimony of a poet's crisis. It put literature back at zero point, it inaugurated the twentieth century with a question about its raison d'être (and of art in general, if we consider Hofmannsthal's pet formula of the "indecency of the brush stroke"). Magris goes farther and traces a line that runs from the zero point of the *Letter* to Kafka's "Conversation with the Drunk Man," in which things are no longer where they used to be and cannot be expressed in language, and to Musil's *Young Törless*, with its talk of a "second life of things, secret and elusive," of "a life that is not expressed in words and yet still is my life"; for Musil it is indeed "this second or third or fourth reality," hidden behind the facade or under the surface that paralyzes the possibility of speech. I would venture even farther than Magris. Ultimately what was Joyce's *Ulysses* if not an effort to adapt language to the disintegration of things into ever smaller parts? But here we are entering areas which, as I once wrote in my journal, border on the self-destruction of literature, self-destruction in an act of sublime, cosmic gibbering. As to Hofmannsthal's *Letter*, it can be summarized as a renunciation dictated by the discovery of "how little, how terribly little can be said with words!"

Seventy-five years after the publication of the *Letter* we are at the opposite extreme. Not a paralysis of the possibilities of speech, but rather their elephantiasis. We are infested and eaten away by words; the mad idea is gaining ground that "words can exhaust all, absolutely all of reality." With the result, exquisitely formulated by Gombrowicz, that "the wiser, the stupider." The revival of Hofmannsthal's text, a writer's vow of silence, is an instinctive reaction of fear that ought to have been expected. Ours is an age that has lost its center. Literature (since that is what we are talking about) began with a declaration of asceticism of the word only to become, after many turns and experiments, dissipation of the word. Hofmannsthal's Lord Chandos broke his pen because it seemed impotent in the face of reality seen from too close up and the mystery that was hidden too deep behind it; he chose to "flow into" in the world with his lips sealed. Thousands of contemporary pens briskly cudgel us with reality as if there were no longer any mystery to it. To regain the center between reality and mystery, and to give literature back its weight and its dignity, there has to be a wish and a will to write, despite everything, in a language every word of which tries to answer questions that are put to us every day by an unknown judge. Do you think it is too late? Yours, G.*

NAPLES, NOVEMBER 3, 1984
[INNER EXPERIENCES]

It is very late, the city has finally quieted down, outside my window the leaves on the bushes and trees glisten after the rain, and the sky is shaking off its frayed clouds.

I have been reading recently found excerpts of Lev Chestov's diary:

"Inner experiences, even the simplest, are either so sacred that nature itself guards them jealously or so paltry that it is not worth revealing them to others." Sacred or paltry, in both cases they are allergic to the written page. But they have a form of their own, on the order of a disorderly fragmented confession whispered in thought. These admissions, like the shreds of dream after waking, are not lodged in articulate language. So what are they? A semi-devotional stammer aimed in darkness at a single invisible and silent listener: in periods when it is intense, a diary remains untouched.

.[. . .]

NAPLES, JANUARY 14, 1985
[WRITING AS A FORM OF PRAYER]

"Writing is a form of prayer." Auden refers to this thought of Kafka to explain his decision to destroy everything he had written. "Anyone who truly addresses his prayers to God does not want others to hear them."

A brilliant but strained interpretation, yet the wisdom of Kafka's observation remains. Every authentic piece of writing ultimately takes the form of prayer, I am convinced of that. A prayer in the broadest sense, let us say, is the equivalent of submitting questions to the Creator. However, an authentic writer — believer or not, on his knees with his head humbly bowed or on his feet with a glint of challenge in his eyes — should not be conscious of the fact that prayer is flowing through his voice like an underground stream, sometimes clearly audible and sometimes muffled or totally soundless. When he is aware of it, prayer becomes a form of literature, generally bad literature. A few days ago, to compensate for a trip to Assisi that was postponed for various reasons, I read Julien Green's book about Saint Francis. It is, indeed, prayer in the form of literature. The prayer is certainly sincere, in some points it is even fervent, but it turns the great and dramatic *Poverello* into rustling paper.

[. . .]

MAISONS-LAFFITTE, DECEMBER 6, 1988
[SOLZHENITSYN, CHIAROMONTE, CAMUS, ET AL.]

It is Solzhenitsyn's seventieth birthday. I have written several times about his books. Some years ago *Kultura* published my conversation with Nicola

Chiaromonte about Solzhenitsyn, and it was later included in that outstanding essayist and critic's posthumous book *Silenzio e parole*. Three
extracts of our dialogue strike me today.

NICOLA: "In Solzhenitsyn's books you catch sight of a response — or rather,
the clear indication of a response — to the infernal torment that, even if it is
not imposed by an autocratic system, oppresses every conscious human
being: the torment of living day after day a life without sense, a life in which
the individual feels he is losing his soul day by day."

I: "Simple, sensitive and attentive readers of Solzhenitsyn's books in the
West are moved and forced to think by what they read, because the Russian
writer restores meaning and something like a clear sound to concepts that
seemed irremediably outworn: soul, human personality, good and evil, justice, honesty, love, truth, the thirst for immortality. In other words, admiration for Solzhenitsyn expresses a latent and often unconscious rebellion
against a world that (in the words of Witkiewicz) 'kills in human beings any
intuition of the future, any capacity to integrate the separate moments in a
construct of life in the long term, and pulverizes the self into so many
moments each separate from the other . . . so that it will all the more easily
submit to any mechanical discipline.' "

NICOLA: "For the literati Solzhenitsyn's novels are nobly documentary,
and that is all. Now it is common knowledge that contemporary literati have
no particular respect for either morality or truth. It is no accident that it was
an Italian writer who invented the formula of 'literature as falsehood.' It is a
much more traditional formula in Italy than it might seem, but it can be
applied to almost everything that is written today in the West. Did we not
hear recently that an eminent French intellectual, Michel Foucault, was
called to the honors of the Collège de France, and in the austere walls of that
institution gave an inaugural address in which the 'desire for truth' was considered a form of repression of freedom of speech?"

On the occasion of Solzhenitsyn's birthday, one wants to ask if any trace of his
books still survives in the West. In the minds and hearts of his readers, yes, I
have proof of that. For the literati they remain "nobly documentary," perhaps
something slightly more than "noble" (in other words, powerless), since they
are now clearing a channel for the streams of the Soviet glasnost. But I do not

think that Solzhenitsyn and those who are akin to him in spirit, however different from him as well — such writers as Camus, Orwell, and Pasternak, for example — put an end to the harvest of "literature as falsehood," the literature of barren subtleties, ever new approaches and tastes, novels that might equally well be published or not, and pen-and-ink party games in which "serious" is a synonym for "boring." We go back to Solzhenitsyn and his like through unfortunately fleeting reference to their weight and substance. That is why this writer who is merely serious, merely fully conscious of the writer's calling, is sometimes accused of wanted to play the "prophet."

Overwhelmed by his enormous volumes, cycles, and "nodes," we are inclined to overlook his "slighter works." Who knows, they may give an even better idea of the class of writer Solzhenitsyn is. "Matryona's House," a story about "the righteous person without whom no village or city may survive." "An Incident at Krechetovka Station," a story about a human soul poisoned by the venom of "revolutionary vigilance." "The Easter Procession," a picture of the Feast of Passion and Resurrection disturbed and reviled by young hooligans. In all three stories, Solzhenitsyn touches the depths of the depravity of Soviet life in the "raging torrent of epochal historical processes." He does it in a way that is modest and frugal, weighing every word, his voice subdued and solicitous, as if he wanted to caution "experts" on contemporary Russia: as long as you do not understand, as long as you do not see the actuality of my country in seemingly slight events and images, as Chekhov tried to see the truth about last-century Russia, your would-be "expertise" will be lifeless, soulless inking of paper that is too clever by half. This warning is no less timely today, when legions of "experts" glide over the surface of Soviet life, content to construct diagnoses and quick to project "prognoses," and make no attempt — God forbid! — to glance even a bit below the surface. Solzhenitsyn is the writer of deep Russia, which lies silent under the ice and rarely awakens. When it does awake, however, there will be a terrible icequake.

DECEMBER 8, 1988
[SOLZHENITSYN]

In our conversation we also talked about the artistic merits of Solzhenitsyn's prose. I quoted Pasternak's view that "art never seemed to me an object or an aspect of form but rather a mysterious hidden element of content. . . . Works of art speak in many ways: with subject matter, theses, situations, characters. But they speak chiefly through the presence of art. The presence of art in *Crime and Punishment* is more overwhelming than Raskolnikov's crime."

What is this "mysterious hidden element of content" that gives the sense of the "presence of art"? Whatever else we might try to say about it, it certainly does not depend on the inherent wealth or poverty of the narrative material. Flaubert dreamed of describing the basest things as if they belonged to history or epic. An apparently absurd undertaking (he added), yet the only one worthy of a writer's efforts and the one that determined the degree of originality and artistry. In a letter to Louise Colet he made a strange comparison, The artist must raise everything to a higher level; he is something on the order of a pump, which dips into the deepest layers of things, sucks up what is at the bottom, and brings to light something unremarkable and disregarded. The comparison may be too clever, but the meaning is sufficiently clear. To transform what is featureless, even banal, into the unusual; to elevate the gray quotidian and glut it with unexpected colors.

The "presence of art" makes it possible to set Flaubert's "A Simple Heart" side by side with Solzhenitsyn's "Matryona's House," two masterpieces of transfiguration that take earthbound realistic description into another dimension.

Translated by Ronald Strom

Jan Józef Szczepański

(1920–2003)

As a very young man, Jan Józef Szczepański was drafted and fought in the
short September 1939 campaign, witnessing the destruction of the Polish army
and the collapse of the state. He then became an active member of the
Resistance and belonged, when the war ended, to the incorruptible ones, to
those who never struck an ideological compromise with the communists. He
dwelled on the fringe of the writing community, gravitating around an
important—and relatively independent—liberal Catholic weekly in Kraków,
Tygodnik Powszechny, a haven of moral and political integrity.

In his writing, though, Szczepański was more a stoic than a Catholic; his
main interest lay in gauging the morality of history. In his novels and short
stories he tried to render justice to the complicated world of modern Polish
history. Both in his writing and his comportment he had a well-deserved
reputation of utmost honesty. One of his intellectual masters was the writer
Joseph Conrad, with his idea of Faithfulness (in this Szczepański was not
alone; for his generation, abandoned by political leaders, Joseph Conrad
Korzeniowski was a surrogate spiritual father).

The text published in this chapter has an exceptional status in
Szczepański's work: it is a philosophical essay in which the author tries to
answer unanswerable questions, in which he displays his metaphysic—a lonely
writer's credo. The addressee of the essay, Julian Stryjkowski, was an influential
fiction writer of Polish Jewish origin.

LETTER TO JULIAN STRYJKOWSKI

Dear Julian,

I hope you'll forgive me this mystification of sorts: the appearance of privacy I'm allowing myself to lend a text intended for publication by using your name.

I needed just this kind of form. The form of an intimate conversation or even a confidence, because the things I want to talk about won't bear the acoustics of the open forum, where the criteria of pragmatism and "common sense" hold and where anyone who can't offer doctoral credentials in some highly practical science can easily be shut up by an accusation of "mysticism." The golden age of philosophical dilettantism is over, and there are no longer any accredited authorities behind you if you don't have a patented method at your command; what's more, if you don't represent the interests of one given ideology or another, you're a usurper who in the best case deserves to be ignored.

However, I owe you an explanation for why I chose you in particular. First, because you and I are so very different. We grew up in different traditions, in different atmospheres. We broke away from different faiths. We worked for different causes. Occupations and despairs of different kinds fell to each of us. So if we share the same anxieties (we both know we do) and also, I think, similar longings, then those anxieties and longings are fundamental, more important than differences shaped by circumstances — they are the kind that are worthy of, and demand, reflection.

As you can easily guess, another reason I'm addressing myself to you is a certain conversation we had walking down Wiejska Street in Warsaw — one of those conversations people have who happen to be walking in the same direction, people who are friendly, respect each other, have more than one interest in common, but who are far from intimate. It sometimes happens that a pleasant conversation suddenly takes on an entirely unexpected turn. Some question, meant only to satisfy a moderate curiosity, elicits an answer that goes slightly beyond the boundary of conventional reserve and then (because nothing happens, no alarm signal, no embarrassed reflex disturbs this freedom) words throw off the mask of euphemism, try to measure up to what is most important and most difficult to name. And then silence follows, because it turns out this is a conversation for which a whole lifetime won't be enough.

Something of the kind happened to us on that walk. And what I'm writing now is another attempt to face up to the silence in which we are sunk by our petty weakness.

I said then, and you agreed with me, that our task — our calling even — is to beat against a wall in which there is no opening, to search for what we will never find — neither we nor any human being. There was once an American TV series: *Mission Impossible*. It piled up dangers and difficulties apparently impossible to overcome but vanquished in the end by the hero, thanks to his phenomenal intelligence and undaunted courage. Our mission is truly impossible, because there's no genius or bravery that would allow us to force the boundaries imposed by the reach of our five senses. And yet — I'm profoundly convinced of this — engaging in that effort doomed to failure is our responsibility and the most important one at that. Probably the only important one, because it is what our vague sense of human dignity comes down to.

Literature is above all what I have in mind. That is what we were talking about back then. What is it really for? What should it be?

Joseph Conrad defined its function as "rendering justice to the visible universe." Visible, so only the universe accessible to our human senses. It would seem that this limitation, put with unmistakable emphasis, soberly set the conditions for the trial, permitting only the testimony of concrete things that can be verifiably measured and excluding all metaphysical speculation. But the Conradian formula doesn't in the least guarantee the serene self-confidence offered by moving in a familiar and neatly inventoried space. Above all, we don't know what code of law underlies this justice. And from where the judge derives his authority. Because if he delivers judgments on matters of the visible universe, he himself must stand outside that universe — as every judge stands outside the trial he is adjudicating — and what's more, he must be armed with an infallible measure of truth and falsity. Is taking up such a position not a usurpation? In any case it is a mission impossible — which Conrad no doubt knew perfectly well. He also knew, however, that usurpation is the artist's calling.

The codes we live by — both those contained in articles of law and those written in the verse lines of revealed truth — are subject to trivialization in the service of short-term interests. We have always had and will always have a sense of the incompleteness of those norms, and even of their deadness in the face of the unreliable, ultimately elusive element of reality. Literature must cast doubt on it, if only because one of its first duties is the struggle for man's sovereignty, his liberation from the pacts he concludes time and time again — depending on the circumstances — with himself and with the world. We know what those pacts are for. They create an appearance of meaning in our existence. They are a kind of theater flats, artificial horizons screening off the real ones to which we aren't brave enough to raise our eyes. In order to feel safe in life, we limit the scope of our perspective and that thin allotment we try to sow as closely as we can with duties, prohibitions, and claims that require no further questioning. That is our visible universe. But if anything important happens in that universe, if dramatic changes take place in it, and we humans vaunt ourselves on a history different from the history of the biological survival of the species, it is because we never manage to believe to the end in the single binding force of our fictions.

A panicked fear of becoming aware of the true proportions of things makes us seek shelter in sober practicality and in the entrenchments of all kinds of orthodoxies. However, this leads inevitably to the trivialization of our existence. In the wings, amid artificial scenery, it becomes narrow and tawdry — all for the sake of our safety. There's something indescribably depressing about this. Because if there is only a world "from here to there" and beyond the walls of the air-conditioned cell of our visible universe there extend astonishing, infinite realms — it comes to the same thing.

Orthodoxies are crumbling with growing rapidity these days — religious as well as ideological ones — and a man feels more and more defenseless against the pressure of outer darkness. The rational practicality of "here to there" cannot save him, because even he needs principles deeper and more enduring than any short term. Principles on the measure of the whole human being and his eternal unrest. Without them, without those principles, there's only arbitrary method, a contract without dignity, whose execution might equally well be entrusted to animals or machines. A world functioning "from here to there" without reason or purpose is an unnecessary world, and so a trivial one. If we are conscious of this, it is also a tragic world.

What justice was Conrad talking about? He didn't grant himself the right to appeal to Powers inaccessible to his experience. His honesty forbade him to do so. But on the other hand, a sense of dignity — that mysterious and sublime human realm — didn't allow him to consent to life in a trivial world. The parable of a journey across immense expanses, at the mercy of the blind forces of nature and their caprices, was not merely a rhetorical figure for him. He knew well what human insignificance was and he knew that insignificance carries in it a potential for greatness. So he saw "rendering justice to the visible universe" as a judgment on its human matters from the point of view of that potential.

But what is the essence of that potential? On what is it based?

Honoring Conrad's resolve not to overstep the boundaries of the visible universe, it must be stated that the consciousness of the existence of those boundaries must have been a fundamental matter for him. Here the sea analogy is once again helpful. The solitude of the seaman in the middle of the indifferent ocean couldn't mean a senseless erring. It was a trial. A trial of the sense and order that we carry inside ourselves without knowing their essence. Something we call honor, fidelity, courage — not self-interest. For in the visible universe we are bound by the laws of some Higher Order, whose origin we can't trace, but which determine our exceptional place in nature's plans. Of course, Conrad didn't say this directly. Within the confines of a ship's narrow deck, surrounded by a small crew, a seaman was a relentlessly conscious part of the equation: on the one hand, a thinking, short-lived particle — on the other hand, an enormity, eternal and strange, apparently chaotic, though perhaps subject to an enigmatic harmony, magical and terrible, in the face of which he had to be something, be himself, in order not to dissolve in chaos. And in all likelihood it is precisely in that necessity of preserving one's difference, putting up opposition in the brief moment of a confrontation (and the most unequal confrontation imaginable) that the potential lies.

How to define it more closely, without resorting to words that don't lend themselves to being filled with visible content in the visible universe? Isn't this fear of words something along the lines of a superstition? After all, nothing is its own explanation. Every life, every concept requires more and more explanations, and these finally slip past the borders of our field of vision, past the sphere of options available for determining causes. So if the word "metaphysics" sounds so suspect and naive to us, if it embarrasses us even more than it embarrassed Conrad, we ought to realize that reducing the meaning of the world and our own existence to rational models of social, economic, or political utility, we are continuing to cultivate metaphysics, even if clutching another dictionary.

It seems a hopeless enterprise to look for precision in Conrad's formulation. However, it holds a dazzling flash of intuition. Because he took the thing whole from the most profound personal experience. From that awareness of confrontation. And that awareness is what became his point of departure for a code. Rendering justice to the visible universe, then, lies in catching it in the dramatic perspective of the dimensions that, revealing our infinite smallness, demand that a man be humble and simultaneously give him a right to be proud.

I did not manage to answer your question as to whether I am a believer with a simple Yes or No. This gets me into trouble, because generally we think that a straightforward affirmation or contradiction are the proof of our inner maturity. But I suspect that much more often they merely indicate resignation — the choice of an agreed convention instead of a conviction. They are taken as credentials of some kind of fellowship or partisanship, because one is supposed to belong somewhere, not remain in isolation. Quite often the character of these choices is merely social or political, and one can only accept that if one accepts the trivial arbitrariness of our existence. But a refusal to declare oneself on one or another side in the name of reason (since pronouncements on questions beyond the reach of our minds are a barren pursuit) is also a capitulation dictated by pettiness and convenience. The profession *credo quia absurdum* requires a heroic humility of which we are less and less capable, and the proud Conradian "it must be so" denying us the right to metaphysical consolations is also beyond the strength of most of us. Moreover, the scientific skepticism of today, which has spread as an attitude far beyond the circle of those engaged in scientific research, undermines both faith and systematic doubt. We live in times of great disenchantment.

Yes. We were supposed to be the happy inheritors of the hopes of those enlightened prophets who tore down the bastion of the obscure superstitions of the past and raised an altar to Reason. Our times are the times of the fulfillment of their utopia. Is it necessary to repeat here that neither the deepening of the mystery of the atom's structure nor tearing ourselves from the earth's orbit has clarified for us who we really are and what is the meaning of our existence? Or that all our splendid achievements haven't taught us the art of a life worthy of reasonable creatures?

We were talking about literature. About the calling. And here, in the realm of these questions, these anxieties, we're probably closest to the crux of that question. That's why your question about whether I was a believer was not a digression from the subject. The more as it didn't touch on any formally defined denomination. We were raised in different religious systems, so if I heard an "I am too" or "neither am I" from you, it wouldn't refer to anything like the Holy Trinity, the Immaculate Conception, or the Resurrection of the Flesh — or any of the many things over which the Christian's reason (and with it, his good will) stumbles, but rather something universal and fundamental to humanity. About an irreducible stance. I think to a certain degree this situation between us is typical. Finally, the era of chosen people is coming to an end — the time of an exclusive realm of single and incontrovertible truths. This troubled world of ours, full of fanatical antagonisms, is already too small for us to resist consistently the erosion caused by relativism. Perhaps we all partake a little of a true intuition? Or perhaps others' truths are truer than our own?

In *Austeria* you wrote about the Hasidim not as a cool observer or as a mocker, but as one profoundly moved — by a very complex emotion, because it contains pity, regret, delight, and perhaps even a touch of envy. One feels that the ecstasy of those people, grotesque and beautiful (like the raptures of exotic cults, mysterious to the uninitiated), is for you something close, exerting an irresistible attraction, and at the same time, something irrevocably lost and no longer acceptable, although still more worthy of love than of condemnation or scorn. You seem to say: "They were happy, but that kind of happiness is a closed chapter now."

Have you noticed how strong the temptation is in today's world to reopen those closed chapters? Only — this is the odd thing — it is the other's books that most tempt us. (I know a thing or two about this — it's no accident that I studied Native American cultures.) It looks a bit as if the principles of rationalism and criticism were only binding within the sphere of our own tradition. In fact, we've always used them inconsistently and rather superficially, making them the instruments of new myths at the first opportunity. But as far as the religiosity of contemporary Westerners goes, it is disturbed above all by the varied consequences of the great disillusionment I mentioned. We feel acutely the fallibility and limitations of our reason, but we want to base our hopes on something more certain, we can't erase the effects of the revision carried out in a spirit of unpunished license after the breaking of manifold taboos. It wasn't only our system of Christian dogma that faltered. The history of the Church, too, manifested itself to us as a human affair — in all its human poverty.

One of the reasons for the growing interest in Oriental cultures in the West is the lack of a sense of personal responsibility for their history. Those who suddenly discover the path of salvation in Zen mysticism, in yoga, in the belief in transmigration of souls, don't feel the need to look into the nature of Buddhist theocracy or the perversions of professional asceticism, or the moral value of the caste system. It is as if they purchase their new faith in a duty-free zone, without the surcharges of practical life.

Fashion and snobbery play an important role in this, of course. Beat singers having themselves photographed in bhikshu robes at the feet of a bearded guru are not only doing it to get media attention. With those outward accessories they wish to enlarge and deepen their personality, in the naive conviction that every greatness and every depth is a matter of image, and that a person is what he sees reflected in others' eyes. So there are fashionable prescriptions for being fascinating. Techniques of seduction, an arsenal to which exoticism and mystery have belonged for a long time.

But even those trivial manifestations of coquetry testify to real anxieties and longings. If people in the computer world turn to exotic mysticisms, look for signs in astrological charts or practice voodoo, it is because their sense of reality doesn't coincide with the boundaries of the visible universe and all the forms of protection against the fear this causes, all the systems constructed by their own civilizations (revised and compromised so often in the lap of those civilizations) have lost their authority and emotional freshness. It seems to me that here one could formulate something in the nature of a psychological law. Faced with problems whose solutions are beyond our power and having the choice only among unverifiable hypotheses, we instinctively tend to reach for the least verifiable hypotheses. This law would only apply to the civilizations like ours (the Mediterranean), where two systems of interpreting reality — rational-empirical and religious — have long functioned alongside one another, at times in contradiction, at times aiming at an unattainable synthesis. Weariness of this controversy inclines us to seek salvation in regions unravished by any such battle and so remote that one can move around in them, after discarding one's old customs, with the joyful readiness of the discoverer of new worlds.

And here the time has come for the next question, which wasn't really put in our conversation, but which lies inevitably in wait in the course of these reflections. You could have asked me if I see skepticism as the only possible stance for a thinking person today. As a stance guarding both against a conformist fideism (the result of resignation) and a frivolous embracing of "others' books" (because they are still untouched by the disillusionment of our intellectual experience). In this instance I wouldn't be able to give you an unambiguous answer either. The imprecision of these labels becomes glaringly clear whenever we try to make them coherent principles of our inner life. In practice it's hard to draw the line of demarcation between skepticism and indifference, and it is only a short step from indifference to cynicism. The soberest inhabitants of the visible universe — those who see every anxiety about its true nature as a symptom of sickly feebleness — tend to explain the arbitrariness of human existence in terms of the action of simple mechanisms like sexual needs, ambition, or greed. It is as if these and other elementary urges are the source of all our actions and the foundation of our mental constructions.

It's relatively easy to derive a whole psychic and intellectual superstructure from morally neutral biological laws and even from automatic physical and chemical processes. Regardless of this, a consistent secularization of human life seems an impossibility. To rob a person's consciousness of its transcendental dimension is to cripple and corrupt him. Having come to believe he is only an animal, he will be a particularly dangerous and cruel one. But he is rarely able truly to believe in this. History, on the other hand, offers many examples of substitute cults growing spontaneously from a substratum of rationalist worldviews and ideologies. They are prosthetic limbs meant to make up for the loss of a vital spiritual organ in the human organism — artificial limbs generally of dubious value, because they serve limited and quickly outdated aims. But the most tragic consequence of a loss of faith in some higher meaning of existence is contempt for the world. It is born from an unavowed intuitive conviction that the world could and should have such a meaning (because there is in us a presentiment of perfection), but since it is only an arbitrary and blind mechanism, it resembles a gigantic fraud. And here begins the Célinian Journey to the End of the Night. A journey through evil and ugliness, vulgarity and the insane futility of everything — toward senseless annihilation. We know where the journey led that unhappy writer. It is probably not a coincidence.

Céline, too, rendered his justice to the visible universe — and to himself as well. But how different that justice is from Conrad's. And how different the universe.

Who still cares about Céline — that pitiful outcast — who once basked in the bright light of scandal (now so dim!), he who thrilled with his moral provocation, the arrogant denouncer of pious hypocrisy, later the shameful victim of the void that he carried in himself and with which he threatened his contemporaries as if it were the shattering force of destiny? And why should he be mentioned alongside Conrad, who is draped in the severe toga of unshakable righteousness? Or maybe no one cares about Conrad these days either?

Writers' voices — and both of them were true writers, despite their differences — do not sound in a vacuum. The France of the great debacle of 1940 and the France of Vichy were Céline's France. And Conrad's forgotten voice sounded with unexpected force in the murky shadows of the Polish underground. So for people of our generation the combination isn't accidental. We were talking about literature, after all, and its mission, so hard to define. No, I'm not claiming in the least that Céline or any other novelist bears the responsibility for France's ignominious defeat or that we owe it to Conrad that thousands of young Poles found the strength in themselves to fight in a seemingly hopeless situation. I only want to say that literature carries the potential both for offering shameful justifications and for issuing splendid challenges. If I mention such a strangely matched pair, it is because at the beginning of their diverging paths lay skepticism. Only one of them (more consistent in his Latin reasoning) arrived at a void, the cynical and despairing negation of all values, while the other, denying himself the privilege of appealing to authorities inaccessible to reason (in which there was not only pride but also humility) attempted to find an unattainable higher order in himself, in human beings, and to make of it a weapon against the chaos of the visible universe, to make it a law. These days we don't hasten to legislate or to judge, or even to instruct. Maybe because in recent times too many attempts have been made to put various gospels in our mouths, and surely also because our time runs at an increasing pace and the effort required to keep ourselves afloat in its current makes it hard for us to assume a hieratic stance. We belong rather to the species of nervous and uneasy witnesses. We feel that without our testimonies the world would lose its shape. Without them the continuity of memory would break (in spite of archives filled with meticulously recorded facts), the imagination that allows us to perceive comprehensible patterns in reality would wither and the only moral sanction would be the utilitarian demands of the moment. But the weight of responsibility terrifies us. Giving testimony means trying to determine the truth. If the truth were known, we wouldn't be necessary. And we aren't needed by those who think it's not worth bothering, or by those who imagine they possess the truth and require only confirmation from us. We have to play the fool and expose ourselves, knowing our helplessness and at the same time not giving up hope.

I speak about these things in somewhat heightened language, maybe even elevated language, but they are quite elusive and don't lend themselves to matter-of-fact description like an analysis of a clinical case or an account of a sociological process. In our work we let ourselves be led more by instinct and although we know it serves a constant sharpening of collective consciousness, we are rarely aware of the essence of our motives and aims. We can only define them by approximations, comparisons to events and concepts from the sphere of universal and prosaic experience. But if the writer's fulfillment of the function of witness can be taken literally, the reasons for undertaking it and the hopes connected to achieving it are hard to approach without allegory. Is it not the case that by taking on the role of witness we declare our (often unconscious) faith in the existence of some Tribunal?

We don't really feel called to sit on it, as Joseph Conrad and many of our predecessors did, but it seems to us that a duty rests upon us to aid the far-reaching labors of that highest, dimly perceived authority with an accumulation of proofs of the truth about ourselves — for the defense, the prosecution, the appeal for pardon . . .

In public, usurping the powers of attorney of our fellow human beings, we are in fact doing what a majority of people do inwardly on the sly, wrestling with the meaning of their own lives. For a human life takes the form of a trial and each of us subconsciously waits for a verdict. Only some of us passionately want to penetrate the meaning of the proceedings, to behold the face of the Judge. We long for this to become our personal experience; understanding that we ask too much, in the deepest recesses of the spirit we still wait for a revelation that would finally put an end to our unrest.

I write these words not without fear and with cautious hesitation, feeling like a man in a dark room, creeping around on tiptoe, groping the walls and furnishings uncertainly. I'm aware of my arrogance in using the plural as I lay out this situation and thereby draw you into it. But the literature testifying to our times offers repeated proof of this drawn-out waiting. We are waiting for Godot with Samuel Beckett. Each of us in his own way. Humbly or rapturously, in hope or in fear, with resignation, impatience, in despair, anger — often with a laugh of defiance or scorn.

What else can I tell you? Probably just that I deluded myself when I started this letter — as I do every time I sit down to write — in the hope that I would suddenly find a magic formula. And that — as I usually do — I feel disappointment. This particular kind of disappointment that doesn't indicate a sense of defeat but something like a new awareness of the horizon and the state of my own powers. You could put it this way: "Of course, you didn't manage and never you, but once again you made an effort. Don't be discouraged, go on trying, because only that labor justifies your existence." So there's also a kind of satisfaction in it. A kind of consolation. And because this time I attained it with your help — please accept my expression of gratitude.

Translated by Alissa Valles

Anna Kamieńska

(1920–1986)

Under the Nazi occupation of Poland, Anna Kamieńska participated as a teacher in underground education. Before the war she had studied pedagogy; after the war she graduated from the classics department at Lodz University. She then moved to Warsaw, where she collaborated with several literary magazines. Kamieńska published many volumes of poetry. She was also active as a translator of poetry. Later on, she also published books of essays, commenting on poetry from biblical and classical perspectives.

The history of Kamieńska's poetry is a history of a slow, honest evolution toward religious conversion. Her poetry has nothing to do with any intellectual fashion, although the twentieth century knew some moments when religion was hip. Her religious leanings were accompanied by intense reading of the Bible and Christian and Judaic philosophy, and were deepened by mourning the death of her husband, Jan Spiewak, also a poet.

The pages presented in this chapter are taken from Kamieńska's beautiful *Diary* (or *Notebook—Notatnik* in Polish) of which there are two volumes. These volumes count among the most moving and perspicacious poets' diaries. Short entries having to do with poetry and spiritual life radiate force and freshness that only genuine contemplation can convey.

Diary Entries

1970

The "cipher" of contemporary poetry — the desperate desire to preserve the values of art, while it seems everything is being frittered away in cheap utilitarianism. Opposition to the easy use of goods produced by industry, purchasable, buyable.

It's a spasmodic defense of the art of remaining oneself in an epoch of advertising, posters, mass-produced books, pulp attacking from all sides.

The essence of contemplation is in listening to music.

Effort and inspiration — in art. Labor and grace — in spiritual life.

This analogy makes sense to anyone who knows the torment of waiting for "inspiration," for that strange opening of the imagination and the mind, when it's as if someone were writing for us. One can't feign this state or fake it. It's either there or it's not.

Poetry is a presentiment of the truth. It's the vestibule of faith. It's contemporary poets who have turned it into a juggling act.

People only open up to themselves for brief moments, like flashes of lightning. At times it requires a single word. It isn't necessarily happening where confessions pour out in a flood tide. There are little words, simple, surprising, perhaps disguised. One must be sensitive to them.

Perhaps this sensitivity to another person is called love?

With poetry it is sometimes the same way. There are dark closures to the world of poetry. And there are dazzling openings.

Or perhaps it's just I who am so gagged and "dazzled"?

The way a source strains toward the light, toward the air. Its laboring work, its effort, its black passageways like despair.

That's the way a poet looks for words. With muscles, gestures. That's how

J. wrote poems. He paced, muttered, gestured, as if gathering, summoning words.

Mickiewicz. Bread. A man's power. Energy. Open words. Though he is a classicist, there is more power of health in him than in the "Romantic" poets.

I wasn't searching for God at all!
I was searching for my Departed.
I will never stop saying this and being amazed by it.

Poetry is not liked in Poland. What are the reasons for this? Maybe one of them is that we always associate poetry with slavery. Its function has been too closely tied to recompensation for all the losses of the age of slavery.

There are empty days, when I can't work. But a day like that leaves me as tired as if I had done heavy labor. Inwardly there is that grinding of stones. That state is tiring insofar as I try to struggle against it, though it may be a state of blessed creative attention. That is the most difficult work, when we are creating ourselves, giving birth to ourselves, or maybe we are dying with great effort. For that inner birth is also a death.

On that road distances are not measured in meters or kilometers. It's space on a different scale.

And again about poetry: A poem is a mysterious organism. Words can't lie next to each other like hooked fish. One has to weld them, send some kind of energy flowing through them. Everything in a poem pulses, moves, and yet remains within defined borders.

J.'s poems are like that, his living spirit is struggling inside them. I hear him. He is struggling inside the poem.

December 27

Solitude is always solitude toward someone. That is what is important: who is absent in our solitude. When it is solitude toward people in general, it is only a void.

Solitude toward a single person, someone close, is something else. The person's absence fills our solitude, gives it color. Even a painful longing is some form of presence.

There is also solitude toward God, the fullest kind. That solitude is our freedom. That presence in solitude is difficult, an internal attainment, carved out like a poem.

1971

We were making the final decision in a poetry contest. My criteria of judgment are different from the others'. I notice this all the time, with a certain anxiety. Where I look for a human face, the predicament of a human being faced with every manifest reality, others look only for a "good poem." It's not hard to make "good poems." It's very hard to be somebody. Yes, but that being somebody has to be reflected in good poems. That's true. And so we go round in a circle. When these varied criteria are applied, the forms of poetry that are perhaps less spectacular but more profound usually disappear. Expressiveness — that's another criterion.

Poetry has occupied me my whole life, but in the end it turns out I don't know much about it. I emphasize what is gray and as if unformed. This worries me, because I still believe in the possibility of an objective evaluation of poetry.

Poems have left me. These periods of aridity and emptiness are terrifying. My writing doesn't matter in the eyes of my excellent colleagues anyway. But I don't write for them.

November 1

The idea of a poem about Job. The thing is beginning to grow in me. A contemporary Job. God who is silent. Present in every place and in various shapes — Satan. Paweł said to leave out the ending, it's artificially tacked on, that Job is given back all his goods. Then I thought, I'll do it the other way around, starting from that ending. From Job who is happy once again but already crushed, incapable of happiness, broken. Job's happiness. Job's second happiness.

The task of so-called religious poetry is to cleanse "religion" of the stereotype. And that's why that stereotype has to live in it, one must branch off from it.

1972

Poetry as a cemetery. A cemetery of faces, hands, gestures. A cemetery of clouds and the sky's colors, a burial ground of winds, branches, of jasmine (that's from Świdnik), a statuette of a saint in Marseille, a poplar on the Black Sea, a burial ground of moments and hours, sacrificial cemeteries of dreams. Your eternal rest in the word, eternal resting place, eternal light of memory.

A cemetery of sunsets, running with extended arms, a child's skimpy dress, winter, blizzards, steps on the stairs, tears, a letter with a great confession, silver faces, a shoemaker's shack, parting, pain, weeping.

Everything interred, buried in the amber tombs of the word. The sea, tenderness seeping from someone's eyes, parting; I believe in God, arrivals and departures, solitude harder than death, sweet as death. Unrest and calm. City streets. A monk brushing his belly against a woman tourist in the catacombs. First communion. First love. First storm at sea. First night.

A dog's eyes, a lover's eyes, the eyes of a dead man not yet closed, glazed with a tear. Memory's scree. Mummies, statues with hacked-off arms and legs. A deer, coming out of a grove, standing and watching. A footbridge over a river, amid a goose's flapping and bare legs, meadows in bloom. Grandfather's death, his moustache in the coffin. A dog's howl.

Because there isn't a priest running with holy oils after every fallen leaf. The collective grave of childhood, where lie apple cores, broken glass, my dead friend Basia Bartmańska, my father's angry brow, my grandfather's hand offered for a kiss, the longing for holiness, nettles, a public restroom, spiders, being tickled by boys on dark stairs in a suburb.

That sun and that rain, mother, mother, that sky and tree. The spring is still tightly wound, I can't completely uncoil it.

My mother, dying in my childhood dream, my mother dying and me watching her die, and seeing how she is dying and I am staying alive, whole, almost indifferent.

Warmhearted mother, you who take care of people.

And so many lives like the rings of a tree, like geological layers. I lost God in the darkness of my twenty years. Anthony, saint of lost things, help me find the Lord God I lost! Saint Anthony is standing in the courtyard taking contributions for the poor.

January 26

Of course, only a poem came out of my "Job's Happiness," no play or epic. Short breath, everything just tied itself into a poem's knot.

Tadeusz Różewicz is always writing about the "death of poetry" (that great corpse), about the "new" fall of man. Those pronouncements seem to me to spring from a certain historical naiveté. How many times have the death of poetry and the end of the world not been proclaimed! Every epoch has its menace. On the world's scale, at any given time everything has always been falling apart, dying. Our age is not exceptional from that point of view, though its perverse vanity would seem to favor it.

Silence from excess, not from a lack of words.

In poetry I always need concrete things, a pushing oneself off from the world. I don't amount to anything on my own. But I trust people, animals, birds, phenomena, things. Built into their community, I can hope that I manage to touch the intangible, see the invisible, catch the elusive. I myself only mean something as a part of the world. I have no monopoly and no elevated status. That is what a need for the concrete in poetry means.

March 27

Poetry is only a means of maturation for me. That's why I'm not even ashamed of weaker poems. They are stages, a passageway, a self-definition.

April 3

Poetry should train itself in prayer. Poetry should turn to a destination that is always farther than man. It's like a principle of spiritual dynamics, that a spiritual effort has to aim higher than the goal.

When poetry addresses itself only to the so-called ordinary man, it immediately withers and dries. Poetry seeks higher reasons for the human world, in the olden days one would say: reasons of beauty. I don't say that. I would say: reasons of meaning. If a poet stubbornly answers the question why he writes with "for myself," then that is really the only thing he wants to express.

The greatest poetry in the world — the Sermon on the Mount.

August 8

There's a division in me between me as a living being and me as a writer. I don't fully identify with my writing self. I'm not a poet. Sometimes I recall only with some effort that I'm supposed to be a poet.

Where does this come from? The lack of a writer's identity? What I write is only an imprecise expression of my being, which itself is more important than writing. Approval is nice, like being petted on the head. Disapproval is unpleasant, like rudeness on a tram. I won't kill myself over a bad review. I won't be happy because of any award. There is something stubborn in me, something constant and categorical, which despite everything looks forward and gives me a sense of worth independently of what I do.

Like Katherine Mansfield — I voice myself more by my own life, by my existence, by that inner flow that creates me and that I create. I carry and am carried.

It would be ridiculous and wrong if "Poet" were written on my gravestone. My stony name expresses me most fully. Perhaps because it was loved.

For a while I have noticed that I easily write of myself in the past tense: I was, I wrote, I loved. No, not that. I was, I wrote, I love. Only that is the present tense.

Translated by Alissa Valles

Julia Hartwig

(b. 1921)

Julia Hartwig belongs to the generation that pursued its university studies underground. Under the Nazi occupation, Polish universities were not allowed—nor for that matter were high schools tolerated—but an efficient network of underground education quickly developed. Hartwig lived these difficult years in Warsaw (where she met Czesław Miłosz).

After the war she went to Paris, where her long-lasting romance with French literature originated. She published books on Guillaume Apollinaire and Gérard de Nerval. Much later, in the seventies, she lived and taught in the United States. Her late husband, the acclaimed poet and translator Artur Miedzyrzecki, accompanied her there. After this period the two of them published an important anthology of American poetry in translation. Hartwig also described her American experience in a memoir.

Her poetry has kept the flavor of a personal quest for a delicate existential wisdom. Her poems grow out of a rich understanding of both Polish and European traditions. She is widely regarded as one of the leading women poets in Poland, along with Wisława Szymborska, Urszula Kozioł, Krystyna Milobędzka, and Ewa Lipska.

A FEW WORDS ON POETRY

It is hard to separate poetry from the poet, from his person. Regardless of
how much a so-called lyrical I speaks to us directly from a poem. You might
even say that poems are not written with a pen but with a personality. The
richer the personality, the more interesting the poems.

Critics often categorize poets according to whether there is more culture
or nature in their work. Pierre Reverdy, one of the leading poets of the generation after [Guillaume] Apollinaire, said that poetry is born of a wound
inflicted by other poets' poetry. And so born of culture, not of nature and its
young sorrows, although nature and culture will be its unfailing nourishment.

If the attitude to reality is the nerve center of every aesthetic, whether in
literature or in art, visible reality has always been a constant point of reference for me. I accept the visible world in all its wealth and menace. Sometimes I am in agreement with it, sometimes in a painful quarrel. It does not,
however, deceive by its shape. The truth about it, the image of it accessible
to us, at the same time carries us in the most extraordinary way into an invisible sphere. Through contact with it, the transformation of external reality
into internal reality is accomplished. The experience of reality thus becomes
a kind of transcendent experience. I don't deny that this attitude toward the
world might be seen as a sort of reality mysticism, that doesn't scare me. I
believe that you can describe a thing, a sight, a situation, so that the reader
understands that they have other, hidden meanings. Here poetry sometimes
unexpectedly coincides with the description cultivated by phenomenolo-
gists, of whom Enzo Paci writes that they aim at a forever new discovering
"situated between the dark infinity of perception and the complete infinity
of what is real."

That double view "at" and "through" is at the same time a kind of intuitive cognition. Even scientists admit a cognitive function to poetry, even if
it is of a different species than scientific knowledge. Sometimes it is a tempestuous process and its attainment doesn't always result from a harmonious
state. In Rimbaud, the process is accomplished by a "deregulation of the
senses," while Apollinaire on the contrary feared above all a fall into madness; in turn, Roethke expected to find truth precisely in a state of madness,

and asked: "What is madness if not the dignity with which a soul doesn't agree with the world, with a predicament?" Nerval's visions come from a man who returned again and again to psychiatric care; Michaux describes his narcotic visions without embarrassment, and the whole of his work can be regarded as a kind of magic.

All these excellent figures with big names may seem suspect from the point of view of the health of society. But their work, moving beyond the area of beauty, contributes to the broadening of our knowledge of the world and of man.

The need for understanding, for a response to what we write, pierces the darkness and looks for an intelligible expression for itself. That's why, although [Jack] Kerouac's slogan "Write so the whole world understands you" may sound frivolous, it's worth taking to heart. And it is not at all in contradiction with Braque's statement: "Only one thing is important in art: that which can't be explained." Because understanding in art is not always an intellectual act.

The readability of poems is connected to the way they are structured. As for myself, I build a poem on a sentence, almost never on a verse line that I would call "free," such as is typical, for instance, for futurism. The sentence as a logical and coherent unit, as used in common speech, is easier for the reader to receive. But poets who use common structures don't do so to make the reception of their poems more accessible. It is their natural way of for-mulating a poetic idea, in accordance with this and not another sense of rhythm, or as is sometimes said, in accordance with breathing.

It would be terrible, however, if simplicity necessarily meant the banal-ization of thought and an avoidance of what is difficult to express. There can be a truth hidden in darkness that we ourselves don't understand or don't want to look into. After all, a search for irrational knowledge is yet another way of writing.

A poet is defined in equal measure by his attitude to the word and his atti-tude to reality. Between the word and reality there is a clear interdepend-ence. A poet cultivating a concept, a poet cultivating word games, treat lan-guage in a different way; a poet for whom the word is mainly an element of aural harmony and artistic perfection treats it in another; in yet another, the poet for whom the word properly chosen is, above all, the carrier of poetic meaning, the expression of a certain reality, however transformed by the imagination. I confess that I belong to the latter group. This poetic meaning, this intellectual discipline, depends to a great degree on the suffusion of a poem with intelligence. For irony, which is so often employed by contemporary poetry, is nothing but the daughter of intelligence.

Joseph Brodsky was a poet who proclaimed a religion of the word as the active principle in a spiritual renewal. Like him, I am deeply convinced that the defiling of language, sloppiness, imprecision, and the impoverishment of language testify to a lack of culture and are ominous signs for societies.

Different views exist on the subject of the future fate of poetry. Some are inclined to believe in its future; others are extremely pessimistic. Poetry has also known different phases in different eras: an expanded readership and popularity or complete neglect. It has often happened that feeble poems which spoke to the moment were most read; it has also been the case that poetry with a long flight capacity, as in the time of Polish romanticism, managed to live up to the historical moment. It seems wise, however, not to put too much superstitious faith in poetry's popularity. Its number of readers is generally limited. But those readers tend to be faithful.

Translated by Alissa Valles

Tadeusz Różewicz

(b. 1921)

A great, prolific poet, Tadeusz Różewicz, born in a small town in Poland and always avoiding political and cultural centers (he is one of these poets who need the quiet ecstasy of provinces), has been an indispensable part of the contemporary Polish literary scene. He made his name right after his first collection, *Anxiety*, appeared in 1947, and since the late forties, he has remained gloriously active and almost always listened to. Różewicz's poems start under the sign of a philosophical premise: after the barbarous war—in which he took part as a Resistance fighter—and the Holocaust, poetry had to change radically. The metamorphosis he proposed is characterized by (a) simplicity and (b) sincerity. Beauty and formal (rhetorical) sophistication ceased to exist; they were among the casualties of World War II. Sometimes the results of this self-imposed strangulation are stunningly beautiful (because of their simplicity), sometimes a bit tedious (also because of their simplicity).

Różewicz has written several poetic plays and not many essays. A classical piece of his programmatic writing is "Preparation for a Poetry Reading," from which we learn a lot about his ideas and phobias.

PREPARATION FOR A POETRY READING

1959

My "poetry reading" will take place tomorrow at 7 P.M. It was a mistake to agree to this performance. Now I have to go there: to read and talk. What am I supposed to talk about? I'll read poems. I know I read badly. Monotonously. Sometimes someone says "Louder!" and then I'm irritated and nervous and I read softer, I don't enunciate words; I know those words so well, I know what's coming. "We know you don't like doing readings, we can have an actor do it." How do they know I don't like reading? I prefer reading myself, then I don't have to listen to my own poems. I look at the student sitting in front of me. I'll tell him the truth, that I don't know anything and that I have nothing to say. He won't believe me. If he believed me . . . he'll think I'm laughing at him. So we sit at a table and talk about the organization of this "poetry reading." "You see, this is a difficult crowd, they're in technical studies. We need something that will grab them." — "I won't bore you, if I see you're bored, I'll leave after five minutes." — "You're joking, the thing is just to choose the right texts."

I'll sing, if the need should arise. I had a performance like that once. It was in Mongolia. Poets sing there. They're shepherds. I listened to their poet. He accompanied himself on a one-stringed instrument and improvised. He sang. About wild horses, steppes, lost sheep and lambs. You know what's the worst thing about the work of contemporary poets? The material that we produce is so slack. It doesn't hold anything. It lets everything through. It has really ceased to exist. It's scattered, sometimes there are just a few scraps. For many years, from 1945 maybe, I have worked on building poems. I didn't build life, just poetry. It seemed to me that you could build poems from elements that last. Again, I'm confusing poems with poetry. Of course I'll come and I'll do the reading.

Now I have to prepare myself for the performance. I haven't yet turned on the lights. I'm standing in the window looking at the moon. The poet and the moon! It appears that this year's Nobel laureate, an Italian, wrote a long poem on the moon and a lunar spaceship launched by the Soviet Union; it appears that the Vatican wasn't "enthralled" by the poem. Poor moon and poor poet, Nobel laureate. It's not easy for a poet to "sing" in our time. You could say something jokingly on the subject of the moon and lovers. The worst thing is really that young people come to see a poet, hear him, talk to him.

Poetry has to consummate a given place and time. If it does, it is perfect. How easy it was to create poetry and describe poetry, while it existed. Poets still use this kind of phrase: "As long as poetry hasn't died in me, I can't be unhappy." As if they didn't understand that there is no "poetry." They are like children. Worse: They are merely childish. Poetry! If they're not comparing a fist to an eye, they don't feel like poets. What empty gibberish: "As long as poetry hasn't died in me, I can't be unhappy." What confidence in oneself and in "poetry." What if "poetry" died in you a long time ago and you feel happy? Is poetry in you as a kind of foreign body? Poetry? The happy knew where poetry began and ended. Critics could pinpoint the place in a poem where there was poetry. They feel unhappy if they're not describing poetry. Until you feel unhappy, "poetry" won't be born in you! That's better. But there are even poorer poets. They say: "Poetry is like a bell" or "Poetry is a moonlit night." They make comparisons. They clutch comparisons as a drowning clutches driftwood. They already know what poetry is. So they can create poetry, have poetry in them. They can feel happy. But there is no poetry. They sense this, but they don't want to touch on the truth. They're afraid. The old and the young.

I'm not going to the Third National Festival of Young Poets. I'm not going to the poetry festival because I don't know what poetry is. I wrote poems for many years. Was I creating poetry? I always felt that contradiction in me. From 1945 on. I wanted to reach poetry and run away from poetry. Destroy poetry and build poetry. It didn't have anything to do with writing so-called new poems. "New poems" is a pitiful way of referring to poems recently written. The people who publish new poems in journals every two or three months are wrong. But they're blind. "No poet would dare now to say 'poet' in answer to an inquiry as to his profession." Some poet has poetry "in him" like you have a speck of dust in your eye. You can't see very well. Sometimes you can't see a thing. An aging teacher has poetry in him and knows it. He also knows what that "poetry" looks like, what it is . . . if he has it in him and talks about it, so he knows how "it" looks. He can talk and write about it. He wrote a book about "poetry." When he started writing it, by the way, poetry still existed. So he was performing a useful task. He didn't notice the absence of poetry. He gathered momentum and goes on writing. . . . He writes about what no longer exists. He was a whole world smarter than his contemporaries. He formulated a precise and perceptive theory, it seemed — but in our time his theory grew numb. It was shouted out as if by a stallholder on the Krakó marketplace, under the statue of the Poet. Once cohesive material was united by words.

But if he said after a moment of silence: I'm a dog not a poet, I'm like a dog owner and his dog at the same time. A dog! What have we literati not come up with to keep the public interested! The poet a dog. You think I'm exaggerating? But I heard a young man call a poet a pig once. A pig polluting the air of his native country. But then, how flat that all sounds, how pretentious. Who condemned me to such a life? I didn't choose it. I was chosen. By whom?

I will try to give a clear answer to that question. I don't remember when and about what I wrote my first poem. Nor do I remember why I wrote my first poem. I'm not going to manufacture "legends." No one "chose" me or "called" me. One thing is certain: One day I wrote my first poem. Was I working on its form, its shape, from the first poem? I don't remember. When and why did I begin to work on form? I don't remember. Who compelled me to do it? I don't remember.

Is formal perfection, is every form a mystification? Poetry can only be cultivated by a constant compromise. May it perish. Clumsy, frightened, venal, a fool's cap on its head. You see the road to Calvary. Calvary in a jolly little town. Is that the road of contemporary poetry?

How silly the drama of poets. For they are aware that they are unnecessary. Only a blind person can still write poems and achieve something. Chatterbox, clown, egotist, play-actor. So that's all. After twenty years. Is that how the account stands? It's not closed yet!

But why are the leaders afraid of us? Why aren't they afraid of scientists, astronomists, dentists, singers, dancers, doctors? They are afraid of the weakest ones. They are frightened of people of the word. Of that soiled,

trampled, worn-out word. They're frightened. They know that in the beginning is the word. No, that's not true! That's a lie.

Leave me alone. I'm not a poet. I don't have anything to say on the subject. I have to deliver a collection of stories to a publisher before the end of
December. I signed a contract. That's my work, after all, that's how I make
my living. I live by the pen. That sounds good. There's something of the
bird-man in it. Yes, it's true that lines are counted in a piece of work.

Why am I fleeing from that way of working, the poem? I'm scared. I'm
scared of that work. And yet I am always ready to sacrifice every amusement
for it, every free moment, every day and every night. I'm scared. If you only
knew how scared I am of the words I've written. I don't want to look at
them. From a certain moment on they are dead, they decay. It's already a
conventional ornament. Words. New romanticism. Truth. A fashion for
artificial despair.

And that waiting for the opinion of critics, experts, friends, enemies.
What will they say? I remember that after a book came out that I had written dying of despair, after those poems were published, a certain lady wrote
that my black despair was so black that you couldn't believe in it, it was
ridiculous. . . . I was stung by that judgment. . . . Hadn't my despair been
genuine?

An end to it! An end!

This is what the realm of poetry looks like. This is what poetry in me is
like.

To spit out the names, the names, the titles, at last. Everything.

Works of art should be published anonymously.

Is that what I have to bring to these young people? My insides are pol-
luted by the excrement of literary chickens and eunuchs. That toilet soap,
the most clean-shaven literatus of an average generation! Shaven from the
inside. He dabbled in Dostoevsky. He threw up onto the pages of a literary
magazine. Emptied his stomach. His insides are made of paper. That tin
model of a mediocre literatus should one day be laid to rest in a gallery of
curiosities. He should be kicked hard enough to make him feel alive. I'm
sorry, I'm getting carried away. I have to talk to you about poetry, about
beauty. But I'm talking about something that can't be defined, I'm talking

about mediocrity. About the repulsive in life and in art. Forgive me, I'm filled with ugly sentiments, I don't belong to the blessed who are filled with "poetry"; I let myself be carried away by my feelings. I haven't said anything for so many years. . . .

I couldn't work out the program for this "poetry reading." I chattered on and on. I started by saying that I had nothing to say. It turns out things are not that bad. It's true that I'm talking crap, but I'm talking. I have to spit him out. Right here in this hall. I will vomit up the lukewarm literatus in public.

You say this is his most "personal" work? His truest? Mediocrity can't be true. He feigns remorse for sins, he feigns anger. That ponce never got himself a voice of his own. When he confessed his sins, he was as little truthful as at the moment he committed them. Even his lie wasn't a true lie. And you're going to tell me here that that ponce finally wrote a personal work, about himself. He was never either a true socialist realist, or a rationalist, or a communist, or a writer, or a human being — he was always a true superficiality, he wasn't even a true swine. He's too much of a coward.

You goggle at me and ask: "Who are you talking about? Call him by his full name. Someone from Kraków or Warsaw? Why do you hate him so much?"

I won't tell you. His full name! It's not the person that's important but the phenomenon. How could it come to pass that someone mediocre, average, smooth, lukewarm became the chronicler of our present age? Are there no real people? Let's flush this toilet. I paced the room and shouted. Flush it! Flush it! Flush it!

I had to get my material together. Somehow I had to arrange the program for this "poetry reading." But maybe I won't go to the reading. I'll call them, to tell them I'm sick. Or I'll run away, leave town. Young people will understand this kind of behavior more easily anyway. But I don't know who to call. Nor do I have a telephone. No, dear friends, I don't have a phone. And you know why I don't have a phone? I don't have a phone because I have nothing to say on the phone. What I have to say, what is most important to me, I can say tonight or in a week or a year.

In the meantime, in turns out that there has been a big hand-painted poster on the door of the students' association for the past twenty-four hours. Tomorrow at 7 P.M. my poetry reading will take place at the association. Did you ask for water? Me? I didn't ask for anything. I thought you were shouting "flush it," so I thought you wanted water with your coffee. No! I'm fine. True, I shouted. But that's a completely different thing. Sometimes I yell or talk. This was about a guy. Who are you talking about? Nobody! Everybody. Leave me alone. I'm calmed down. Despair is easier than calm, said [Stanisław] Brzozowski; that sick hysterical genius was right. Despair is easier than calm. I will be calm. I'm already calm. Instead of writing a treatise. Dispensing with surface modernity, dispensing with dead aesthetics, instead of all that I'll write a few dirty phrases on a wall. I'll leave a bad testimony to myself. I'll show myself in the worst light. Cultured people chatter on about poetry. I howl.

I read all this and started to yawn. You waste your time, spend it on garbage instead of creating "beauty" and "poetry." And bathing in that "beauty" all your life, milking that beauty, feeding people those banquets of inspiration and imagination. I'm starting again. I have to pick things to read. Say a few words about myself, about my work. About poetry.

I stare grimly at the wall.

I took out an exercise book from my drawer and began to write: "Poet," my debut, editions of my books. Making these notes bored me. I looked in the file where I kept my "new poems." Drafts. It turns out you can't destroy poetry. It is reborn in the most misshapen forms. It grins from the very pit of prose. I yawned. This outburst wore me out. The ponce wore me out. A writer, a poet, should have a little pride. Can you have "a little pride"? We have to regain pride, honor. I threw dirt and deprecation at others' heads with a generous hand. But I stoop to pick up a pea. My head is strewn with ash, my body is covered with a paper bag. I have a ban in me. A ban on writing beautiful poems. My arms are dangling. But all of this isn't suitable for a "poetry reading." After all, no one plays a happy tune at a funeral. It's all from fear. You have to have a little dignity. Can you have "a little" dignity? Some things have to be cleared up at last. There are ballrooms and public toilets. No one throws up in a ballroom. Although, sadly, various writers have been doing this for ages. And I committed this error. Perspective! For fifteen years I was an orderly, a maintenance man, a gravedigger, a charwoman, a construction worker, and suddenly I woke up with my finger in the pisspot.

Don't complain. Struggle on. There are all kinds of oddities in the world. Amusing, marvelous, ravishing, putrefying, beautiful. You have to maintain a perspective. Subtexts! Subtexts! Sometime I'll write something about myself. I'll explain.

I don't care about aesthetic values. That's what our classicist is all about, our stylist, the distinguished translator, that one there who hasn't spoken a true word for fifteen years. His whole style is made out of plaster! The sage. I have to stop writing. This chattering. I'm beginning to rave. I may be ill. I may only be in despair. Ambition. Boredom. Lies. From all this, "pure beauty" and "poetry" are supposed to crystallize, and so on and so forth. It makes you want to cry. But you can't. Ladies and gentlemen, various prominent experts and fine critics write of me often in the papers as an "excellent, remarkable, wonderful poet." But not one among those gentlemen ever stumbled on the trace of a wounded man looking for shelter. Not even a human being, no more than a creature. The man who was murdered in Auschwitz. Of course, I'm speaking "symbolically."

All those discussions about aesthetics, poetry books, lyrics, metaphors, "schools" — into the garbage, into the garbage, into the garbage bag! Here you don't have to compare and transpose. You have to touch with your hand. My rage obscures everything and harms me. I have to break off these notes. I can't use this for a poetry reading.

I want to say a few words to you about my generation. "The death-infected generation." Not just infected, consumed by death. Poisoned by death. We're alive. God, I'm so stupid. Because I "love" poetry. And people are not like that. I'm thinking of the literati — they're unhappy people. You can't go on living like that. Where does so much scorn come from, so much hatred felt for those . . . It will pass. It will wear off.

A minute ago I read those notes concerning my poetic work, my person, my views on poetry, dead aesthetics, and on the environment in which I stand with my left foot. Of course there are literati who are stuck in it with both legs, arms, up to their eyes. You could say they feed on it and live off it. However, I have to keep my left foot there in it. That's how it was to be. Let's return to the matter at hand. I looked through those notes. Are they the accurate reflection of my interior? Is that what I look like? But is it not a falsification? Is this what the interior of a contemporary poet in this country is like? Is this what my insides are like. Do I have the right to show myself in this light? It's a garbage can. What will happen when I tip this garbage out? It will be empty. What might be put in the place of the dump? What will grow in that interior? In me. Perhaps the tree of poetry?

I will read you the poem "Jacob's Fight with the Angel."

The shadow of wings grew
the angel roared
and his moist
nostrils touched
my eyes and mouth
We fought on earth
tamped with newspapers
on a garbage dump where
spit blood and bile
lay mixed up together
with the dung of words
The shadow of wings grew
but they were soft wings
covered with fur
pink as mussels
warm and pointed
on either side of his head
amid clouds
our fury covered
a playing field
he overcame me finally
pinioned twisted dazzled
optimistically
he was entering the heaven of poetry
I caught his leg
he fell on my garbage dump
by the wall
in this little spot
where in the midst of filth
a hampered slave

of reality
messes around
our bodies were covered
with sweat
the breathing was thick and broken

This piece isn't finished. It hasn't been included in any collection yet. It's living among my papers and growing, maturing. Best at night. Everything you correct, alter, stylize is already literature. Writers have been employing crazy speech for many years, that was supposed to be poetry. By now some of them have learned to say what they mean. But they still defile themselves with those "beauties" who make "poetry."

Sometimes I think my hatred of poetry, my scorn, has its origin in romantic love. I broke off my notes. I sat at my desk. There was a calendar on the wall. Yes, 1959. I stuck newspaper photos on the wall between two windows. Poets feel better than others the powerlessness and feebleness of a man in the modern world. They play the fool out of despair.

Before I get up in front of you, I have to sort out a few things. I can't speak about poetry, which is currently characterized by the fact of its dissolution, disappearance. The fate of poetry readers dwelling in our cities has to be considered. When I talk about poetry, I'm thinking of the poetry created for the present moment. What is going on with readers? City dwellers, the relations between them, the lives of people in cities, this is the fabric on which we stitch the green rose of contemporary poetry. The fabric is so fragile that it falls apart in our hands. The threads don't touch, don't intertwine, don't mesh, don't cross.

We create the "rose" not on a strong canvas but in a void. Sociologists have taken note of this phenomenon. Poets haven't. They haven't noticed and they go on playing. Poetry can't be dropped into a vacuum, it has to catch, it has at least to rebound from the bottom to make its way back to the surface. In the meantime, people are moving apart, are so remote from each other that between one hand and another, one heart and another, an infinite void gape. Until the people who live in today's big cities begin to weave a new, strong fabric of life, poetry and art will fall into a void. Infantile poets amuse themselves. In the meantime —

Great cities
are emptying out
cities are growing
these seas of heads
oceans millions millions of bodies
shoals of people
so close one right beside
another so near
you see wrinkles skin
teeth and hair
we feel each other's bodies
leave our prints on each other
shreds of words
at times you can assemble
fragments of another life
but
in this reservoir
we begin to feel more and more alone
the distance between people is growing
under neon lights
in the glare in the crowd
we live as if on an island
inhabited by a very few human
beings
we remain with a handful of intimates
but even they leave us
each goes his own way
Some take with them
their jobs women children
motorcycles fridges TVs
others their diseases
their sins
gluttony sloth
organic debris
nails instead of claws

dentures instead of jaws
some leavings residues
of faith
something like god
something like love
others
don't have anything
yet others talk about art
chatter about poetry painting
yet others
have bread meat a knife a fork
they leave us
we live on islands
and look for traces of humankind
where has it gone
when was it here
at times it seems to us
we are being called summoned
a human being is calling to us
we listen
run to the window
run out onto the stairs streets squares
rub up against each other
look around feverishly
come home
exhausted
some people live
using only a few words
an ever decreasing number of words
until in the end they fall silent
go off to their caves
carrying off their prey
the weaker stay
at the bar at tables beer-stands
the even weaker

lean on shadows ideas words
but the shadows are see-through
you see death through them
so we go off
and no one admits he's dying
better not to cause confusion
and maybe they don't notice
so everyone lives forever
only the whites gleam
from between slits in faces
remember we were open
in the face of the worst oppression
the pain and joy of others
easily penetrated our interior
your life ran toward me
from all sides entered me
now we are covered up
with armor impenetrable shields
from between the slits fissures
in faces the whites gleam

Translated by Alissa Valles

Miron Białoszewski

(1922–1983)

Miron Białoszewski spent his entire life in Warsaw. The city was his inspiration, his Dublin and his Florence. His most famous prose work in fact is *A Memoir of the Warsaw Uprising*, a book written by a noncombatant recording the atrocities of city fighting in 1944 as seen—and heard—by a young artist with a passionate interest in poetry and music but none in the art of war. The book, a fruit of many years of meditation and work, appeared in 1972.

Białoszewski made his debut in poetry relatively late in his life, in 1956. The communist government was imposing on artists its doctrine of socialist realism, which was deadly for his poetic talent, which represented a highly original blend of "urban mysticism" and linguistic quest for a freer idiom. Białoszewski was a mystic relishing the serendipity and approximations of the spoken language, the tension between the roughness of the language and a quest for the modern sublime.

He became well known as the creator of an experimental poetic theater whose location was a friend's tiny apartment and whose actors belonged to a wide circle of friends and admirers. As the leader of such a circle, this hermit-like poet exerted quite an influence on the Polish intelligentsia. In the second half of his creative life, Białoszewski turned more to prose writing. Through quasi-diaries in which he used his very individual idiom, he tried to capture the fabric of human life and speech.

BAŚKA

It's warmish. Raining. From a window high up, people. I look at them, watch them from an experiential-descriptive need. For pleasure, as in love. And people are walking along, getting rained on, thinking and wanting something or other, feeling pain.

In art sometimes I feel pain, too. But my pain is shameful compared with what happens in life. It can't be any other way, if art is to have weight. It has to seize on the worst. With that shiver of pleasure. It's cruel, shameless. A kind of divinity that has the option to prolong its existence at the cost of everyone who comes its way. Omnivorous.

Baśka [. . .]owa was once shocked by someone's producing a few poems right after a sudden death.

When Baśka was in the Pionki hospital toward the end of May 1962, I stayed at her parents' house outside of Pionki. During the day I would walk over to the hospital. Baśka's mother didn't really want to let me. She wanted to spare her. Her mother gave me various delicacies to take to the hospital for Baśka, so that she would at least eat something. She didn't think the end was so near, though she and Baśka's father had greeted me on arrival with the words, "Oh, Baśka, bad, be lucky if she lives through May."

The last day I came in quietly, Baśka was lying motionless in a separate room.

She looked terrible, as if she were dying.

She opened her eyes.

I glanced at the chair. On it were two stanzas of a translation of Tsvetaeva's "Separation" I had done with Olgierd.

"I was too weak to copy out more. Adam was right, I'll be dying and still talking about Sandauer."

She had revived so much that I told her, "When I came in you were lying there as if you were dead, but now you're all different."

"I rest that way by turns; I watch the window; sometimes it reflects the view near the hospital, a bit of the woods . . ."

Baśka's brother-in-law arrived. Her sister Lusia dropped by.

When we were leaving, arranging Sunday visits the next day, Basia yelled, "Only please, not all at the same time!"

She said to me at a certain point, "If I agree to a traditional funeral, it's so there won't be confusion, not to hurt anyone."

The previous year she had taken me in a cab to the church and to the graveyard in the country, to show me where she would be buried. In the fall she gave me some of her papers or additional documentation to find out if she could be buried in Warsaw in the tomb of her grandmother in the Evangelical cemetery. It turned out that it would be a big hassle, a lot of paperwork.

"Too bad," said Baśka, "so let it be in the country."

It was that phrase of hers I remembered at the time we were discussing where she would be buried, if not in Pionki. Obviously she's buried in the country.

The long day was darkening. Basia wanted to eat something. "Maybe she can make me an egg?"

I brought an egg to the nurse. There didn't seem to be a ward attendant. She cooked it, brought it to us. Baśka tried it. "What did she do with it? Go, bring it back to her."

I brought it back. The nurse on duty took it all in without any resentment. "I'll do another one."

Baśka said, "I'm tired. I'll give myself a eukodal."

"Is that good?"

"I have to."

She gave herself an injection. Almost in the dark. She was talking while she did it. That maybe part of it had spilled. After a moment of revival, "You know, I'm feeling bad now, weak . . ."

"I'll get the nurse."

"No, no, wait. . . . My heart is going crazy."

"I'll call Lusia."

"No, no." Lusia, Basia's sister, is a lung doctor.

It was now completely dark. Baśka said, "Give me your hand, look." She put my hand to her heart.

It was pounding like crazy.

She whispered something.

"What?" I bent over her.

"I'm terribly . . ." I didn't catch the rest.

"I'll let Lusia know." I flew out to the nurse on duty.

Lusia and her husband, a general physician, got there in a few minutes. By car. They gave her injections. It helped a little.

"That's until tomorrow."

"Bye."

Lusia drove me to their parents' house in the country. She smoked one cigarette after another. Saying nothing. In the end I muttered something. Lusia said, "Man, she's dying."

She didn't want to see her parents.

"Just don't say anything to mother."

"No."

Their mother later held it against me a bit.

"God, I would have gone to see her to talk to her a bit."

I myself hadn't taken what Lusia said about dying so literally.

After a grim conversation we all went to bed. I was spending the night in a connecting room between the living room and the porch. On one side there was an empty room, where Baśka had always been up to this point. On the other side an empty room where she had lain most recently, before being carried to the ambulance on a stretcher.

For a moment I looked into that last room of Baśka's. I saw a ghost of a deadly figure in a quilt. Quickly warded off. The wind was blowing. Strong and warm. The doors of the room with the bed kept opening by themselves. In the end I blocked them with a chair. I lay on bedding on the floor and wrote about what was going on in a letter to Adam. The doors banged and banged.

At some point I got up to go to the bathroom. The day was peering in. Silence. Water was dripping from the tap. I stopped, motionless, across from the bathroom and the window. I remembered once coming back from the bathroom and saying to Baśka, "The tap's dripping, write a poem about it."

She wrote about the dripping and about herself.

At that moment the dripping increased alarmingly. In complete silence. I heard a car. Coming closer. It stopped. *Lusia's come by, that's bad*, I thought.

I heard a car door slam.

I stood at the little window. I waited for Lusia to come in the gate. I couldn't hear any steps. Why was it taking so long? Nobody came in. Silence. No sound of an engine. Nothing.

I kept waiting at the bathroom window, astonished.

Had I imagined it?

I went back to the camp bed. Lay down. Wrote. Fell into a light doze. Suddenly I was woken by a quick knocking at the door, someone running around, crying.

"Quiet!" Baśka's father shouted.

Baśka's mother, crying and wailing, "My God, Basia!" She opened the door to Lusia.

Lusia fell into the room, stood in the doorway.

"It's over, Miron."

She had driven over just now. Basia had died at four, after four. She and Mira, her other sister, had rushed to the hospital at once; they had been sleeping by the telephone in their coats. Baśka had been sitting up, her head swayed. Lusia began to cry. Baśka said to her, "Silly."

She pointed to the little radio a girl in the hospital had lent her. "Remember, the radio . . ." Then she lost consciousness.

Lusia ran to get the priest. "Don't tell mother he didn't get there on time." Mira held Baśka's hand.

"At one point I didn't know if I still felt her pulse, or just my own. Just think, me, and I'm afraid of the dead."

Translated by Alissa Valles

Wisława Szymborska

(b. 1923)

Born between Tadeusz Różewicz and Zbigniew Herbert, Wisława Szymborska, not unlike her peers, was shaped by the years of war and occupation and by her perception of the grandiloquent war-generation poets like Krzysztof Kamil Baczyński and Tadeusz Gajcy (who in turn were born just a few years before her). Szymborska's main aesthetic enemy has always been what she regards as stiltedness, the "too much" of traditional poetry. But her mature poetry draws also on her experience with socialist realism, which she endorsed in her youth—out of conviction, as she later commented. Her wonderful, warm skepticism—an entire, fully developed, humanistic *weltanschauung*— was probably born out of this occurrence.

Cherishing her independence, relying on her wit and wisdom, Szymborska journeyed safely through the shallow waters of Communist Poland. She has lived her literary life in Kraków; a private person thriving on friendship and good conversation, she nonetheless never stopped being elegantly involved in the vicissitudes of modern political history. One may consider her poems a fine dialogue with the ogre of politics.

In the late seventies Szymborska became involved in the dissident democratic movement, always keeping a serene distance to its ardent leaders. The Nobel Prize of 1996 caught her by surprise. Now she had to unfurl once again her techniques of being herself, of keeping her privacy. Once again, Szymborska has succeeded in that.

THE JOY OF WRITING

1967

Why does this written doe bound through these written woods?
For a drink of written water from a spring
whose surface will xerox her soft muzzle?
Why does she lift her head; does she hear something?
Perched on four slim legs borrowed from the truth,
she pricks up her ears beneath my fingertips.
Silence — this word also rustles across the page
and parts the boughs
that have sprouted from the word "woods."

Lying in wait, set to pounce on the blank page,
are letters up to no good,
clutches of clauses so subordinate
they'll never let her get away.

Each drop of ink contains a fair supply
of hunters, equipped with squinting eyes behind their sights,
prepared to swarm the sloping pen at any moment,
surround the doe, and slowly aim their guns.

They forget that what's here isn't life.
Other laws, black on white, obtain.
The twinkling of an eye will take as long as I say,
and will, if I wish, divide into tiny eternities,
full of bullets stopped in mid-flight.
Not a thing will ever happen unless I say so.
Without my blessing, not a leaf will fall,
not a blade of grass will bend beneath that little hoof's full stop.

Is there then a world
where I rule absolutely on fate?
A time I bind with chains of signs?
An existence become endless at my bidding?

The joy of writing.
The power of preserving.
Revenge of a mortal hand.

Translated by Stanisław Barańczak and Claire Cavanagh

THE POET AND THE WORLD

1996

They say the first sentence in any speech is always the hardest. Well, that
one's behind me, anyway. But I have a feeling that the sentences to come —
the third, the sixth, the tenth, and so on, up to the final line — will be just as
hard, since I'm supposed to talk about poetry. I've said very little on the subject, next to nothing, in fact. And whenever I have said anything, I've always
had the sneaking suspicion that I'm not very good at it. This is why my lecture will be rather short. All imperfection is easier to tolerate if served up in
small doses.

Contemporary poets are skeptical and suspicious even, or perhaps especially, about themselves. They publicly confess to being poets only reluctantly, as if they were a little ashamed of it. But in our clamorous times it's
much easier to acknowledge your faults, at least if they're attractively pack-
aged, than to recognize your own merits, since these are hidden deeper and
you never quite believe in them yourself. . . . When filling in questionnaires
or chatting with strangers, that is, when they can't avoid revealing their profession, poets prefer to use the general term "writer" or replace "poet" with
the name of whatever job they do in addition to writing. Bureaucrats and bus
passengers respond with a touch of incredulity and alarm when they find out
that they're dealing with a poet. I suppose philosophers may meet with a
similar reaction. Still, they're in a better position, since as often as not they
can embellish their calling with some kind of scholarly title. Professor of
philosophy — now that sounds much more respectable.

But there are no professors of poetry. This would mean, after all, that
poetry is an occupation requiring specialized study, regular examinations,
theoretical articles with bibliographies and footnotes attached, and finally,
ceremoniously conferred diplomas. And this would mean, in turn, that it's
not enough to cover pages with even the most exquisite poems in order to

become a poet. The crucial element is some slip of paper bearing an official stamp. Let us recall that the pride of Russian poetry, the future Nobel Laureate Joseph Brodsky was once sentenced to internal exile precisely on such grounds. They called him "a parasite," because he lacked official certification granting him the right to be a poet . . .

Several years ago, I had the honor and pleasure of meeting Brodsky in person. And I noticed that, of all the poets I've known, he was the only one who enjoyed calling himself a poet. He pronounced the word without inhibitions.

Just the opposite — he spoke it with defiant freedom. It seems to me that this must have been because he recalled the brutal humiliations he had experienced in his youth.

In more fortunate countries, where human dignity isn't assaulted so readily, poets yearn, of course, to be published, read, and understood, but they do little, if anything, to set themselves above the common herd and the daily grind. And yet it wasn't so long ago, in this century's first decades, that poets strove to shock us with their extravagant dress and eccentric behavior. But all this was merely for the sake of public display. The moment always came when poets had to close the doors behind them, strip off their mantles, fripperies, and other poetic paraphernalia, and confront — silently, patiently awaiting their own selves — the still white sheet of paper. For this is finally what really counts.

It's not accidental that film biographies of great scientists and artists are produced in droves. The more ambitious directors seek to reproduce convincingly the creative process that led to important scientific discoveries or the emergence of a masterpiece. And one can depict certain kinds of scientific labor with some success. Laboratories, sundry instruments, elaborate machinery brought to life: such scenes may hold the audience's interest for a while. And those moments of uncertainty — will the experiment, conducted for the thousandth time with some tiny modification, finally yield the desired result? — can be quite dramatic. Films about painters can be spectacular, as they go about recreating every stage of a famous painting's evolution, from the first penciled line to the final brushstroke. Music swells in films about composers: the first bars of the melody that rings in the musician's ears finally emerge as a mature work in symphonic form. Of course this is all quite naive and doesn't explain the strange mental state popularly known as inspiration, but at least there's something to look at and listen to.

But poets are the worst. Their work is hopelessly unphotogenic.

Someone sits at a table or lies on a sofa while staring motionless at a wall or ceiling. Once in a while this person writes down seven lines only to cross out one of them fifteen minutes later, and then another hour passes, during which nothing happens. . . . Who could stand to watch this kind of thing?

I've mentioned inspiration. Contemporary poets answer evasively when asked what it is, and if it actually exists. It's not that they've never known the blessings of this inner impulse. It's just not easy to explain something to someone else that you don't understand yourself.

When I'm asked about this on occasion, I hedge the question too. But my answer is this: inspiration is not the exclusive privilege of poets or artists generally. There is, has been, and will always be a certain group of people whom inspiration visits. It's made up of all those who've consciously chosen their calling and do their job with love and imagination. It may include doctors, teachers, gardeners — and I could list a hundred more professions. Their work becomes one continuous adventure as long as they manage to keep discovering new challenges in it. Difficulties and setbacks never quell their curiosity. A swarm of new questions emerges from every problem they solve. Whatever inspiration is, it's born from a continuous "I don't know."

There aren't many such people. Most of the earth's inhabitants work to get by. They work because they have to. They didn't pick this or that kind of job out of passion; the circumstances of their lives did the choosing for them. Loveless work, boring work, work valued only because others haven't got even that much, however loveless and boring — this is one of the harshest human miseries. And there's no sign that coming centuries will produce any changes for the better as far as this goes.

And so, though I may deny poets their monopoly on inspiration, I still place them in a select group of Fortune's darlings.

At this point, though, certain doubts may arise in my audience. All sorts of torturers, dictators, fanatics, and demagogues struggling for power by way of a few loudly shouted slogans also enjoy their jobs, and they too perform their duties with inventive fervor. Well, yes, but they "know." They know, and whatever they know is enough for them once and for all. They don't want to find out about anything else, since that might diminish their arguments' force. And any knowledge that doesn't lead to new questions quickly dies out: it fails to maintain the temperature required for sustaining life. In the most extreme cases, cases well known from ancient and modern history, it even poses a lethal threat to society.

This is why I value that little phrase "I don't know" so highly. It's small, but it flies on mighty wings. It expands our lives to include the spaces within us as well as those outer expanses in which our tiny Earth hangs suspended. If Isaac Newton had never said to himself "I don't know," the apples in his little orchard might have dropped to the ground like hailstones and at best he would have stooped to pick them up and gobble them with gusto. Had my compatriot Marie Sklodowska-Curie never said to herself "I don't know," she probably would have wound up teaching chemistry at some private high school for young ladies from good families, and would have ended her days performing this otherwise perfectly respectable job. But she kept on saying "I don't know," and these words led her, not just once but twice, to Stockholm, where restless, questing spirits are occasionally rewarded with the Nobel Prize.

Poets, if they're genuine, must also keep repeating "I don't know." Each poem marks an effort to answer this statement, but as soon as the final period hits the page, the poet begins to hesitate, starts to realize that this particular answer was pure makeshift that's absolutely inadequate to boot. So the poets keep on trying, and sooner or later the consecutive results of their self-dissatisfaction are clipped together with a giant paperclip by literary historians and called their "oeuvre" . . .

I sometimes dream of situations that can't possibly come true. I audaciously imagine, for example, that I get a chance to chat with the Ecclesiastes, the author of that moving lament on the vanity of all human endeavors. I would bow very deeply before him, because he is, after all, one of the greatest poets, for me at least. That done, I would grab his hand. "'There's nothing new under the sun': that's what you wrote, Ecclesiastes. But you yourself were born new under the sun. And the poem you created is also new under the sun, since no one wrote it down before you. And all your readers are also new under the sun, since those who lived before you couldn't read your poem. And that cypress that you're sitting under hasn't been growing since the dawn of time. It came into being by way of another cypress similar to yours, but not exactly the same. And Ecclesiastes, I'd also like to ask you what new thing under the sun you're planning to work on now? A further supplement to the thoughts you've already expressed? Or maybe you're tempted to contradict some of them now? In your earlier work you mentioned joy — so what if it's fleeting? So maybe your new-under-the-sun poem will be about joy? Have you taken notes yet, do you have drafts? I doubt you'll say, 'I've written everything down, I've got nothing left to add.' There's no poet in the world who can say this, least of all a great poet like yourself."

The world — whatever we might think when terrified by its vastness and our own impotence, or embittered by its indifference to individual suffering, of people, animals, and perhaps even plants, for why are we so sure that plants feel no pain; whatever we might think of its expanses pierced by the rays of stars surrounded by planets we've just begun to discover, planets already dead? still dead? we just don't know; whatever we might think of this measureless theater to which we've got reserved tickets, but tickets whose lifespan is laughably short, bounded as it is by two arbitrary dates; whatever else we might think of this world — it is astonishing.

But "astonishing" is an epithet concealing a logical trap. We're astonished, after all, by things that deviate from some well-known and universally acknowledged norm, from an obviousness we've grown accustomed to. Now the point is, there is no such obvious world. Our astonishment exists per se and isn't based on comparison with something else.

Granted, in daily speech, where we don't stop to consider every word, we all use phrases like "the ordinary world," "ordinary life," "the ordinary course of events." . . . But in the language of poetry, where every word is weighed, nothing is usual or normal. Not a single stone and not a single cloud above it. Not a single day and not a single night after it. And above all, not a single existence, not anyone's existence in this world.

It looks like poets will always have their work cut out for them.

Translated by Stanisław Barańczak and Claire Cavanagh

Zbigniew Herbert

(1924–1998)

Born in Lvov, a city that after 1945 was incorporated into the Soviet Union, Zbigniew Herbert led a difficult life of an eternal and itinerant student until 1956, when his first collection of poems finally appeared. As a young man, he hesitated between poetry, art history, and philosophy. His life remained peripatetic even after 1956, an important year for Poland as it marked the end to the excesses of Stalinist cultural policy. Herbert lived then in Warsaw, Paris, Berlin, Italy, and the United States (he taught for a year at the University of California, Los Angeles). He was driven to travel by his immense appetite for the ancient and modern beauty that is scattered throughout the museums, architecture, and landscapes of western and southern Europe, food for his imagination.

Herbert invented a new tone in poetry, a music filled with tragedy, irony, and goodness. His "Mr. Cogito," the speaker in many of his poems, is a brilliant and sometimes melancholy commentator on twentieth-century madness. Herbert's poems turned out to be readily translatable, so he found a home for his brilliance in other languages as well (especially in English, German, and Swedish). Still, he never enjoyed a Goethean peace of mind; tormented by sickness and bad luck, he became a beloved and nationally worshipped poet only posthumously.

Henryk Elzenberg, one of young Herbert's masters, is the addressee in the letters that follow. Elzenberg was an independent philosopher and a sage.

LETTERS TO HENRYK ELZENBERG

OCTOBER 22, 1951

Dear Professor,

On my way to Warsaw I stopped for a few hours in Toruń in the hope that I would be able to see you and thank you for your Intellectual Patronage up to this point. I also came to ask you not to strike me from the student register, as it is very important to me to stay in touch with you. In Warsaw I will be at the mercy of Marxified philosophy and trashy pseudo-cosmopolitanism in which an innocent provincial can easily lose his way.

I would like very much to take my exam with you and work under your supervision.

I would be very grateful if you could let me know through Dr. Voisé if and when you will be in Warsaw.

If it won't be before the holidays, I will permit myself to bother you in Toruń.

Respectfully
Zbigniew Herbert

PS My apologies for the form (and content) of this letter, written on the stairs.
PS Professor Czeżowski, whom I saw, asked me whether writing poetry doesn't get in the way of philosophy. I told him I was ashamed and that I would do my best to kick the habit.

NOVEMBER 2, 1951

Dear Professor,

Thank you very much for a letter particularly important to me in a time of trial and doubt. What you say about philosophy is very consoling; it comes close to my own feelings and gives me hope.

I put to myself — in answer to your letter — the question what I really look for in philosophy. The question is rather Faustian and perhaps it would be more appropriate to ask what philosophy demands of me, what responsibilities the discipline lays on me.

The answer to the first, more my own version, turns out to be extremely compromising for me. I look for emotion. Powerful intellectual emotion, painful tensions between reality and abstraction, yet another rending, yet another, deeper than personal, cause for sorrow. And in that subjective cloud, respectable truth and sublime measure are lost, so I'll never be a decent university philosopher. I prefer living through philosophy to brooding on it like a hen.* I would rather it be a fruitless struggle, a personal cause, something going against the order of life, than a profession.

I now have all sorts of practical worries and because I had to apply for a place to live in Warsaw, I had to give my studies as the official reason for my residence, which entailed a formal transfer to the university here. It was an act of despair. Will I be able to stay in contact with you despite all this?

[. . .]

Respectfully,
Zbigniew Herbert

BRWINÓW, DECEMBER 16, 1951

Dear Professor,

Because my affairs are becoming more settled one way or another (if you keep one eye shut), I'm thinking of my studies. I would like very much to take Part II of History of Philosophy and with you; if that turns out to be impossible, I may not take it at all because Prof. T. J. Kroński arouses in me a complete aversion to philosophy. I would be ready for the exam in mid-February 1952, and it's now a matter of how to approach the secretary Ms. Jeśmanowiczowa (who frightens me).

I've even chosen a philosopher. It will probably be Blaise Pascal. But is he a philosopher? Ha!

I've been reading Lucretius recently. I'm studying a little Latin and, if the truth be told, for Lucretius alone.* It started with my picking up *De*

---

*Everything should be an offering to someone. One can't study anything in general. One must always dedicate. If I studied Greek, it would be for Homer and Plato. [Footnote is Berbert's own tongue-in-cheek commentary.]

rerum . . . and finding with horror that I couldn't understand it. But the poem I liked a lot — a spear's flight. I'm also attending Prof. Krokiewicz's lectures on Lucretius. However, he truly is a very unhappy poet. Tied to the philological chariot, I batter my weary head, stripped of poetry — naked and disgraced. I'm becoming very fond of him. Your essay and that one philosophy seminar of mine brought me very close to him.

I also read Marcus Aurelius in translation and your book on his ethics. I think of him not without sadness and disappointment, and before that sentiment fell into logical theses, I made a note of the impression:

To Marcus Aurelius

Good night Marcus put out the light
and shut the book For overhead
is raised a gold alarm of stars heaven is talking some foreign
    tongue
this is the barbarian cry of fear
your Latin cannot understand*

Terror continuous dark terror
against the fragile human land

begins to beat It's winning Hear
its roar The unrelenting stream
of elements will drown your prose
until the world's four walls go down
As for us? — to tremble in the air
blow in the ashes stir the ether
gnaw our fingers seek vain words
drag off the fallen shades behind us

Well Marcus better hang up your peace
give me your hand across the dark
Let it tremble when the blind world beats
on senses five like a failing lyre

Traitors — universe and astronomy
reckoning of stars wisdom of grass
and your greatness too immense
and Marcus my defenseless tears

Translated by Czesław Miłosz and Peter Dale Scott

That's enough lyrical gabbling. In your last letter you wrote about four intelligent people (Polish literature students?) who don't understand what I write: That number should be increased manifold. And I'm afraid that the small handful of those who are my only hope are carrying out some sort of program of benevolence toward me, by encouraging me and dissipating my solitude. Those long-suffering souls get the "fruits of my spirit" by mail. Gutenberg was not invented for me.

In closing, I permit myself to wish you healthy and peaceful holidays with profound respect,

Zbigniew Herbert,
your pupil

MAY 30, 1952

Dear Professor,

I apologize sincerely for not having given what are called signs of life. But there hasn't been much to be proud of. Much more to hide and to make me blush. One thing in particular: a philosophical crisis. I realized I made a mistake in choosing my direction of studies. My last hope of becoming an intellectual is shattered, and there's nothing to sustain the illusion. I wanted to write a long letter (it was to be bitter and tragic), with the request to strike me from your list of current students and with a request to keep me on the list of unofficial students in rebellion against philosophy.

My lamentable spiritual state is probably a result of my conditions of life and studies here. Professor Kotarbiński's seminar was a torment of a kind I hadn't known in all the time I spent studying accountancy, civil law, and canon law. There was also Professor Kroński, who even when he uttered idiocies didn't enliven the doctrine. I went to Professor Ossowski's lectures on culture, but time and again that notion, so dear to me, got buried under an avalanche of sociology. I fled to Classics, where they read Homer and Horace. I listened to Book 6 of the *Iliad* and tried to catch the meaning of that wonderful poetry, covered with assiduous philological commentary.

Totting up the balance of this year, I see a great disproportion between intentions and their realization. But where do I get my capacity for self-justification? It whispers to me that in all this tug-of-war and messing about, there is a search for authentic philosophy, for the kind that comes from the deepest experience. And it's not so important whether you find truth (in this I'm a skeptic), but what philosophy does to a person.

I was urged to study Thomism. I started going to readings of the *Summa*. And, indeed, many things began to fall into place and become clear. I felt happy and free. And this was the first signal that I should run away, that something in my human substance was being distorted. I felt the pleasure of judgment and classification. But a human being is better defined by words beginning with "un," after all: unrest, uncertainty, unconformity. And does one really have the right to abandon that state?

For in essence the whole question consists in a choice, a simple act of will. On one's knees. After that it takes care of itself. A person assimilates a foreign body, identifies with it. And, in fact, it's most often a matter of chance — of spending a certain number of hours with books of a certain kind. One becomes a doctor or an electrician in a similar way.

I write all this confusedly and badly. I have a fever and feel under the weather. But this whole confession, if you will receive it, is an unworthy attempt to find succor. Apart from that, having chosen you as my Master (an absolute and irrevocable act), I feel obliged to give an account of myself. And, finally, a concrete question: Despite all this, I would like to take the exam in modern philosophy in the first half of July. It will be my only chance to save this year, which I've wasted in so many ways.

I've been immersed in *Hamlet* for the past month. I'm writing something on it. It will be an attempt to show Hamlet "de-Hamletized," not as Goethe saw him.

I'm reading a little poetry. French, above all. I hit upon this fragment of
the poem "A Madame Lullier":

> *Dans ces moments chacun oublie*
> *Tout ce qu'il a fait en santé:*
> *Quel mortel s'est jamais flatté*
> *D'un rendez-vous à l'agonie?*
>
> *Délie elle-même à son tour*
> *S'en va dans la nuit éternelle,*
> *En oubliant, qu'elle fut belle*
> *Et qu'elle a vécu pour l'amour.*
>
> *Nous naissons, nous vivons, bergère,*
> *Nous mourons sans savoir comment;*
> *Chacun est parti du néant:*
> *Où va-t-il? . . . Dieu le sait, ma chère.*

Who would have thought that was written by Voltaire, the same man who is
so loudly condemned by priests. My God, we don't even know how religious
we are.

[. . .]

Zbigniew Herbert,
your refractory pupil

SOPOT, JULY 9, 1952

Dear Professor,

My warmest thanks for thinking of me and for your letters. The first was
precious because it opened up Taine for me; up to now I had thought him a
good positivist. I read his *Philosophy of Art* a long time ago but without great
excitement. I don't like philosophy that explains, I love the kind that makes
one's head spin. I put in this confession so that you won't be deluded:
Nothing will come of me.

I'm all the more ashamed of my epistolary tardiness — for which I apologize sincerely — and not being ready with my modern philosophy. The doctor said I had to interrupt my studies and go somewhere to rest — I've been
very worn out lately, a silly typhus fever I acquired during the war caught up

with me — so I packed up and fled home, yet again, weaker, more deprived of illusions about myself, but in spite of all that, with my stubborn "No" and my irrational rebellion.

I'm harrowed by literary obsessions. Once I started writing a novel; I've been carrying two stories around for a year and even . . . but I won't tell you, it's a terrible embarrassment to attempt anything in the theater. The characters come to me in the night with faces like hanged men, with upturned eyes and fettered hands, stifled by silence. I have to let their blood from time to time, otherwise they will die without a trace or a memory, and this way I can use their blood to write of them that they existed.

I'm reading *Hamlet* — I think I already wrote you about that; I would love to write some sort of piece on him: that he didn't Hamletize, that he was a philosopher-existentialist, that to be kind he had to be cruel, that he suffered the torment of full consciousness, a torment close to madness.

I'm writing all this so you'll see that though I neglect my philosophy, I am nonetheless trying to think for myself, messily, obsessively.

I'll be ready with the material in August at the latest (subtracting four weeks for the recommended rest period), and then I would come wherever you summon me.

I'm waiting for you now, because Waldemar wrote that you were on the way to the Northern coast by way of Miedzyzdroje and Ustronie Morskie. I would be very happy to help in any way: I could carry your suitcase, buy tickets, take care of small formalities, stand in attendance, be a companion.

As I haven't pestered you with poems for three months, I send one such as nobody wants to publish. It's called "My Father":

> My father adored Anatole France
> and smoked choice Macedonian
> in the bluish clouds of an aroma
> he savored a laugh on narrow lips
> and back in those distant times
> when he sat leaning over a book
> I said: my father is like Sindbad
> at times it's hard for him with us
>
> upon which he set off On a divan
> on the four winds Anxious we ran

after him in atlases but we lost him
In the end he returned and took off
his smell put on his slippers again
the jangling of keys in his pockets
and the days like drops heavy drops
and time passes but doesn't change

one Christmas curtains were opened
he stepped through the windowpane
and didn't return I don't know if he
closed his eyes for grief or didn't turn
to look back at us Once in a foreign
magazine I saw a photograph of him
he is governor of an island on which
there are palm trees and liberalism

Translated by Czesław Miłosz and Peter Dale Scott

Thank you very much for everything for which thanks are due; I send warm regards. I await your absolution and a date for a meeting.

Zbigniew Herbert — your pupil

WARSAW, JUNE 4, 1954

Dear Professor,

I'll begin with some information on my external life, in order to explain my tardiness in correspondence. From mid-January I've occupied the position of senior assistant in the Economics Workshop of the Central Bureau for Research and Projects in the Peat Industry. The institution has a grand name and the position is supposed to be important, but it's essentially eight hours of arithmetic and boredom. A month ago a peat course started and the work in fact runs from 7 A.M. to 5 P.M. Ten hours. After that, you only want to sleep and sometimes worse.

In the past month the balance of what I've written and thought comes to almost nothing. I don't even care that much anymore about my so-called inner development. It's not just about me, but about the cardinal principle:

that existence doesn't determine consciousness, or at least not always, not for everyone. But there you go, evidently it's "too much wind for my little sail."

In the realm of inner life — to continue my practice of confiding in my Master — I can convey that I am still in a deepening crisis regarding the orthodox and official layer of Catholicism. What [T. S.] Eliot in one of his poems conceived in the figure of a hippopotamus in a swamp of whom one must remember, or rather believe, that he will one day be playing a harp in Heaven — this is what gives me the most trouble. I began to put together my own pocket religion, God help us, some sort of eighteenth-century deism. I was appalled by the results, which initially I intended to bring together in systematic form. What to do with this religious luggage? It's hard to go it alone, but no means of locomotion is entirely satisfactory. And besides, all the different means of locomotion have different prescriptions. Some cast me off because my luggage isn't hefty enough to legitimize my journey; for others my luggage is too heavy, and in the end there will be yet others who will say that I'm smuggling things not entirely religious in my bags, like psychology, the cult of humanity or culture. At the same time, I don't feel comfortable with the idea of a private religion (a conversation in sign language with the Absolute), and I need the sacramental gesture, the smoke and fumes of animal sacrifice. I don't know where all of this will lead me, but in any case I decided not to hack anything off for the sake of a system's slick symmetry. Coherence isn't necessarily an intellectual principle, it often signifies fear, a closure to another image of the world. In the end one can live with two images; one practical, for everyday use, another dazzling, for when hypotheses are proven true, when one goes from darkness into the light, or from the half-dark into a great darkness.

I'm trying to gather material and reflect on two great poetic myths: the Arcadian and the other, its opposite, I don't know what to call it, Heraclitean, Grailian, or Faustian. The first is the Epicurean garden; the second, the sea and skepticism. I think these divisions have already been made, but I'll try to put it on paper anyway, so I can formulate some things important to me along the way.

I thank you again for Omar Khayyam and apologize for the delay in sending the book. In closing, a request: A year ago I sent you a little poem (I think untitled), ending with a temptation and an exorcism. I seem to have lost it, and because I think I will manage to publish a collection in the fall, I would like to copy it for myself, so I would like to have it, if it would not be a great trouble.

I send warmest regards.

Zbigniew Herbert
All letters have been translated by Alissa Valles

THE ART OF EMPATHY:
A CONVERSATION WITH ZBIGNIEW HERBERT

RG: For me one of the key words in your poetry is the word "not." The definition of a concept, an object, a person is often based on a negation. Something is not something else. For example: "It did not require any strength of character"; "I remained in the city which is not a city"; "Virtue, an old maid, repeating the great No." As I understand it, these negations have a profound meaning in your work.

ZH: You are the first critic to ask me that question, which I think is a crucial one. My poems aren't normally my bedtime reading, unless I'm preparing for some poetry event. And once, when I was putting together a little selection of that kind, a little anthology, I noticed — as when one sees oneself in a mirror for the first time — that I use the word "not" too often. I don't like it in people who are always negating things, and I don't like the impulse in myself. But there is probably some meaning in it, because I'm not a great believer in the subconscious. Evidently I try to define something not directly but by a negation. By seizing on the negative part of an existence, an object, I avoid unpleasant marks of arrogance, self-confidence, and at the same time I surround the object, the lyrical situation, the emotion, in some way, right?

RG: But isn't there sometimes a moralizing aspect hidden in that "not"? It's a little like a father saying to a child: "Don't do that."

ZH: But I ask you to consider how hard it is to build a positive ethics, constituted of imperatives that we could accept. The decalogue is based on

Interview conducted in 1986 by Renata Gorczyński.

"not." I have a profound sense of taboo — that is, I don't know what is good, but I know exactly what I shouldn't do, what is forbidden. In my codex that is expressed by negation. So maybe that's when it is seen in the best light; on the other hand, I am terrified reading my own poems, in which I find so many "not's" because I'm scared as hell I will be suspected of nihilistic sentiments of some kind. They can call me whatever they want, only not a nihilist, for the love of God. I wouldn't want that.

[. . .]

RG: So can one take it that the lyrical "I" in your poetry has a lot in common with the author?

ZH: I just don't know what that lyrical "I" is. Stanisław Barańczak tried to explain it to me, he laid it all out very well. But a reader wants an author to identify completely with his poems. He doesn't think poems can be a working hypothesis or an idea, you can't take that seriously. An author has to stand behind his poems. That's the difficult fate of the Polish poet, who is a slave of what he says. He can't say: "Leave to poets a moment of happiness, otherwise your world will perish." I'm quoting Miłosz. Nobody is going to accept that. We made a kind of pact with our readers, which I would like to respect. But I also try to make it clear that the author doesn't appear in his own person. He creates a certain poetic persona, which — sadly — is better than he is. Because I think man isn't who he really is — who knows who he is — but who he would like to be. This is my fundamental discovery in the sphere of psychology. That's why I feel sympathy for elderly people who make themselves look younger, for people with bow legs who happen to like dancing. I sympathize with people who have bad voices but never let an occasion slip in company to sing the Virgin's Prayer. It's moving, this striving, this attempt to outstrip oneself, that's what literature is. It's a longing for a better "I" that I thought up, and that then takes its revenge on me. Because people say: "Look, he writes like this, but he lives like that — what's that all about!"

RG: I get the impression that in many of your poems there's a warning not to divide oneself into body and a sphere of spirit, because it will cause a reaction like an avalanche.

ZH: That's a pertinent remark. And maybe I'll start from an experience that was crucial for me. Namely, in the first year of philosophy we studied psychology. We went to a class at a school, sat in, and our professor instructed us to observe a particular child, so as to make up his profile later on. You had to distinguish the child's volitional, emotional, and rational responses. That holy trinity, Aristotelian psychology, very helpful in distinguishing certain features. But I thought I couldn't define the little boy whose behavior I was studying. He kept putting something under his desk and taking it out again, shuffling something around. Was that a volitional, emotional, or rational action? In other words, at a so-called higher level, these things should be treated differently, not as a simplistic dichotomy. My friend Jan Lebenstein says that you don't paint with your hands, but with your liver, your disappointment, despair, hope, fear, and everything that I wouldn't attribute to one of two categories: body here, spirit there. I'm more for incarnation, concretization. My concept of God is vague; on the other hand, when I think of Christ and the Passion — those are concrete things to me, moving, overwhelming, arousing anger and love. They are mixed and ambivalent feelings. Anger, because was such a great sacrifice necessary for our terrible humanity? If there were no testimony in the Christian religion, if there were no Gospels, I probably wouldn't be able to move in this world.

[. . .]

RG: The imagination — you write in one of your poems — is an instrument of compassion. Why is it? How does that work?

ZH: You know, for me it wasn't a problem of the imagination. I'm still speaking for myself. It wasn't the strange marriage of beings — half-women, half-fish, centaurs, which I happen to like a lot . . . That's just a kind of medium. In general, writing is not a medium of expression, of expressing oneself, but an art of empathy — that is, an entering into others. You can't write novels, which I don't read much anyway, because I don't have a taste for them, unless the author manages to divide himself into several characters — a protagonist, an antagonist, or whatever they're called. That's elementary from my point of view and doesn't require further explanation. It's probably my lacking, because I don't have that kind of reliable capacity for fantasizing, that kind of imagination. The ability to put oneself in the position of another person is very useful in life.

[. . .]

RG: In the poem "To Ryszard Krynicki — a Letter" you wrote that not much would remain of the poetry of the twentieth century. You mention

Rilke, Eliot, and you also answer the question that arises as to how this came about: "We came to believe too easily that beauty doesn't save." Is the Platonic connection between the good and the beautiful then not an abstract mental construction, something that your famous poem "The Power of Taste" would also suggest?

ZH: Yes, that is an accurate reading, only with the caveat that the line is an expression of regret. "Too easily," I should have added: "Sadly, we came to believe too easily." But I'm still searching. My master, Professor Henryk Elzenberg, searched for a common definition of the good and the beautiful. In the end, ugliness is evil in the sphere of beauty, evil is moral ugliness. In common speech those two words: "ugly" and "evil" are used interchangeably. That's not a coincidence. It appears in every language I know. So I submit that there's a connection between goodness and beauty, that those who serve beauty perform the good. In our times there is a tendency to avoid the beautiful. Beauty has become a synonym for aestheticism, has become a shameful thing. From the beginning, the reception of my poetry in Germany was suffused with uncertainty — what is he doing, going to Greece and writing about it? That's what the Romantics did or people with sexual problems, with certain proclivities. That's almost a standard reaction. Common, wrong and insulting, but that's how it's taken. So the restoration of a belief in beauty, to use a pompous phrase, how else to say it — in aesthetic values, is a condition of man's happiness and his goodness — and one shouldn't be ashamed of it. We too easily fell into the ugliness that surrounds us, into the moral ugliness of all totalitarianisms. This great subject of culture — and not only European culture — has to be dealt with. People wanted to express something through beauty — it seems, the good. When sacred art existed, it was simple: A temple was built for the glory of God. Now everything has been stifled. I think the subject will be tackled, and in different areas — architecture, good painting, good poetry, which serves man, gives him courage, and says: "Look, we can sing."

RG: "The Power of Taste" speaks of a rejection of total doctrine not intellectually, because that would be attainable only to a few, but with the aid of the senses, the body. Should one deduce from this that the body is wise?

ZH: Ah, yes. I would risk that claim. In any case it's wiser than I am. It revolts in a scientific way, so to speak. There is simply a limit to endurance.

On the other hand, in the sphere projected by our imagination, we are always thinking that we are without limits, that our possibilities are inexhaustible, but the body here . . . The body is wise.

RG: So one should trust it . . .

ZH: Not permit it too much, not allow it everything, but at the same time listen to it. I'll give you an example from architecture. In Italy I can tell right away what was built for Mussolini. It's not even such bad architecture. But in our communities, for lack of a better word, it's not without reason that this sort of ugliness emerges. The ugliness is simply astounding. My eyes, senses, body don't accept it. It's just not on the measure of man, you don't have the feet, measures, modules, which exist in great cathedrals. It's not the gigantism, it's the proportions. You have to start from the elbow, the foot. In classical buildings the foot is the human foot.

RG: And then a cathedral is elbows and feet multiplied by X.

ZH: Yes, so many times a human being. And then we find a home in the cathedral, we trust in it. Then the universe was logical and not infinite. It was built in seven spheres, created by God, you could know it and describe it. And those concepts could be translated into everyday language, and from that, consequences flowed for man.

RG: Adam Michnik, analyzing your poem "Apollo and Marsyas" in his *History of Polish Honor*, thinks that Marsyas is a symbol of the tormented soul, and its inexorable experience is pain and suffering. But it seems to me that that poem contains above all a warning: Every notion of incarnate perfection — whether in the image of God or the state — is dangerous, because it leads to totalism.

ZH: Michnik has one interpretation of the poem. What you're talking about is a kind of complement to it. In any case I would resist the Romantic model, which is not my model. I recognize the weight of suffering and experience — of physical suffering as well as spiritual — but I wouldn't recommend it. A wise person said to me recently that at moments when a person is alone and suffering, let him try to bring that suffering as a sacrifice. That's very good advice, very practical. I can't do anything with suffering, but I can ennoble it in some way by an inward act. In any case I am in no way a supporter of the view that we are ennobled only by suffering. In a human life there has to be a balance of suffering and joy, because that is what gives fullness to humanity. On the other hand, a person who only suffers in the end withdraws into himself. The Book of Job, that masterpiece, really says everything about suffering, about revolt, about the overcoming of revolt and about acceptance. It is very instructive seen in that light.

And as for the question of totalism, of totalitarianism, I think it is born of terrible arrogance. [. . .] I would derive it from pride, the mark of Satan, who wants to create the kingdom of God on Earth. And from those good intentions, it turns out, frightening things emerge — concentration camps, exile. And it seems to me that we can't do without a dash of skepticism — that old ridiculed liberalism and the acknowledgment that another being, no matter how we empathize with it, is another being, with its rights and its precepts. Of course, I'm not speaking as some parish priest, because I feel guilty of violating these principles, but I acknowledge them. On the other hand, when someone has that only true road to the happiness of humankind, it ends fatally. And those guys — I'm against the death penalty, but maybe not against imprisonment — should be discreetly isolated from society in some way.

RG: You write a lot about the necessity of humility, of overcoming one's pride. This theme appears in "Prayer of Mr. Cogito the Traveler" and in the poem "Old Masters," where the greatest painters of the Middle Ages leave their work, but we don't know their names or even traces of their biographies.

ZH: Although it might sound paradoxical, I'm for anonymous creation. Let's try not to be Dupont or Schmidt, let's just write in someone's praise. Of course it's impossible, but I have the impression that we got rid of some sort of world soul in favor of individuality. We lost our communion with the generations, which could only leave their achievements as they do in archeology — only objects, only works. Even the bones have disintegrated. I feel close to that and that's why I would like to understand anonymity as humility. On the other hand, art orders me to be better than my friends, better than the guy next door, and we can't do without names. But I think that after a fasting period of about a decade, those who were only writing for their names would fall by the wayside. I think great poets have an enormous need to speak, not necessarily to have it be added to their account. They approach objectiveness by anonymity, I would put it that way, by the fact that they don't intrude with their whole individuality, with the lesser part of it. Apart from that, what distinguishes me from another makes me the other's opponent or even enemy, seen from the point of view of competition, which is always a kind of battle.

[. . .]

RG: Why do you so often reach for ancient history, for Antiquity? Is it because you are looking for a kind of model of human action, because it is easier to see there? Not yet lost in the commotion of gods, voices, layers of history?

ZH: History simply interests me. Which is to say man, eternal and changing at the same time. That very basic question, a fundamental one — whether man retains his nature, or whether he will change so much that he loses the possibility of communicating with other generations? The danger has always been changes of style, philosophy. But at least in the sphere of European culture, there exists a certain continuity. So I rented this mythological attic and made myself at home, no one can kick me out of it.

RG: Apollo is probably the cruelest of your gods, guarding his perfection jealously against all rivals. You present him as the god "with nerves of artificial fiber." In another one of your poems Mr. Cogito meets him on the road to Delphi, where he is carrying the severed head of Medusa, saying to himself: "A conjuror must plumb the depths of cruelty." And in the poem "In the Workshop" you write that God created a perfect world, scientifically perfect, and that for this reason one can't live in it. On the other hand, the artist creates a world that is good because [it is] filled with flaws. So we have two views of the artist — one under the sign of Apollo, in that highest, most perfect embodiment, and the other who — so to speak — paints a bowlegged perspective . . .

ZH: There's a certain contradiction here, I don't at all try to avoid it. I assert with regret that I will not found any school, will not create any coherent philosophical system. These are two images of art. One is Apollonian: Deprived of compassion, it wishes to deepen cruelty. And in the artist there is a kind of mark of cruelty. Take descriptions of death, for example. Why did poor Flaubert work himself so into a sweat over dying, why did he want to describe it so precisely? Or Rembrandt, painting a portrait of his sick wife. To fix the features of a face, when death is already taking up residence in a person. That pure artist is truly Apollonian, and the other didn't even correct his own paintings. I was writing a little tongue in cheek. He simply gives birth to a world. People don't see in geometrical perspective, that's an illusion. On the other hand, a little street painted as it is seen with a naive eye, smoothes over reality, removes hard edges. Those are two aspects of art — that pure kind, and the kind that agrees to imperfection, to its own incapacity, to flaws, to its own character.

RG: I have the impression that there is often an attempt in your poetry to humanize God, as in the poem "Mr. Cogito Tells of the Temptation of Spinoza."

ZH: There is the God of the philosophers, the God of the common man, the God of poets. That doesn't mean that there's polytheism, only that people have different roads to him. Just as the parish priest says. I really missed my calling. And to Spinoza of all people, a philosopher who really created an ethics without God — so geometrical — a God comes who says: "I want to be loved by the simple and uneducated, they truly hunger for me." Recently I got a letter from Józef Czapski, with whom I have very close, warm, and friendly relations. He wrote to me that he remembered a gathering of women in Kazakhstan who had come out of the camps and were praying before an ineptly painted Mother of God for their homes to be saved, their husbands and children to return. And the excellent Józef Czapski writes: "But they must know that nothing will be what it was before, that their homes were burned, that their husbands perished." In the face of such acts of faith I don't make light of them, but I myself can't attain to a fall to my knees. I was asked once in Poland at a poetry reading: "But what is God to you?" Suddenly, this question. I answered: "Incomprehensible." That's the only answer that came spontaneously to mind as a confession of faith. Because if I can imagine God, of course I humanize him. And why do I love Greek mythology so much? Because it's something halfway between the God of the philosophers, between the God of Plato and the God of Socrates above all, who is already pre-Christian, with the prefiguration of a single God; and at the same time all those erotic escapades, hunts, and metamorphoses of gods, in which — I have the impression — the Greeks of the enlightened period hardly believed anymore. It was already more of a rhetorical figure. I write apocrypha in which the gods complain about having to be eternal. How much happier are humans, who have a finite path from-to. I like reading philosophy — everything is clarified there, everything is derived from concepts. But it doesn't convince me. It's a need of both mind and heart. My model is Pascal — a mystic and a physicist.

RG: But also Descartes, from whom Mr. Cogito has his name, not just as the author of *Discours sur la Méthode* but also as a man who had a great mystical vision.

ZH: Right, right. Those three dreams of his . . . An extraordinary business. Simone Weil wrote something that struck me very much, that where we find contradiction, we find reality — great, ontological reality. That contradiction, I think, is so fertile that one should not be ashamed of it, for that is precisely where the mystery resides.

RG: Where does the interest in the object in your poetry come from? In the chair, the house in the suburbs, the table, the stone?

ZH: You can simply deduce it genealogically. In the period when everything was going crazy, changing, I turned to objects, to create a kind of private ontology. Białoszewski, whom I didn't know then, did something similar. We didn't know anything about each other. In the middle of that world of chaos, that shrieking of ideology, we tried to make an ontology from simple objects, which are equal to themselves, which don't change. I'm for values. They have to be constant, you can't say: "Oh, we live in a different epoch, everything has changed." There has to be something enduring, otherwise motion loses its meaning. You can step away, you can move closer, but I like a few enduring things. And probably that's why I was taken from the first for an old reactionary. Of course, I like them from self-interest, so I have something to go back to, so I don't chase endlessly after novelty with a bouquet of flowers. That's where my attitude toward still lifes comes from — a few objects, a pipe, and it lasts. It's the triumph of objects over us. Before it was Vanitas, a symbol of evanescence, but I come across those objects which the Dutch painted in antique shops. They outlived Rembrandt.

RG: And that's why you bring still lifes to life so often?

ZH: Yes, I would like to enter the painting and say to those objects: "Well then, you are spirits." That's connected with a certain experience from my childhood. I wrote a poem in connection with it about my sister, in which I realize that in fact I could have been anybody. I could have been the fat man walking around in the funny bowler hat, I could have been a little dog, or a wall. You know, that had nothing to do with philosophy, it was something elemental. I had the feeling that my individuality was not absolute, certain, finished, that it was by an accident that I was born into the Herbert family. I could have been that child in the courtyard with whom I played, that daughter of the Jewish shopkeeper with whom I was so in love — she was my first love. Here we return to empathy, which for me is something completely natural and even, let's say, a precondition of writing.

RG: In "The Monster of Mr. Cogito" you recommend mimetism as a method of self-defense in the face of nothingness or nihilism; take on the shape of a stone or a leaf. How can that be translated into a more concrete piece of advice?

ZH: How to translate it? Well, it's a kind of consolation, that after me the world will continue anyway, if someone doesn't blow it up. Objects will be renewed, oaks will blossom. Nothing began with me — only my life — and nothing will end with me. Because if there is existence, then I am an exchangeable, unimportant fragment. It's a kind of attempt, difficult for me as well, to reconcile myself to my own disintegration into physical nonexistence. Here I remember Rodin, whose secretary was Rilke. Rilke said that he couldn't write anything, that he was having trouble, and Rodin's answer was: "You know what? Go to the Jardin des Plantes and study the animals there." Thanks to him, fine poems arose. Which is to say, one must go out from oneself to the object. I know it from myself — always whining and bellyaching, but going in that direction, along that road: studying the object, not oneself, contemplating something which is outside of me. That philosophical surprise, that something *is*, just as I *am*.

RG: Poetry is equal to memory — that is, generally speaking, the meaning of "Report from a Besieged City." Memory rescues from nothingness, which also manifests itself as amnesia. But great poetry is surely also a prophetic gift. In your opinion, can it anticipate the course of events?

ZH: Whether poetry is prophetic? I really don't know. But it does seem to me that by a certain necessary concentration — I won't call it inspiration, vision, but concentration on unsolvable problems — a poet sometimes succeeds in something, something appears to him. And in general poets have presentiments. The catastrophists, with Miłosz at the front, and some others divined a real threat that hung over the world. Others didn't perceive it, because the world doesn't want to be under threat. But poets have presentiments because they're vigilant. Others are asleep — give us a break, it's all right, what are you scaring us for. So it seems to me. Poets on the other hand are sensitized to the smell of sulfur. Others need sulfur clouds to get the idea, but they can sense its smallest components in the air. You know, I can feel the air thicken at times of terror, which I lived through both during the occupation and later. I couldn't explain it scientifically, nor do I even try to, but my senses perceive danger and death very powerfully. I'm not a fortune-teller and I wouldn't read tarot cards, but I have published poems that later turned out to fit the situation. That's not to my credit, I was just meditating while I worked on them and I managed to hit on something.

[. . .]

RG: It's well known that you don't like to be called a "moralist." In the poem "Knocker" a moralist is someone who knocks on a board, which answers yes-yes, no-no. The moralist has the makings of a decent totalist.

ZH: That's true, there's no big difference between a moralist of the inquisitorial type and a totalitarian. My master, Professor Elzenberg, about whom I spoke before, wrote about this. He wrote an essay that was a revelation to me, "Brutus, or the curse of virtue." However, there is a difference in argumentation and a difference in motivation, which is very important. If a man condemns another man to suffering in the name of some superhuman ideal, it is a different matter from condemning someone to suffering in the name of a purely human, so to speak, order. You have to make a slight distinction. The consequences are terrible in both cases. But why I don't want to be a moralist? Because while I desire enduring values, love still lifes and Vermeer's *View of Delft*, I would also like to submit to those changes that are also the changes of my body. That is, I want to live through old age in a dignified fashion, if it is given to me to do so. Kornel Filipowicz wrote in one of his poems, an excellent one by the way, that some ask God for fame, others for money, but I ask to be spared old age. That is a terrifying anxiety I have now. Looking at the fate of others who are not luminous figures, I am also afraid of fragility, the sense of vulnerability, and as a result of it, committing an error that could strike out a whole life.

RG: Could you define your poetry in one sentence?

zh: When a person decides to take the frightening step of publishing, he has no idea what the consequences will be for his life, for his health. Writing, painting (I might not include music) leave their mark on the soul. They make it either better or worse, but never leave it indifferent. Here my younger colleagues will say: "He's all right, he got prizes, he's sitting in Paris and giving us advice." Nevertheless it is choosing danger, choosing fate, a more difficult life. I would like what I write to be the reflection of some human life — unimportant, undistinguished, mine — and through that the life of my generation, my relation to my elders, to my masters. That is a duty of continuity and — apart from my terrible character flaws — a duty of fidelity. Oh, that's what I would say, that my poetry is about fidelity; in general it is about a certain virtue of endurance, of affirming life in all its complexity. And I still hope that one day when I see that I'm slipping on the page, I will have the courage to say to myself: "No thanks, I step down." There's that eternal question of Mauriac's: why did Rimbaud stop writing? Well, because he had said everything.

Translated by Alissa Valles

Sławomir Mrożek

(b. 1930)

Sławomir Mrożek is so famous in Poland that his name has become synonymous with absurd situations (and these, especially under communism, though
even later on, have never been in short supply in Poland). A modest and
obedient journalist in the early fifties, the peak of the Stalinist period, he
soon after became a brilliant and sought-after playwright who through witty
allegories portrayed the contradictions of a life in the shadow of Karl Marx
and Joseph Stalin. Influenced by *le théatre de l'absurde* but also by Witold
Gombrowicz, who was an absurdist *avant la lettre*, Mrożek was able to
contribute a fresh tone, a personal touch, to the existing tradition.

Mrożek had lived for many years in Italy and in France, where his talent
matured (his best play, *Tango*, was written then) and flourished. He also
wrote several stupendous short stories that had the density of philosophical
parables. Mrożek returned to Poland in the late nineties and though not very
prolific now, he is considered an institution, a writer emblematic of sardonic
humor and moral sanity. His letters in this chapter were written in the sixties,
from his Italian home in Chiavari; the addressee is Jan Błonski, one of the
outstanding literary critics of postwar Poland.

Letters to Jan Błonski

Chiavari, March 1, 1965

Dear Janek,

So I moaned and complained shamefully and was rude enough to stay on with you too long, all on account of my soul and its future life. I could have stayed on longer, because it turns out the soul isn't like that and is quite eager to stick with life as long as the body can go on sitting around inertly, drinking and chattering on about the soul. My trip back was good; on the way I also visited Gombrowicz, who is fitter but still ill. He's gained quite a bit of strength, but he wasn't up to any tricks, he only argued with me, though quite gently. I had a photo taken with him as a souvenir. He said again that I shouldn't sublimate myself, because my calling is to remain an artist in an impure state — those were his exact words, an impure state — that I'm an artist of this world only and of temporary effect, that I merely express my time and that that's good for me, so I shouldn't try to be serious because for me nothing very useful would come of it. I'm not writing this with complete irony, because all that he said wasn't entirely deprecating, though it's clear he places an artist in an impure state lower than one in a pure state, though still pretty high.

In any case, whether my state is pure or impure, I can only ask myself questions like that in moments of leisure; when it comes down to work, I don't have strength or time to wonder about it, so I can only find, not a solution, but respite from this worry, in some productive occupation.

He also said that I shouldn't get into theory or any sort of reflection, because I'm not suited to it and theories do me harm. I'm not sure if he said that in deprecation, or not entirely; he wasn't completely clear from that point of view. This aversion I have to theory, or rather my organic inaptitude for theory, philosophy, he once ascribed to my typical Polishness, and he may have been right, but it didn't sound very flattering. Nor do I have any particular idea how it works or what to think about it. And anyway, think about it or not, it probably doesn't matter very much what and how I think about it, when it comes down to it; work is too absorbing.

As you see, work is what is supposed to entertain me, in it there is hope.

Meanwhile I haven't been doing anything very salutary; up until now I've somehow been unpacking. I'm asleep — a resident's life, it seems, would suit me best. There's nothing I really want very much. Either stand around, or sit around, or go to the kitchen to see if there might not be something good to eat there.

So nothing much of interest. If I could I would pour out my troubles on the spot. As it is, the questions I've been asking myself so intensively have worn me out. I'll stop and hope to save something up for the next letter.

Thank you again for having me in Sarcelles. I send my regards to the whole household.

Your S.

CHIAVARI, MAY 5, 1966

Dear Janek,

[. . .]

Janek, I don't know if you are even slightly susceptible to the tendency I'm about to describe, but if you are, you will have a discussant in me. Axer and Brandys demonstrated this tendency to me with crystalline clarity, each independently of the other. And it seems to me quite universal in Poland. They don't like some things, some things disgust them, but in fact they say: Poland the people is one thing and what is going on over there is another. Poland and the people have tremendous values, and for their sake everything should be forgiven. When I asked them what this was all about, what independent values these are, the first answered youth and hidden biological strength, the second something that seemed to end up meaning the people who read. And here I don't agree. Because I think that "the people," the life of the people, is not some abstract spirit of the people or some mysterious biological force, but it is concrete everyday life, and this concrete life is manifest is concrete forms, in structures, in how things work, in every nail knocked into a wall by a Polish carpenter. This life of the people is fully expressed in the kind of nail and wall, and the hammer too, in the reason for which this hammering takes place; in the psychic state or mental state of the one hammering, only and exclusively there is the life of the people. So you can't cut off what's going on there, what's there, from some spirit, make a waterproof division, and if such a division is made, it is only in bad faith, in order to [get] oneself a passably peaceful conscience and a little unfounded hope. You can't separate the system from the people, because the people live in that system whether they want to or not, they express themselves only through it, it is it — but the system is not the people. In every way the authorities are surely right to give speeches about the victory of socialism in Poland. If I put on a pair of green pants, for example, I can't keep telling people all day that inwardly I'm against green pants and therefore they aren't green. This kind of behavior leads to national schizophrenia, which we observe in so many of the people we know. That something is wrong is obvious from the achiness, the oversensitivity, and moral insanity that are growing so frighteningly strong in our national environment.

To know it is the only prescription for one's own health, to know, not to fool oneself, because that kind of facilitation doesn't facilitate but ends in the ruin of one's own inner life. Almost all visitors from Poland give me the impression they are half stuffed, half paralyzed, and their shocking uniformity of responses, thoughts, phobias, and likings, their inner divisions into a series of conceptual cages that don't interconnect and sometimes contain concepts in total contradiction with each other, without any synthesis, without the ability to make connections, without the ability to see even their own contradictions — this uncanny spectacle of something like former people, captured by a mysterious Doctor N-hu or B-hu, who passed through this doctor's laboratory and came out freakishly dissected. And the horror is amplified by the fact that each one of them is convinced of his absolute autonomy and the originality of his thought, his inner life, his personality. I don't want to become a cripple like that, just as I don't want to give up my arms and legs. And I don't write this to blame them, or derive any self-satisfaction from it, as if because I see them this way, I'm obviously different. It was precisely in Poland that I learned not to bother about Poland, let alone what was going on in the rest of the world. Only here I learned to worry, not just about Poland and the people living there, but about everything going on elsewhere. Which is just a return to life, to normal responses, retrieving oneself from that paralysis, that sleep, that poisoning by the stench given off by the general rot.

Unfortunately, I appreciate very well the significance of a person's situation, how a situation forms and conditions — "unfortunately" because it deprives me of many illusions about my autonomy. Although at the same time I can't agree that a person is just a situation. Nevertheless, I know it's hard to be different in Poland, because there are laws of adaptation, of mediocre endurance and so on, though much in us and in our environment cannot be justified that way. Adaptation is one thing, but pride, craving for importance, vanity, envy, exaggerated love of comfort, ascription to oneself of the highest values — in other words, everything extracurricular — cannot be forgiven, because it isn't necessary. I know I'm too weak for life in Poland. My strength is of the kind that doesn't help very much in those conditions. Everyone is different, everyone has to work it out for himself. You're different and have a different kind of strength and weakness. I retain the memory of a time in the fifties during some group discussion when you suddenly started to yell at Polewka, when his stupidity became unbearable, especially together with his sense of his own power, his untouchability, his nonchalance and dogmatic correctness. You shouted: "It's because of people like you that we're stuck in this idiocy," or something like that. In any case it was very sharp. You turned red, and you obviously weren't watching yourself; the atmosphere turned heavy and menacing. We all knew who Polewka was, what all of this was, there in that dining room that was still Bavarian, there in Kraków, there in Poland. You may have paid for that explosion with a sleepless night. But whatever the price was, whatever fear you felt later, because maybe you did, I tell you now, it paid off in some way, if only because I still remember it to this day, and I remember having to make a confrontation between your performance and myself, having to look hard at myself, my fear even of having witnessed this and having silently agreed with you.

In general, I've eaten a lot of shit in my life. You can eat it without permanent damage while you're still young and have a strong stomach. But later, when you're grown up . . . This is what amazes me, that old men who have nothing left to lose tremble so for themselves. Only young people can lose everything, for that reason I'm not afraid if they pay a lot to keep all kinds of possibilities for themselves. One explanation is that in older people the past stiffens into a substance whose loss seems to them the equivalent of the annihilation of the world. What does Iwaszkiewicz have to lose, for example? Maybe it doesn't occur to some people until the last minute that they're going to die, this is what characterizes youth. Whether I like it or not, I already know more or less from time to time that I'm going to die and it's only a matter of time. Which doesn't mean I want to lose everything right away either; I just don't have the same reckless strength to spend on self-preservation, preservation of my outward self, whole, without the slightest damage. Maybe it comes partly from the fact that I don't have children, that must influence a person, even later on, not in relation to the children.

In general, I often observe aging that is only biological — it's as if some people don't notice they left their youth behind, which often makes a comical and pitiful spectacle. An old man telling me he has a young heart is for me an immature, underdeveloped old man.

Getting back to the subject: I don't feel strong enough to live in Poland with full clarity, or even the clarity I achieved here and which I see as the most valuable achievement of emigration. I would have to retreat into pure mysticism, which doesn't suit me, because apart from anything else, it seems I was born a writer who by nature can't fulfill himself through mysticism alone, through mystical experience; or I would have to lie a little to myself, which would be a pity, even if technically I could manage it. I should live in a country, in that reality which yields to me, a Pole, with the least resistance, without additional veils, without all of what foreignness is, and which stands between me and reality here, because when I say "reality" I mean reality in general, not some Polish or Italian reality: Countries and peoples are only forms of reality in general. I should, but I can't, and here lies my dilemma. Responsibility falls to those who present themselves as the only stewards and representatives, which is what I most hold against them, this usurpation. When someone deprives me indirectly of my country and my people and more than that, presents himself as me. Because the system man presents himself as me, you, he appropriates us, and it's the worst crime, almost a crime against nature, to whistle your own tune, something entirely your own. That's unforgivable, because you can't forgive it when someone empties you, drains you of yourself, your own personality. In a funny way this is even evident in the letter from the embassy I quoted to you. In it they prove to me that it's not me but someone else.

I'd like you to write me something back. I'd like even more to see you before you go back to Poland.

Your S.

Paris, September 4, 1971

[. . .]

One of my secrets, which can now be filed away in the archive, was a feeling of strangeness that plagued me in Poland from my childhood. Strangeness and thus nonadaptation, nonadaptation and thus terror. The fact that in a certain period I was considered a super-Polish writer, essentially a pork chop and Kosciuszko guy, was due to my success as a mimic, though not only, because in that there was also the tormenting gnawing of my own nightmare, magic tricks, spells. (Here there's no need to say I come from Fredro and Mickiewicz and so on; that's where I'm supposed to come from — I had and have only the stuff I was raised on, only the school I went to, only the literature I was formed by. But I'm not talking about props, about the cultural material I was given, I'm talking about myself, so let's leave aside the obvious.) It isn't and never was a specific strangeness related only to Poland. I would have been a stranger wherever I was born. But it's particularly difficult to be a stranger in Poland. So now I can be openly, fiercely strange; now I simply have the status of a stranger and don't speak the language of the community I live in, the situation is clear and honest. That's also why in emigration I'm finally at home. And that's why it's hard to ask me (I often hear these questions): How do I bear emigration? The word "bear" isn't appropriate. I don't bear it. For me it's a state a little more natural than life in my own country. (I write a little more natural because I don't know what a natural state is and can't imagine it.)

I'm writing roughly but I trust you to understand me. What I just wrote might sound to an unmusical ear not like desecration, but just false. That is, it might be understood wrongly. After all, a stranger isn't either an enemy or an ill-wisher or an indifferent, or a person without ties. My search for a state of open strangeness — maybe it can best be explained as a search for a state in which the pressure of identification no longer nags. So everything, everything remains beyond identification. And if I'm reproached that it doesn't look good not to identify in this situation, I say, I can't even identify fully with this body sitting here and writing on a typewriter, even with my writing, and I'm supposed to identify easily and unproblematically with something much thinner and paler than my own body and my own literary works?

My fundamental arrogance lies in the fact that I tore myself away to correct my fate. I was born where I was born, and in my view I was born in the wrong place. God, not because I'm better and all that is inferior — I'm too old and experienced to think anything so stupid. Just in the wrong place, awkwardly, without fitting in. Anyway this is not about Poland alone. It started from the crib, or from my own family, and whatever I came across as I grew up was somehow not right.

And all my life I've been like an eel born in the Sargasso Sea and cutting through that sea to get somewhere else, a hemisphere away. No, in the end I couldn't accept, take on the fate of a Polish intellectual, in Poland, in the second half of the twentieth century. I call it arrogance, because there may always be a punishment for it. But in the last analysis I didn't take off one coat to put on another, though some coat or other might have struck my fancy along the way. And now I'm truly without a coat, quite stripped documentwise. So much so that I begin to suspect that somewhere in all of this it was not about an exchange but about a fundamental *dépouillement*.

If that was what I was after, I succeeded at last. I'm almost completely naked and the wind is blowing. Where are the times when it contented me to write satires on *polonité*? And where are the times when writing, literature, or art seemed to me a way out, a means, the only instrument and in general a primary thing? Such dimensions and expanses opened up before me, always anticipated and felt, but thought through so very slowly, so gradually, with years and experience, to the point that it turned out I'm not at all such a so-called natural-born artist. By that I mean one who stubbornly, passionately, maniacally does what he does and only that, not feeling in what he does the part that is limited, small, imperfect, ridiculous, and ineffectual. I'd like to be, I'd like to be very much, but I'm afraid I'm not like that. And I'm left with only one false situation — me as a professional literary man.

Apart from that it seems I got my own way. Equidistant from all possible points, alone, without luggage, without a past and without any way of imagining the future. Quite literally patted down by myself, conscious of my own parts and their functions, scantily dressed. What is supposed to come from all of this? I have no idea.

Of course I know what I've written is also a kind of myth, a current myth about myself. But I'm no longer capable of spontaneous myth-making.

Rather, it's an honest myth, because it's conscious and the only possible one for the moment. Anyway, how to express anything without some sort of coherence that is without myth — I don't speak of myths with any scorn, because one way or another they serve for something — how can you point to anything without them? You mentioned receding from passions. I wish them well; sadly they can't be the primary material for me any more. They're like an old sofa to me now: I've sat on it so often that the stuffing and springs are popping out.

It's age, but I don't want to complain about my age. I was given it to live through so that I would live according to it. Why should I pretend and look for something that doesn't exist at my age, something already beyond it?

[. . .]

Translated by Alissa Valles

Ryszard Krynicki

(b. 1943)

Born in a Nazi labor camp in Austria, Ryszard Krynicki began his writing life under the sign of language poetry. His early master was Tadeusz Peiper. Soon this purely artistic choice was complicated by his perception of social reality. Events in the spring of 1968, when nonviolent student manifestations were brutally crushed by the "socialist police," slowly made their way into Krynicki's poetic thinking and a few years later brought him into the orbit of a newborn democratic opposition.

Accordingly, the formal pattern of his poetry had changed too: his poems, once long, capricious, bursting with the energy of linguistic wit, became much shorter, almost aphoristic, gnomic—simple, yet with an uncanny force of sudden poetic discovery. Along with his friend Stanisław Barańczak, Krynicki became one of the favorite poets of those in the solidarity movement who cared for words; Zbigniew Herbert was also worshipped by these same readers.

Krynicki's creative life is not free from long periods of silence, however. A collection of his poems appeared in 2005, though, and confirmed his high place in the pantheon of Polish poets. He's a fine translator of German poetry; his translations of Paul Celan, for instance, are among the best in any language (if such a statement can be made).

An Interview with Ryszard Krynicki:
"Some I, Looking for Its Thou"

KM: We're talking in Poznań, where you've lived for many years. But you're moving to Kraków. Is there a place on earth you could call your own? And what does it mean to you?

RK: I never managed to settle in Poznań, though I've lived here, with intervals, for almost thirty-seven years. I use the past tense, because inwardly I already took leave of this city a couple of years ago. We're living on our suitcases, or more precisely on our boxes of books, which you had to squeeze through, in a rented apartment, and we're waiting to move to Kraków. It's probably too late now for me to put down roots in Kraków, but I hope at least that I'll be able to relate to it in some way and that I won't feel isolated there and that even if it had to come to that, I'd be able to bear it more easily. I've had to move many times in my life, and every time I took it very badly, because in the process I always lost some papers, souvenirs, photos, books, and letters. I don't think I could survive another move, so this one by necessity has to be the last.

I have to admit that your question touches on a very sensitive point in my soul, because I always suffered from a homelessness complex. Usually people have some place of birth to which they are attached whether they like it or not and which is a point of reference. There's some courtyard where you played with other kids, some little homeland, and so on. With me it's different. So I couldn't write my "To Go to Lvov."

KM: What are your roots in literature? That's a question about your masters and your way of dwelling in language.

RK: I take it you're asking not so much about to what extent I feel rooted in literature, whether I found my place in it, as much as about what I owe to literature, about influences. There may be some paradox in this, but the biggest influence on me has been from books that, being great works of literature themselves, at the same time cast literature, or living through literature, under suspicion: *Don Quixote*, *Madame Bovary*, *Auto da fé*. I've always tried to distinguish literature from life. But I owe almost everything to lit-

Interview conducted in 1998 by Krzysztof Myszkowski.

erature and certainly, almost certainly, I would be a different person if I hadn't read Kafka and Bruno Schulz, not to mention Sophocles, Shakespeare, or Dostoevsky.

I would also be a different poet, if a poet is something one is, if in the mid-sixties the poems of Tadeusz Peiper had not seized my imagination, together with the sonnets of Mikołaj Sep Szarzynski. A strange combination, but evidently possible. I'm almost sure, though, that Peiper would not have printed me in *Switch* if I had lived in his time. Julian Przyboś on the other hand wanted to publish me in *Literary Monthly* with his own introduction, but I decided against it, though I respected him very much and admired (and still admire) his "Hearts' Equation," because I didn't want to give the impression that I was part of his tradition. I think you can have only one master. In my case it happened to be Peiper. I was his late (and tardy) pupil, his "blossoming system" was to me what the sonnet was to my neoclassicist contemporaries. I see that with time little remained of that fascination of mine, and anyway even at the time when it seemed to me that I was the last Peiperist, I was solely and exclusively Krynicki, no more but also no less. What remained is an attachment to some poems from "A" and "Living Lines," to the journal *Switch* and to the "Switch Library," and if you wanted to look for a continuity in my life, you can't not see that the a5 poetry series is some kind of continuation of that series. In another time, another place, in other circumstances, but nonetheless a continuation, unless it's obvious only to me.

On the other hand, just once, in my poem "In Transit" from 1982, I dared to call Zbigniew Herbert my master, which doesn't mean that I am his follower in poetry. I'm ashamed to admit it, but there was a time when — as a Peiperist — I rebelled against his poetry, because I believed that it was merely neoclassical, and I had to get rid of my literary prejudices first and hear "The Envoy of Mr. Cogito" in Kraków in 1972, to realize how great and rich that poetry is. I permitted myself, once and anonymously, to call him my master, like a student of Zen Buddhism. Luckily masters don't answer for their pupils, as I may have said somewhere before, but it doesn't hurt to repeat it.

Besides, it's a thing with great poets that we sometimes have to rebel against them. So I also rebelled — it seemed to me, not always without cause — against Czesław Miłosz, and traces of that remain in some of my poems, as there are two literal quotes from his poems, when I couldn't find words of my own. I can say that of that great trio, I have never rebelled against Wisława Szymborska, and from the time that I read poetry consciously, I've always awaited her poems with great anticipation. I return to them often and I am always finding something amazingly new in them that I hadn't picked up before.

KM: And non-Polish poets? Who are the most important ones, the most necessary to you? And do those loves or fascinations have an influence on the choice of poems you translate?

RK: My answer will be incomplete, and uncertain, I'll admit in any case that although I have great admiration for great, completed works — it's hard not to admire the *Songs of Songs* or the *Divine Comedy* — I have always been drawn to short, fragile, transitory, gnomic, enigmatic writings, often things preserved only in fragments, scraps, single lines. And so, recognizing the greatness of the *Iliad* and the *Odyssey*, I like to go back to the Pre-Socratics — part-poets, part-philosophers — and I find more in the songs of Milarepa than in the whole *Ramayana*. Etcetera. I'm moved by Ancient Egyptian love songs, some of which I know in Anna Akhmatova's translation. I adore Issa, though it's hard for me to believe that he wrote three thousand of his haiku. Of poets closer to us, twentieth-century poets, I admire Trakl, Rilke, Apollinaire, Jacob, Khlebnikov, Tsvetaeva, Mandelstam, Auden, Amichai, Natan Zach, Kunze, Brodsky. Gottfried Benn too, although I also feel a great resistance reading some of his poems. As you see they are different poets, different worlds. Often it is just a single poem, like "My Mother's Prayer before Dark" in Miłosz's wonderful translation. Nelly Sachs and Paul Celan are particularly dear to me; I've been trying to translate their poems for more than twenty years. With varying results, because many of Celan's poems, so deeply rooted in the German language, in my opinion don't permit translation into Polish; in any case no one has yet managed it.

I'm not a professional translator, I don't translate on commission, and I've known for a long time that I'm not suited to it, not only because you have to translate within a certain time, and I have trouble with time. So I try to translate poems that I would have liked to have written myself. Naturally,

I'm limited as a translator by my knowledge (or ignorance) of languages, though it sometimes happens that I can't resist and I translate from a language I don't know. I do that very rarely; I'd say, only when I don't have another choice.

KM: What do you think of Samuel Beckett?

RK: Knowing you a little I could have expected that question, but I have no answer ready. I don't know his work well enough, though he didn't write that much, nor am I one of his followers. I did see *Waiting for Godot* and *Endgame*, but watching those plays is almost physically painful for me, even when the audience is laughing. I saw *Krapp's Last Tape*, but I remained deaf and blind to it. So I prefer to read Beckett than watch him; the plays too, because the readings are no longer so terrifyingly literal, definite and closed, you don't associate them so strongly with particular actors. I prefer reading his prose, which is close to poetry. Reading him I always feel that he's touching nothingness from the other side.

KM: Painting plays a large part in your life. You publish your books with the drawings, graphics, and etchings by prominent artists. What does painting mean to you? And how do you see the ties between painting and poetry?

RK: I make an effort to refer to the origins of modern art, when it seemed a natural thing that there was a *correspondance des arts*. Now poetry and art have become remote from one another, as if they had ceased to need each other. I try to recall those mutual ties.

KM: And music? I don't find many tropes concerning music in your poetry, which is a rhythmic structure suspended between sound and silence. What does music mean to you and how do you think music relates to poetry?

RK: I am above all a visual person, not an aural person. But even though I'm chiefly a visual person and I can't imagine my life without the possibility of contemplating images, I don't try to describe them in my poems. Sometimes I try to translate them into the language of poetry, not describe them but translate them. That sometimes happens with music too — in the end my early poems owe as much to the blossoming system as to listening to Bach — but I am much more defenseless in the face of music, because at times a great piece of music can hold sway over me like a top hit, and that doesn't happen when I look at pictures.

There are poets who have perfect pitch and whose poems are born directly from music, like Stanisław Barańczak's brilliant "Winter Journey." As we know there are whole epochs, if only romanticism and neo-romanticism, in which the ties between poetry and music are closer.

KM: What is silence for you? In the poem called "You Are" from the collection *Our Life Grows*, the lyrical subject, or you, calls silence his "only homeland."

RK: The lyrical subject, and only that, or some concrete I looking for its Thou, someone who speaks in the hope that his words get across to someone. I take responsibility for each of those I's, but they are not always identical to me. Often they are other voices that I only shape and pass on, not knowing to whom or where.

Silence? It's a necessary component of speech, and for that reason one must take great care not to overuse it.

KM: What does poetry mean to you? In a poem dedicated to Henryk Waniek, "Living Poetry" from the book *Collective Organism*, the lyrical subject says that poetry is "like blood sent to the heart" or that it is something that can save a life . . .

RK: I don't know what poetry is, even though I wrote that poem. Nor do I believe that poetry can save a life. But there are poems that can give meaning to the fugitive moment, and that is already quite a lot.

KM: The New Wave in which you are counted was involved in politics from the beginning: March and August 1968, December 1970. Language games, a moral message: truth, freedom (independence), justice, Poland. The theme of Poland is present in different tones — serious, ironic, sarcastic, humorous — in many of your poems: from solidarity, affection, and participation to the bitter, painful poem called "Nothing more" from *Poems, Voices*. A strong knot? An open wound? What is it?

RK: "A strong knot"? "An open wound"? Sometimes one, sometimes the other, more often the other. What can you feel, living in a city in which a synagogue was turned into a swimming pool? In Poznań it's often said that the Germans did that, as if the war hadn't ended half a century ago. It seems that even communism has fallen.

And the New Wave, I have less and less a sense of what it was. We couldn't be silent any more, that's all.

KM: The poetic-political epigraph to "Independent of Nothingness" (a section from a poem of Zbigniew Herbert, "Meditations on the Problem of the Nation") and the poetic-metaphysical epigraph to *Magnetic Point*, the end of a poem without a title by Nelly Sachs, printed at the beginning in the original version, repeated after 275 pages in a translation with one word changed — it's as if these are two poles of your poetry.

What is that "magnetic point / through which God enters"? Who is God for you? What is faith in your life?

RK: A search. A search and a path.

Translated by Alissa Valles

Adam Zagajewski

(b. 1945)

Born in Lvov in the aftermath of World War II, Adam Zagajewski belongs to a generation that was supposed to witness a gradual rebuilding of a country that had been destroyed by the Nazis. Instead, the Soviet domination, though made milder after 1956 by Polish Communists who were not too bloodthirsty, warped this pattern. Together with his peers, Zagajewski was active in creating literature of social and political critique (the so-called New Wave, or the 1968 generation). His 1974 collection of essays, *The Non-Represented World* (co-written with Julian Kornhauser), stirred public response.

Zagajewski's early poetry and a novel tried to stick to this postulate: to represent the visible world of a society impaired by totalitarianism. His later books, collections of poetry and essays, seem to move toward a different ideal: to represent both the visible and the invisible (whatever that may be). He grew up in Silesia, graduated from the university in Kraków, lived for many years in Paris, and returned to Kraków in 2002. He is a professor of literature at the University of Chicago.

Excerpt from "Flamenco"

1985

I think about form: it is a liberation from confinement, a liberation and joy. I do not understand Gombrowicz's distrust of Form — which, in his opinion, deforms, lies, distorts. In my opinion, form delineates and liberates. Except one must constantly confront it with formlessness, passion, anxiety, fear; these are the various names of chaos, that is, nothingness. For the nothingness we know is not at all, in spite of appearances, nothing. On the contrary, it bursts with an excess of being, substance; all it lacks, poor thing, is form. It rushes all over the world like a tornado basically seeking form, would like to meet up with form — like wind with a sail. But it has great demands: it seeks form to its scale, a brisk, youthful rhythm to yoke it but also to preserve some of the velocity, yes, so it wouldn't have to go straight from the field, from the steppe, into the museum, sober, its pride swallowed. No, it wants to keep some violence as it does in *Carmen* or in *King Lear,* yoked and innocuous, to be sure, but still pretty, it still wants to appeal and is afraid to lose its Asiatic grace. Nothingness is ready to capitulate but presents conditions; there is no way it would agree to everything proposed. For it is a world power — a mobile one, true — and the demands should be taken very seriously. Nothingness surrounds us, attacks us without respite, brings a constant pressure to bear on us, just like the barbarians who for many centuries threatened Rome. Only an energetic politics and readiness for wise compromise can save us. New forms will continue to be a compromise. As long as I live, I create forms. My thoughts are a form. My poems are form.

I am on the side of Rome, against the barbarians — even though Romans have never lived in my country. I would like Rome to know how to renew itself so it would not freeze in the same defensive gesture, and give the emperor's throne to the barbarians. My Rome, mere poems and thoughts. My allies — my confederates who disappoint me so frequently — are forms in existence for a long time, slumbering in someone else's poems, paintings, novels.

I stand on the street. Next to me walk generals, directors, cabinet members, messengers, moneylenders, policemen, pharmacists, women, feminists, high school girls. No form, no matter how perfect, can quell the barbarians. Passionate nothingness fits into no prison. No meaning can become the ultimate meaning, the final meaning, incapable of leaving its stamp on all material, with an abundance of remnants, stores that remained in freedom and will make themselves known to us, will be reborn, will show themselves where no one has expected them, and to the sound of drums will march again on Rome.

Open wide Blake's doors of perception and our eyes will see a fairy tale — rich chaos, an unending war of worlds, the glistening leaves of alders, clouds high in the sky, trains standing at a small station, the ruined Arabian fortresses in Yemen, the quiet of Antarctica, the dreams of a young Chinese woman from Shanghai, the hatred and cunning of people, tricks of rulers, the opulence of flora in June, ruins of sailboats resting at the bottom of the sea, fights and murders during one night in a big city, the weeping of the maltreated, planes over the Atlantic, the flight of the lark, genetic laboratories, sparrows indifferent to the progress of history, our Ego, cruel and magnificent. If one were to open wide the doors of perception and leave them thus, open, we would have to be silent and remain in eternal mute wonder. Luckily, we dispense prejudices, ideas, ideologies, and religions that allow us to simplify this wealth. They allow us to bear the sight of the eternal war of existence, of a furious and wild war revealing itself only to the most peaceful, calm eye of contemplation.

Prejudices, hierarchies, ideas allow us to cup up reality, order it, that is, deprive it of light, of a thousand shades of meaning, its majestic splendor. Sad philosophers come along, they find eternal laws and stable regularities, and they cut through this jungle with the sharp sword of their diagrams. The doctrinaire types come along with their penknives, the professors of a single idea, the politicians of three slogans. If one were to open the doors of perception . . . sometimes they open up by themselves and life becomes unbearable, impossible, full of violence and cruelty. This is what happens when wars begin or end, real, true historical wars; refugees or released prisoners-of-war trudge along the streets, borders are not yet determined, the police — *the* most scrupulous philosophers — have not yet taken up their work, schools and banks are closed, the nights restless, the sunsets bloody, constant fires and robberies. No one knows yet what religion the new prince professes, only gold and bread have any value, and perhaps a woman's body. Then comes the new ruler to calm turbid reality. He prints money, arrests bandits, designates a new god, appoints professors, judges, and editors, cuts away the excess of chaos, illuminates the streets, introduces internal passports, patrols the cities and villages. Chaos retreats deeper, retreats into desires, thoughts, hides in a forest, like partisans, conceals itself in the effervescent juices of plants. It can reappear on the surface at any moment. If one opened the doors of perception it would appear immediately, unchanged, angry, restless.

Systems lock chaos in a cage, in political systems, systems of thinking and seeing. Here we are dealing with the steady rhythm of concealing and revealing; they are decent, good philosophers who try to conceal barbarian reality a bit, while others, pupils of Nietzsche, constantly tear at the curtains, veils, euphemisms and present the multiplicity and the wildness of the world.

It is impossible to live in the open doors of perception, the world is too rich and garish; no one can be mute, one must speak, live, and to do this must forget about the whole growing like bread dough. One must accept a hierarchy and not just any hierarchy. False hierarchies deform reality even more, while others are more faithful to it, they are real. At the same time, one must sometimes return to the whole that confounds categories. Sleep cannot be peaceful while right next to us, and right within us, lies concealed the unexamined kingdom of reality. This is why form is constantly needed and constantly inadequate. Hierarchies and ideas are needed. As are works of art to order the world's chaos in the most impartial way.

I remember a visit to New York, a city that is one of the modern models of the world, inordinately difficult to get to know, to grasp, too rich in nuances, aspects, colors, neighborhoods, races, possibilities, energies. I felt uneasy for the whole day because I was incapable of coping with the excess of this city; I had not method, shortcuts, no theory was enough, no sociology, economy, or history; I was at the mercy of newer and newer impressions with their arabesque flux, of a free, open cognition that does not want to order anything, merely gathers and hoards, greedy, insatiable, eternal. There is a category of perception swelling with images — images attached to emotions, passions, perceptions — which does not settle into a design and becomes deprived of rational categories. This state cannot be tolerated for very long, as anxiety follows along just as if the mind, which is also alternately a decent and cruel philosopher, feared going mad.

Just then I came across a museum, the Frick Collection, and there, in front of Vermeer's *Girl Interrupted at Her Music*, all of a sudden, I felt how reality stopped for an instant and froze in harmonious motionlessness. A painter who had lived a few hundred years ago calmed New York, stopped its quivering, its undulation. A blue tablecloth, next to it the little girl and her mandolin, the music teacher, all suddenly became more real than the overwhelmingly real, unreal city strangling with its excess of features and points of view, with the excess of its breadth and height. I looked at the chairs painted by Vermeer, sleepy chairs illuminated with the soft rays of light that appear only in his paintings. I felt joy, the pleasure of existing — the blue pleasure of existing. Vermeer's painting also simplified the cosmos, but differently: it diminished but did not dissect it. Now everything seemed easy and possible, life could begin anew, somewhat more cheerful and simpler than before, so much easier to bear than ungraceful life in its natural dimensions.

Something had slammed shut, closed. To put it another way: the world was dressed, had put on a blue robe. Before that it had been naked, aggressive, agitated, everything was possible, all questions were open, nothing was obvious or certain, pretty or ugly — simply enormous, growing, mobile, without order. A moment earlier New York had been as new, fresh, swollen, unnamed and dangerous as the underground corridors of its subways. And now suddenly it was quite different, a breakthrough had occurred. Before me a girl is having music lessons, wrapped in a light as soft and blue as the ocean's interior. Suddenly there is tranquility, in me and in all of New York. I was as happy as if I could move into Vermeer's painting and live in it forever, never feeling fear or the burden of questions without answers, never experiencing the tempest of contradictions and uncertainties. Another, different landscape was opening before me, a smooth road among the domesticated, warm furniture. I had a different world before me: furniture lay on the floor tiles as calmly and trustingly as a cat endowed with a sweet, kindhearted intelligence. Even the light understood. This was not an ordinary, external light that stops at the contours of objects, is deflected and returns in keeping with the laws of physics — no, this light seemed to wash over everything, it did not divide, did not isolate, on the contrary, it was fraternal and wise.

How I would like to stay in this painting. Remain in this form. This painting ended history in a certain sense — not all of it, but one of its trends. Which one? Why, this one: a girl and her mandolin, gentle light, the music teacher, the room. This will never be again; it will neither repeat itself nor develop. There is nothing to inquire about, everything is obvious. And the strength of this still painting is so great that for an instant it freezes the velocity of the great burgeoning city.

To inhabit this at whatever price. To stand before the painting as long as possible. The museum guard begins to look at me suspiciously. I should be invisible and step into the blue room, clenching in my invisible fist a ticket to the Frick Collection.

But could I really live here, within the frame of the painting? Is there room for me there? Would I have to become the music teacher? Why, he teaches nothing, the girl knows everything, she does not need instruction. If she wanted to she could easily play not just Scarlatti but Chopin or Scriabin. It is true the girl is a pupil, but she is not learning anything. Everything is ready. The music has long been perfect, the music could be light, could change with the light. And the teacher could sit at the instrument like a pupil. The girl would tell him how to play. But the light would tell him the same. I would have to change considerably to keep these perfect beings company. Wouldn't I begin to yearn for my restlessness after a while? Beauty interrupts anxiety. When I am pursued by the multiplicity of New York, I seek respite and form, but wouldn't I miss chaos? Wouldn't I think that in the tumult of a great city and in the roar of the waves is contained a more difficult meaning, a meaning still awaiting me and which, though it may torment me as it does others, and though it is my opponent, is at the same time the place of a nervous, difficult life. It is the seed hidden in the opulent flesh of the fruit, but hulled from under the skirts of matter and impressions — doesn't the nutmeat wither if stored in the pantry too long?

Suddenly I realized I can stay neither here nor there forever, permanently; neither in the great chaotic city nor in the painting. When I am in one, I yearn for the other. I must act like a statesman, a politician from a small country lying between two mighty powers: the only way out are alliances with one neighbor against the other, and with the other against the first, with art against restless reality, and with reality against perfect art, with form against chaos, and with chaos against form. I must move from place to place, constantly in motion, journeying, seeking form, which is liberation, and formlessness, which frees me from my liberation. I must seek forms and try to create my own and fortify the party of forms, consider myself its proponent, and, at the same time, not trust too much in the lapidary calm of art, and even less entrust myself to the chaos, so sly, dishonest, and malicious.

Where should one live? Constantly in a hotel, boardinghouse, small town, where after a few days I am pointed out as a foreigner? Each town belongs to the party, belongs either to the party of form or to the party of chaos. Activist of both groups are critical toward me, they demand that I finally make a decision and declare which side I am on. I conduct endless consultations with them, sometimes the world finds us in a tavern over empty glasses. Empty wine bottles elongated like El Greco figures tower over the tablecloth or lie on the floor. Who are you, ask the messengers of form. We saw you entering the temple of chaos. You frequent museums — say to me the attacking activists of formlessness. I return to the boardinghouse, pack up, and move on. From the bus I see the morning star, fading in the beams of a rising sun. On the horizon the bruised hills of Tuscany or the Holy Cross Mountains. And again the city and again the street, twilight, and multitudes of people, circulating like clusters of atoms. Men carry their invaluable briefcases concealing the archives of the Thirty Years' War and a sausage sandwich, a bitten apple, and a postcard depicting Saint Peter's Square in Rome.

Over all cities swallows wheel in great invisible circles. They leave no trace in the sky, theirs is a true invisible geometry; if not for the whistling, there would be something completely unreal in the flight. Rain begins to fall, umbrellas unfold like cherry blossoms, again there is more chaos than form, the contours of the city are blurred in the drizzle, in the mist, then in the snow the street vanishes, only occasional women in mourning appear, for only women know what mourning is and what the birth of a child is, and crying in the night when no one hears, and the great sorrow nothing can soothe, which can only be forgotten. And then one must also forget about oneself, die a little, to relieve a too sensitive memory.

Then again the sky grows radiant. I look up and see clouds chased by the wind. The wind plays with them, shaping them this way and that, changing their forms, tearing apart heavy, sullen clouds, tugging at them, drawing long shimmering ribbons out of them, slowing down, accelerating, pushing, forcing them to drift together like a school field trip, then dividing them as if it wanted to talk to each alone, sweeping them away. For an instant the sky is clear, but this doesn't last long; a squadron of cumulus clouds shows itself shyly and grows like a flagship, approaches, one hears sails flapping, the shouts of sailors, whistling ropes. I know that God would have to be both form and formlessness.

Translated by Lillian Vallee

Stanisław Barańczak

(b. 1946)

One of the most energetic advocates of the generation of 1968, both as a poet and as a critic, Stanisław Baranczak spent his early years in Poznan, where he taught at the local university. In the mid-seventies he joined the KOR (Committee for Workers' Defense), a group of courageous dissidents whose determination contributed to the political change that occurred later in Poland (the solidarity movement, the collapse of communism, and so on). In 1981 he moved to Cambridge, Massachusetts, and for many years taught Polish literature at Harvard. A brilliant poet and translator, he has published dozens of collections of English and American poetry as well as drama in Polish translation. He has also translated in the other direction, from Polish to English (the work of Wisława Szymborska and other poets).

Interested in the tradition of "language poetry"—not unlike his friend the poet Ryszard Krynicki—Barańczak created his own poetic idiom in which he was able to express autobiographical elements blended with a larger political vision. His poetry was highly popular and was seen as representing the grievances and aspirations of an entire generation. This, plus his strong critical presence, gave Barańczak a unique position as an intellectual leader. Even his moving to the United States couldn't diminish that fact. As the political realities of Central Europe have evolved, Barańczak's poetry has developed a more personal, existential stance.

The Revenge of the Mortal Hand

1987

It was in the late fall of 1982 that I first heard the news about the death of Grażyna Kuron. She was the wife of my friend Jacek Kuroń, one of the most charismatic leaders of the human rights movement in Poland. I had been close to them during my years in Poland, particularly in the late seventies, when the Kurons (along with hundreds of their "dissident" friends) were working to make the regime's ways a little less inhuman. But in the fall of 1982 I was living peacefully in Cambridge, Massachusetts, where I had moved a year and a half before, while in Poland the first year of martial law (or "the state of war," as it was officially named there) was just coming to a close.

With a rather morbid sort of pride, the military regime claimed in those days that its imposition of martial law had actually been bloodless: several dozen people shot by the police in street demonstrations, nothing to speak about. Grażyna was one of the indirect victims of the "state of war." Jailed in an internment camp, she developed a lung disease. She was released only when her situation was already hopeless: despite intensive treatment, she died in a hospital. Jacek, jailed too, was granted permission to leave the prison for a few days to attend the funeral.

The funeral elegy was one genre I had never tried before, but this time I felt that I simply could not help writing a poem on Grażyna's death. What happened to her was a stupefying blow not only to me but to everyone who had known her: it seemed unbelievable that this brave, strong-willed, good-natured woman who had so cheerfully coped with so much adversity in her life was suddenly gone, had ceased to exist. Why her? Why now and not later? Every death of a friend makes us ask such silly questions, but this particular death was the hardest to accept and understand. Still, even though I sincerely wanted to bid farewell to Grażyna, I wasn't able to write a single word for quite a long time. I lived in agony for several weeks, immobilized, on the one hand, by the sense of the absurdity of that loss, and, on the other, by the sense of the exasperating conventionality of all the words, metaphors, rhetorical devices that the genre of the funeral elegy would have inevitably entailed.

In our illiterate times the classical "Eureka!" would be Greek to virtually everyone, so it is habitually replaced by an icon: a lightbulb flashing above the head of a comic strip hero. Something like this flashed in my head one November evening, when I suddenly found a solution. I realized that the only way to commemorate the death of someone like Grażyna — a death that was so blatantly undeserved, unjustified, unacceptable — was to write a poem which would be a total reversal of all the norms of the traditional funeral elegy; a poem which, instead of accepting the loss, would remain defiantly unreconciled to it; a poem which, instead of shedding tears over Grażyna's grave, would *talk to her* as if she were alive; a poem which, instead of bidding her good-bye forever, would try to fix and preserve her remembered presence.

To Grażyna

To remember about the cigarettes. So that they're always at hand,
ready to be slipped into his pocket, when they take him away once
    again.

To know by heart all the prison regulations about parcels and visits.
And how to force facial muscles into a smile.

To be able to extinguish a cop's threatening yell with one cold
    glance,
calmly making tea while they eviscerate the desk drawers.

To write letters from a cell or a clinic, saying that everything's
    O.K.

So many abilities, such perfection. No, I mean it.
If only in order not to waste those gifts,
you should have been rewarded with immortality
or at least with its defective version, life.

Death. No, this can't be serious, I can't accept this.
There were many more difficult things that never brought you
    down.
If I ever admired anybody, it was you.

If anything was ever permanent, it was that admiration.
How many times did I want to tell you. No way. I was too abashed
by the gaps in my vocabulary and the microphone in your wall.
Now I hear it's too late. No, I don't believe it.

It's only nothingness, isn't it. How could a nothing like that
possibly stand between us. I'll write down, word for word and for-
    ever,
that small streak in the iris of your eye, that wrinkle at the corner
    of your mouth.
All right, I know, you won't respond to the latest postcard I sent
    you.
But if I'm to blame anything for that, it will be something real,
the mail office, an air crash, the postal censor.
Not nonexistence, something that doesn't exist, does it.

I'm reminded of this poem whenever someone asks me if I find
pleasure in writing. In this particular case, perhaps more than in any
other, I'm unable to give a straight answer. The experience that led to my
writing this poem was, needless to say, anything but pleasure. The several
weeks of conceiving the poem were one long wave of mental anguish. And
yet I'll never forget the feeling which, in this mournful context, I'm a little ashamed to admit: the feeling of intense joy that flared up in me when,
still in despair over the insoluble problem of Grażyna's death, I finally
found a solution at least to my literary conundrum. It would seem that
mourning and joy are two mutually exclusive states of mind. What, then,
is there in literature (or maybe especially in poetry) that makes us simultaneously feel the deepest and sincerest pain and equally deep and sincere
joy flowing from the very writing out of that pain? Isn't this joy — let's put
it a bit cynically — a *Schadenfreude* of revenge? Don't we find pleasure in
writing because writing as such, even though it doesn't make the pain
actually disappear, is nonetheless a way of retaliating against what causes
the pain?

The simplest definition of a graphomaniac holds that he is a person who
likes to write. Should, then, the definition of a good poet hold that he is a

person who doesn't like to write poems? If so, I would qualify for inclusion among the greatest. In the more than twenty years of my career, I have written perhaps two hundred poems; I like some of them, but I didn't like *writing* any of them.

Am I, however, completely sincere in saying this? True, the process of writing, especially in its initial stages of groping in the dark in search of a convincing concept, can be real torture; and true, the chief difference between a good poet and a graphomaniac is that writing is easier for the latter, since he lets himself be carried away, unabashed, on the plucked wings of literary conventions. Still, when after much aggravation the lightbulb finally flashes in your head (sometimes accompanied by a huge exclamation point), when you finally realize that a good poem has just been conceived, it is a feeling that can be compared with only a few other pleasures of life — perhaps with only one.

In other words, an outside observer has every right to treat the poets' complaints with utter suspicion. Logically speaking, if writing is really such a pain in the neck, it must be recompensed with some kind of pleasure — otherwise, who would bother to write poems at all? And, since there are apparently thousands of contemporary poets and none of them can seriously count today on any of the more tangible rewards (such as making money or winning a Maecenas' favor), the very joy of writing is most probably the only compensation for the pain of writing.

But wait a minute. Mixing pain with pleasure . . . Aren't we talking about masochism? Would writing poems amount to some kind of perversity?

Why, yes, of course, writing poems is a kind of perversity. And the joy of writing is, in fact, a very perverse kind of pleasure. Just as with every perversity, it results mainly from the deliberate breaking of a taboo, from defiant resistance against a powerful rule or law, from rebellion against the commonly accepted foundations of existence. It's enough to put a verse line down on paper to scoff, in effect, at all the basic laws on which the world rests. For the very act of writing creates another world in which all those laws can be suspended — more, held in suspension interminably by the enduring power of conceit, rhyme, pun, metaphor, meter. No one, I think, has expressed it better than the contemporary Polish poet Wisława Szymborska in the conclusion of her poem "The Joy of Writing":

Is there then such a world
over whose fate I am an absolute ruler?
A time I can bind with chains of signs?
An existence made perpetual at my command?
The joy of writing.
The power of preserving.
The revenge of a mortal hand.

"The revenge of a mortal hand" that holds a pen is perhaps the only retali-
ation against the laws of Nature accessible to a human being. Since in the
real, extratextual world I am unable to change or nullify any of the omni-
present laws of transience, decay, suffering, or death — in other words, since
I can do nothing about the lurking presence of Nothingness in every atom
of this world — the only solution is to create a separate world "bound with
chains of signs," closed within lines and stanzas, subject to the absolute rule
of my imagination. In such a world the flow of time can be magically
stopped, suffering can be avoided, death can be rendered invalid, Nothingness can be scared away.

More important, this artificial world can seem more convincing than reality. After all, what makes poetry different from any other verbal description
of the world is that a poem (only a very good poem, to be sure) strikes us
with its determinateness, inner necessity, essential existence; to an even
greater extent than "each mortal thing" in Hopkins' sonnet, it cries to us,
"What I do is me: for that I came." To put it differently, a truly good poem,
colloquial and seemingly spontaneous as it might be, differs from any form
of extrapoetic speech in that it couldn't possibly be changed: even a single
word replacement, even a slight shift of stress would disturb the balance. As
a consequence, such a poem appears to be endowed with a certain special
force of argument: it proves by itself not only the necessity of its own existence but also the necessity of its own form. And this is an additional source
of perverse pleasure for both the poet and his reader: an encounter with
such a poem breaks another rule of our everyday experience, a rule according to which the world is based on randomness and chaotic unpredictability.

The joy of writing (and reading) poems, then, lies in the fact that poetry
willfully spoils Nature's game; while fully realizing the power of Nothingness

in the outside world, it questions and nullifies it within the inner world of a poem. But what is especially challenging for the twentieth-century poet is, I think his awareness that the same can be done about the power of Nothingness revealed in modern History. Today's world is dominated by the seemingly inflexible laws of History even more than by the laws of Nature (some of which have been at least ameliorated by science). All the historical dimensions of this world conspire to overwhelm the individual with a sense of his insignificance and expendability; what counts is only the great numbers, statistical probabilities, historical processes.

And here again every good poem, by its sheer emergence and existence, appears to be, on its own miniature scale, History's spoilsport. History may compel us to think that the individual and his personal world view do not count in the general picture; and yet poetry stubbornly employs and gives credence to the individual voice (moreover, as if to contradict the law of mimicry underlying modern society, the more inimitable and unique a poem is, the longer it survives in the memories of its readers). History may teach us abstract thinking; and yet poetry insists on seeing things in their specificity and concreteness, on viewing the world as an assemblage of Blake's "minute particulars." And finally, History may demonstrate by millions of examples the continuous triumph of Newspeak, a deliberate and systematic falsification of words' meanings; and yet a single good poem is enough to counter all this tampering with language by making the reader aware of the word's hidden semantic possibilities. A poet who is offended by the course of modern History doesn't even have to write political poetry to find an appropriate response to it. It's enough that he write his poems well.

All this may sound awfully optimistic and self-congratulatory. In fact, I am no exception among contemporary poets: just like the majority of them, I feel much more often helpless and desperate than victorious and elated in my private campaign against Nothingness. I do not stand on a sufficiently firm ground of positive belief to say with Donne, "And death shall be no more; Death thou shalt die," or even with Dylan Thomas, "And death shall have no dominion." Not even a poet (a representative of an otherwise rather presumptuous breed) can be as cocksure as to claim that his word can *really* stop the flow of time, invalidate suffering and death, put a stick in the spokes of History's wheel, make the earthly powers shrink and earthly injustices disappear.

In that sense, to return to my poem, I obviously have not managed to keep Grażyna among the living nor have I wrestled her back from the dead. I have done only what I could, and that is to challenge the power of Nothingness by flinging my poem in its featureless face, by showing it that even though it engulfed Grażyna's life I am still there to remember how much her life meant to me — just as someone may be there after my death, just as something will always be there to exist in spite of Nonexistence (which, as its own name indicates, is "something that doesn't exist, does it"). To spite Nothingness — this is perhaps the essence of the perverse "joy of writing," "the revenge of a mortal hand."

Paweł Huelle

(b. 1957)

The youngest author in this anthology, Paweł Huelle is well known for his fiction, especially for his early novel *Who Was David Weiser?*, a half-mythological story of childhood. The locale of his fiction—Gdańsk (or Danzig for the Germans)—is of utmost importance. An old harbor city, Gdańsk had been between the wars a free city under the supervision of the League of Nations. Earlier, it had been a German-speaking place having strong ties with the Polish crown.

Huelle, who lives in Gdańsk, belongs to a group of talented writers whose imaginations were to a large degree ignited by their city's mostly German history. Gdańsk became a part of Poland only after World War II. This is in itself a rare and commendable phenomenon: the 1945 shift of borders produced not a feeling of bitterness and revenge there, but rather has contributed to the building of literary bridges.

Appropriately, Huelle's essay published below is titled "The Map": indeed, maps have had in Poland—and in many imaginations—a symbolic meaning.

———❧———

THE MAP

It was the dream of my childhood. Not the enormous, colored map with oceans and mountain chains. I had those at school and in the atlas. I dreamed of a map of my immediate surroundings, taking in the hills of Oliwa, wooded valleys and narrow paths between forest tracks on a folding sheet with a magical network of icons and contour lines. The time in which I grew up didn't favor maps, however. Maps were general — like a vague hypothesis — and falsified by an appropriate department, in case they came into possession of an enemy.

Not having a map of my immediate surroundings, I studied my grandfather's map with all the more interest. Those big, canvas-backed sheets, smelling of war, hunting, and adventure, unfolded in the evening in the lamplight, led into an entirely different world. Winniki near Lvov or the surroundings of Drohobycz on a scale of 1:75,000 amazed me with their precision and exotic place names. The Eastern Carpathian mountains, their chains of peaks, valleys, and hamlets were given to me by way of Austrian and Polish cartographers, who made the artistries of the "tourist maps" of People's Poland seem invariably tendentious and despicable. I could make the journey from Strzyj to Sambor many times, the same details always moved me: the wooden bridge on the Dniestr, the inn near Horodyszcze, or the lonely farm whose owners I would never meet. Another thing was also cause for astonishment: My grandfather's maps, which served Austro-Hungarian artillery and staff officers in war, were purchased in civilian bookstores, as the stamps on the reverse side of the canvas testified, along the lines of "Gubrynowicz & Han, Bookstore and Warehouse. . . ." The paradox of my then predicament I owed to history and the era: Never having been in the Eastern Carpathians, I knew them quite well, while on the other hand, though I often walked the forest tracks between the Sambor Valley and Szwedska Grobla, I couldn't even dream of possessing a map of my immediate surroundings, on which the labyrinth of forest roads and paths between Wrzeszcz and Oliwa would finally be presented with cartographic accuracy.

Every year, when the water of melting snow was already flowing down from the hills, I set out on a painstaking journey, equipped with a sketch pad, pencils, a compass, and a ruler. Usually I started out from the road by the Church of the Resurrected: It ran under the bridge of a defunct railroad and

rose sharply upward to a forest glade, which on account of a few postglacial
boulders was locally called the "quarries," though no aggregate had ever been
mined here. On the biggest boulder, some hand had carved a nostalgic
inscription — "Borkowski's love is buried here . . ." From here, roads split off
to Brzozowa Aleja, Weglisko, and Osiedle Młodych, and my sketched map
acquired density. I never managed to calibrate it properly, though, and that's
where the paradoxes originated: The stretch from the church to the glade
took up almost the whole piece of paper, while barely a few inches would do
for Brzozowa Aleja. But the real difficulties came further on, in the tangle of
forest paths around Sambor Valley: the variations in altitude were so significant and the roads so winding, that transferring them to paper always ended
in defeat and a sense of powerlessness. The sketches and the pad ended up
back in a drawer, there to await the next spring, but the desire remained: to
behold all those forest nooks and crannies in contour lines, with a legend and
a key.

After many years, when I only returned to the immediate surroundings of
my childhood in memory while writing stories, the idea of the map unexpectedly materialized. In a secondhand bookstore I saw a reprint of a
German map called *Waldkarte von Oliva und Zoppot*, bought it on the spot,
and subsequently set off on a trip. The map was published in 1936 and much
had changed since that time, particularly in the direct environment of the
forests. However, I noted with emotion that the Präsidentenweg — as it is to
this day — climbs upward from the then not yet existing Church of the
Resurrected, passes the glade with the fallen boulders (where Borkowski's
love had not yet been buried), cuts across Samborowo, Dicke Eiche, trails
along the Reinketal (or rather what is now Green Valley), and finally as
Charlottenweg (now Marta Way) reaches Świerkowa Street in Oliwa.
Thanks to the trip with the German map, I discovered the changeable geog-
raphy of names. The Three Man Hills are now called Głowica, Philosophers'
Way used to run an entirely different route, and the hills behind Pachołek,
with the obelisk of the battle of Oliwa, used to bear the name of Queen
Louisa. But there are also places whose names changed only in language.
Paulushöhe near the Second Manor House is now Pawełek, and Schweden-
damm is nothing other than Szwedska Grobla. The *Waldkarte* . . . isn't a map
without shortcomings: Without contour lines, only showing the main roads,

it might lead astray someone entering the labyrinth of paths at Głowica for the first time.

However, the walker is kept safe from this eventuality by the maps of my immediate environs finally published by Polish cartographers. Perhaps it took the fall of communism for a thing as simple as a good tourist map to wait for us in a bookstore or a street stand. If I set out on a walk from Oliwa to Wrzeszcz today, I have at my disposition the aforementioned *Waldkarte* from 1936, *Oliwa Woods* from 1996, published as a "Via Mercatorum" edition, as well as the two-sided — and in my view a little less thorough — map *Landscape Park of the Three Cities*. Comparing them offers many pleasures and surprises, which I won't go into here, because a final word ought to be said about one Borkowski. Who was he? Where did he live? No one in my immediate environs knows. He carved a inscription on a fallen boulder after the habit of hooligans, and now, after so many years, the broken boulder on the map carries his name. Perhaps this was why the publishers of the *Landscape Park* . . . ignored this name, as if in fear of the inscriptions to follow? They were surely wrong: The hooligans of today dump car wrecks in Green Valley, then set them on fire. Maybe in fifty years someone will call this valley the Valley of Dead Cars, which is something I would not wish upon myself or anyone who loves his immediate environs.

Translated by Alissa Valles

Permissions

Writers/Works Index

ADAM ZAGAJEWSKI's books of poetry in English include *Tremor*, *Canvas*, *Mysticism for Beginners* and *Without End*. He is also the author of a memoir, *Another Beauty*, and the prose collections *Two Cities* and *Solitude and Solidarity*. Among his honors and awards are a fellowship from the Berliner Kunstlerprogramm, the Kurt Tucholsky Prize, a Prix de la Liberté, a Guggenheim Fellowship, and the Neustadt Literary Prize. He is a literature professor at the University of Chicago. He lives in Kraków and Chicago.